Definition
of Suicide

Books by Edwin Shneidman

Deaths of Man (1973), nominated for the National Book Award in
   Science
Voices of Death (1980)

Edited Books

Thematic Test Analysis (1950)
Essays in Self-Destruction (1967)
On the Nature of Suicide (1969)
Death and the College Student (1972)
Suicidology: Contemporary Developments (1976)
Death: Current Perspectives (1976, 1980, 1984)
_Endeavors in Psychology: Selections from the Personology of
   Henry A. Murray_ (1981)
Suicide Thoughts and Reflections, 1960–1980 (1981)

DEFINITION OF SUICIDE

EDWIN SHNEIDMAN
University of California at Los Angeles

A Wiley-Interscience Publication
JOHN WILEY & SONS
New York • Chichester • Brisbane • Toronto • Singapore

Library of Congress Cataloging in Publication Data:

Shneidman, Edwin S.
    Definition of suicide.

    "A Wiley-Interscience publication."
    Bibliography: p.
    Includes indexes.
    1. Suicide.   I. Title.   [DNLM: 1. Suicide.
HV 6545 S558d]

HV6545.S3546   1985   362.2   84-27011
ISBN 0-471-88225-9

Printed in the United States of America

10 9 8 7 6 5 4 3 2 1

Preface

I have meant to write a fairly slim book about an admittedly heavy subject. My intention is to present a series of ideas—clustered around the main idea of the common characteristics of suicide—and to explicate each separate idea just enough to indicate its essence. It is my hope that, taken together, these constitute a new definition of suicide and more importantly provide a fresh view of the essentials of suicide with direct implications for practical preventive action.

If I may be indulged a grandiose reference: Melville, in a letter in 1851 to Hawthorne about the newly completed *Moby-Dick*, wrote: "I have written a wicked book and feel as spotless as a lamb." About this present small volume—not a titanic whale; more like a youthful porpoise—I could say that I have written an innocent book and feel as optimistic (of its possible impact and usefulness) as a cricket.

This is not an empirical book. There are relatively few findings or new data in it; nor does it contain a comprehensive review of the literature on suicide. My goal is to present, as straightforwardly as possible, fresh notes about what suicide *is* and, concomitantly, to imply realistic and practical measures for preventing suicide.

I hasten to assert what will be obvious to any reader: This book is advertently idiosyncratic. It is organized in my special way of looking at the topic, built around books and mentors who have been special to me, and reflects my interest in fiction and literature and my belief in the power of the idiographic (clinical) method (in addition to the nomothetic, statistical method) in the psychological sciences. It is not at all that I am defensive or apologetic about these positions; they have served me well and, on both practical and theoretical grounds, I hold them to be among the most important methodologies available. Simply put, this is a book that contains some ideas that I believe to be the heart of suicide and some suggestions for possible ways to mend that heart.

The driving idea behind this book is the common-sense belief that effective remediation depends on accurate assessment which, in turn, depends on meaningful definition. Prevention rests on assessment; assessment rests on definition. When understandings are inadequate it is unlikely that effective remediations can be found. Curiously, in relation to the age-old topic of suicide, today's first order of business may very well be definition. The definition of suicide is one focus of this book.

The book consists of twenty-six sections, A to Z, under seven larger categories. The contents of Part Four on the ten common characteristics of suicide are my principal contribution to suicidology to date. As the text explains, these common characteristics do not come from Durkheim or Freud, although it is nearly impossible to write on suicide nowadays without leaning heavily on these two giants. In this book, I have seriously attempted not to be a burden to either one of them.

Instead I have tried to be "my own man," borrowing from 35 years of experience in suicidology, leavened by common sense and stimulated by insights and modes of thought other than those traditionally associated with our topic. Specifically, I propose that we examine the implications for the understanding and treatment of suicide from two rich sources: (1) a great American novel which, within itself, contains poetry, song, metaphysics, drama, zoology, technology, and the most profound depth psychology to be found anywhere; and (2) three technical books—none of them about suicide—which have been central to my own professional development and, more importantly, have direct implications for understanding suicide. They are: Stephen Pepper's *World Hypotheses*, James G. Miller's *Living Systems*, and Henry A. Murray's *Explorations in Per-*

sonality. I am proud to have known each of them personally and to have been their friend.

Professor Pepper justified for me, once and for all, my main questions about philosophy and religion in a way that was totally satisfying both intellectually and emotionally. Dr. Miller was my chief in the Veterans Administration in 1947 and is my friend and colleague at UCLA today. In this present book I have tried to apply aspects of his masterful systems theory approach to the topic of suicide. Some things that I have said about the prevention of individual human suicide might apply equally well to the prevention of self-destruction of groups, nations, international organizations—and even to the survival of the civilization of our world.

Henry A. Murray is precious to me in a very special way. Anyone who knows anything at all about me knows that he has been the absolute center of my intellectual life since the late 1940s and that now, in his 90s, he is, if anything, more dear to me than at any time in my life.

EDWIN SHNEIDMAN

Los Angeles, California
March 1985

Acknowledgments

Grateful acknowledgment is made for permission to reprint the following:

Excerpts from "Orientations Toward Death: A Vital Aspect of the Study of Lives" by Edwin Shneidman in *The Study of Lives*, edited by Robert W. White. Copyright © 1963 by Prentice-Hall, Inc. (Atherton Press). Reprinted by permission of Prentice-Hall, Inc.

Excerpts from "Can a Philosophy Make One Philosophical?" by Stephen C. Pepper, "Dead to the World: The Passions of Herman Melville" by Henry A. Murray, and "Sleep and Self-Destruction: A Phenomenological Study" by Edwin Shneidman in *Essays in Self-Destruction*, edited by Edwin Shneidman. Copyright © 1967 by Edwin Shneidman. Published by Jason Aronson, Inc. (formerly Science House). Reprinted by permission.

Excerpts from *Voices of Death* by Edwin Shneidman. Copyright © 1980 by Edwin Shneidman. Published by Harper and Row, 1980, and Bantam Books, 1982. Reprinted by permission.

Excerpts from "The Suicidal Logics of *Moby-Dick*" by Edwin Shneidman. Much of the original version, entitled "Melville's Cognitive Styles: The Logic of *Moby Dick*," will be appearing in a forthcoming publication entitled *A Companion to Melville Studies*, edited by John Bryant, and has been used with the permission of the publisher, Greenwood Press, Westport, CT.

Excerpts from "An Empirical Investigation of Shneidman's Formulations Regarding Suicide" by Antoon A. Leenaars, William D. G. Balance, Susanne Wenckstern, and Donald J. Rudzinski. To be published in *Suicide and Life-Threatening Behavior*. Copyright © 1985 by Human Sciences Press. Reprinted with permission of Human Sciences Press.

Excerpts from *Living Systems* by James G. Miller. Copyright © 1978 by McGraw-Hill Book Company. Reprinted with permission of McGraw-Hill Book Company.

Excerpts from *The Aristos* by John Fowles. Copyright © 1964 by Little, Brown and Company. Reprinted with permission of Little, Brown and Company.

Excerpts from *World Hypotheses* by Stephen C. Pepper. Copyright © 1942 by the Regents of the University of California. Reprinted with permission of the University of California Press.

Excerpts from "Suicide" by Edwin Shneidman in *Encyclopedia of Psychology*. Copyright © 1984 by John Wiley & Sons, Inc. Reprinted with permission of John Wiley & Sons, Inc.

On the less perfunctory side, I wish to thank particularly two individuals: Carol J. Horky, my Administrative Assistant at UCLA, who typed and tightened the manuscript, and Herb Reich, Editor at Wiley, who behaved in every way like a perfect editor and improved the book in the process.

E.S.

Contents

Definition
of Suicide

Part One

Basic Words and Approaches

A

Headnote

We are coming up on both the centennial of Durkheim's *Le Suicide* (1897) and the 75th anniversary of the 1910 psychoanalytic pronunciamentos about self-destruction, and there is a feeling in the current suicidological air that the time is ripe for some thoroughgoing reconsiderations of the nature of suicide—including, of course, the very definition of suicide itself. In this ambitious sense, this book concerns the future of suicide, that is, how, in the immediate years to come, acts of suicide should be understood and how they should be regarded, especially by the academic and professional communities.

In 1930, Maurice Halbwachs, a student and critic of Durkheim, set out to bring the work of Durkheim up to date, but he immersed himself further and further in his own data. As M. Mausse tells us in the introduction to Halbwachs' *Les Causes du Suicide* (p. vii), he was:

> ... forced little by little to undertake new research, to pose new problems, to present the facts under a new aspect. In effect a totally new book was necessary.

But the sad fact is that Halbwachs' book on suicide was not at all a new approach. To quote further from Mausse:

> The greatest part of Halbwachs' new facts on suicide were of the type Durkheim had described and were essentially subsumed by the interpretation which Durkheim proposed.

3

The point is: Bold words do not a new theory make. Many a self-proclaimed iconoclast ends up a tamed hagiographer. I take this as a cautionary for me and as a caveat for each reader.

No contemporary suicidologist can eschew the formulations of either Durkheim or Freud and the psychoanalytic school. There would be no point to do so. Nevertheless, there is merit in studying suicide by wholly independent routes, not neglecting those giants simply for the sake of avoidance, but consciously trying to create useful formulations other than the traditionally sociological or psychoanalytical ones. That is the route I shall try to find.

The improvement we seek in our current understanding of suicide lies not in some demographic tabulation or new psychodynamic formulation. It lies in ordinary common-sense characteristics of suicide that can be readily discerned and sensibly inferred, but are not, on the face of it, immediately obvious. To find these muted characteristics, to speak of them to others, and then to give voice to their implications for treatment and therapy is the purpose of this book. In order to do this we must commence at the starting line. The genesis of wisdom lies in clear and distinct ideas: In the beginning is the definition.

In relation to suicide—admittedly a somewhat intransigent topic—it seems evident that our current definitions (and our current conceptualizations) of suicide are not adequate. To put it another way, the definitions of suicide that we see in textbooks, use in clinical reports, read in newspapers, and hear in everyday talk are just not good enough to permit us to understand the events we wish to change. The basic need, in relation to suicide, is for a radical reconceptualization of the phenomena of suicide. What is required is a new definition of suicide followed by a broadening of many clinical and social activities based on that new understanding.

The hunt for a definition may involve some stealth and indirection. I propose that we begin our search for a meaningful definition of suicide at a tangent, specifically by considering various *approaches* to suicide (however suicide is defined). We shall look first not at the different definitions of suicide, but at the different ways of talking about the word and its near synonyms—at different ways of coming at the problem. That is, we shall look at the different orientations to suicide and the various contemporary disciplines that have considered themselves relevant to the topic. These disciplines or lines of thought have historical roots of various lengths, some (like religion) reach back millennia, others (like sociology) go back merely to the past century, and a few (like our supranational concerns over nuclear destruction) begin only with our generation.

Let us begin by accepting the word "suicide," rather than by seeking an alternative to it or by neologizing one of our own. Then we can simply discuss suicide without being fretfully self-conscious about our ordinary use of that word. In addition, we shall discuss a number of words that, although they are peripheral to "suicide," are nonetheless important to its understanding.

B

The Words

In its essence, diagnosis is a matter of definition. A clear diagnosis depends upon an unambiguous definition. "Suicide" is one of those words that seems to have both a core and a periphery. For most of us the core would seem to be unambiguous enough, almost self-evident. Surely "suicide" is one of those patently self-evident terms, the definition of which, it is felt, need not detain a thoughtful mind for even a moment. Every adult knows instinctively what he means by it: It is the act of taking one's life. But, in the very moment that one utters this simple formula one also appreciates that there is something more to the human drama of self-destruction than is contained in this simple view of it. And that "something more" is the periphery of any satisfactory definition. Are totally lethally intended acts which fail (e.g., shooting oneself in the head and surviving) suicide? Are non-lethal attempts on the life (e.g., ingesting a possibly lethal dose of barbiturates) suicidal? Are deleterious and inimical patterns of behavior (e.g., continued smoking by a person with acute emphysema) suicidal? Are deaths which have been ordered by others or deaths under desperation (e.g., Cato's response to Caligula's requesting his death, or the deaths on Masada or in Jonestown) suicide? All these questions and more constitute the indispensable periphery of the definition of suicide.

Some further thoughts: We know that diagnosis (and in this sense, definition) have an interactional quality. The very attribution of a diagnosis (especially a "label") may serve in some mysterious way to change or modify the person and behavior which it seeks to identify. The appellations "homosexual," "psychopathic," "feeble minded," "schizophrenic," or "suicidal" are not without their reciprocating effects. (The Heisenberg Principle is ever at work in our clinical activities.)

On the other hand, it is true that unlike many other diagnoses—some mentioned above—suicide has a postdictive clear-cut criterion; there is, so to speak, a smoking gun. Operationally, suicide is defined as: dead person—hole in head—gun in hand—note on desk. (The suicide note is not a necessary part of this definition.)

In any comprehensive suicidology, it is important to speculate about the date of the origin of the key word; specifically, why did the word "suicide" not appear until about the mid-1600s, and why then? In this etymological sense, it was not possible, before about 1635, to commit suicide. One could, of course, do harm to oneself, starve oneself to death, throw oneself upon one's sword or off one's roof or into one's well—but one could not "commit suicide." The word, and with it the basic concept of suicide, did not exist.

R. D. Romanyshyn in *Psychological Life: From Science to Metaphor* (1982) argues, persuasively I think, that the human heart did not *beat* until 1628, that is, not until William Harvey described the heart as a pump. Of course, ears had been put to chests for centuries and the heart's action was listened to, but it was heard as thumping or murmuring or sighing or as a living organ. However, it was not until Harvey described that organ as a divided heart—a "right heart" from which blood flows into the lungs through the pulmonary artery, and a "left heart" which moves the oxygenated blood from the lungs through the body—that the heart was seen as a pump, and its sounds heard as a beat.

Harvey's pronouncements are even more impressive when we know that he proposed this radical idea without having observed the capillaries. The empirical evidence for the missing link between the outgoing arteries and the returning veins, which was correctly hypothesized by Harvey, was supplied only four years after his death by Malpighi. But they *had* to be there; their existence was inexorably implied by Harvey's carefully reasoned explanation.

All these discoveries in the human body were given their intellectual permissiveness by a new view of the larger world. Harvey could not have posited a new kind of function for a pump-organ (against all the mysticism that existed about the heart) within a living body if he had not been surrounded by changes in scientific thinking. He was assisted in some way by the insights of Copernicus and the observations of Galileo about a "moving" world, and by the turn from the medieval world of blind faith to the renaissance world of direct observation and inductive logic (exemplified by Sir Francis Bacon's *Novum Organum*).

Romanyshyn (1982) muses and explains (pp. 111–112):

> This blood's movement in space is a new concern which places the Harveian heart in the same tradition as the Copernican earth and the falling bodies of Galileo. By 1616, therefore, the heart which moved as recently as a living organism now has motion as a pump. What could not be seen in 1603 is seen in 1616. In that brief period human existence and the world have changed. Here, again, how are we to understand this change?

> An answer may be found in an event which occurs in 1610. In that year Galileo turns his telescope toward the moon and confirms the Copernican vision. But this confirmation is more than a piece of empirical evidence. It is also and more importantly psychological confirmation. With his telescope Galileo *sees* . . . the surface of the moon which *reflects* the Copernican earth. Through the telescopic observation of the moon the Copernican earth becomes a psychological reality. . . . One can now image a moving earth.

> The Copernican earth appears in 1543, the same year that living human body becomes defined from the side of the corpse. That corpse which lies on Vesalius' dissecting table inhabits the Copernican earth. The moving earth and the human corpse belong together. One is the reflection of the other. Hence Galileo's telescope also makes the corpse a believable reality, a new psychological reality.

And Harvey's mechanical heart animates that corpse . . . to "dwell" on the moving earth. . . .

What cannot happen in 1603 happened in 1616 because in that interval human existence changes. In that interval the early stirrings of modern science in the previous two centuries become a world. A resurrected corpse animated by a mechanical heart and occupying a moving earth becomes psychologically real. An answer to the question of why the pumping heart appears in the seventeenth century (1610–1628) can now be given: it appears because at that time the pumping heart becomes a psychological reality reflected through a new earth and a new body.

It is the paradox of the seventeenth century that the same new psychological realities which permitted and produced the beating heart also permitted and produced "suicide"—for suicide, like the pumping heart, required a secular view of the world in order to come into psychological existence.

In the medieval world, a tenacious belief in God—and in heaven, hell, spirits, goblins, witches, and the immortal soul— was omnipresent. That belief was at the center of the warp and woof of everyman's psychological reality. With this view of the world, and of the universe, it was simply not possible to extinguish oneself forever. One could certainly drown oneself or hang oneself or exsanguinate oneself, but one's immortal soul would then transmigrate to some other existence; perhaps, if one sinfully took one's mortal life, to purgatory or even to hell. But the essence lived on. That was the human condition and the human fate.

But if the sun were the center of our universe; if the heart were merely a pump, if the world were a physical thing (the 1600s were two centuries away from being ready for Darwin's biology and Freud's psychology); if there were no god; if there were no immortal soul; if this life was all there is—then one could truly end it; then one could kill the self; then, and only then, one could commit suicide. The time was ripe. The *zeitgeist* supported this new concept and this new word, this new psychological reality. It was then logical to think of "suicide."

No word can be invented before its time. In general, feelings and actions (especially tabooed ones) run ahead of conventional vocabulary, and it is the self-appointed task of the wordsmiths to bridge these anachronistic gaps. Until they do, the gaps are covered by arches of euphemisms, circumlocutions and outright avoidances. A time of rapid "social change" is a time of dramatic linguistic change, and vice versa. The current "sexual revolution," for example, is as much a radical change in what topics and themes, what *words* can appear in the home-delivered newspaper and on the television screen, as in the patterns of behaviors which they report and reciprocally reinforce. The linguist, David Daube (1972) writes:

> ... the history of the word "suicide;"—and a strange one it is, mirroring the flow of civilizations and ideologies as well as the vagaries of the fate and fame of individual authors.

The surprising fact for many people about "suicide" is that it is a fairly recent word. According to *The Oxford English Dictionary*, the word was first used in 1651 by Walter Charleton when he said, interestingly enough,

> To vindicate one's self from ... inevitably Calamity, by Sui-cide is not ... a Crime.

The exact date of its first use is open to some question. Edward Phillips in the 1662 edition of his dictionary, *A New World in Words*, claimed invention of the word: "One barbarous word I shall produce, which is suicide." Curiously enough he does not derive it from the death of oneself but says it "should be derived from 'a sow' ... since it is a swinish part for a man to kill himself."

The British poetry critic Alfred Alvaraz in 1971 claimed that he found the word was used even earlier (in Sir Thomas Browne's *Religio Medici*, written in 1635 and published in 1642), in the following passage: "Herein are they not extreme that can allow a man to be his own ᴀꜱꜱᴀꜱꜱɪɴ and so highly extoll the end by suicide of Cato."

To understand the word "suicide" we must understand something of our language itself. We deal now only with Indo-European languages, or Standard Average European (SAE)—not Japanese or Urdu or Arabic or Eskimo. I depend here, in this paragraph, on the definitive work about the linguistics of suicide by David Daube (1972/1977). English, as he says, has genuinely separate words for loving and dressing, but not for loving oneself, dressing oneself, or killing oneself. Suicide is dying or killing, but with a twist, where oneself is the object. We ordinarily think of killing someone else. I quote from Daube (1977):

> It is necessary here to draw attention to a fundamental phenomenon: In the case of an act, as distinguished from an object, the verb regularly comes first and the noun later, if at all. People are said "to think," "feel," "speak," "dominate," "buy," "sell," long before these things are turned into "thought," "feeling," "speech," "domination," "a buy," "a sale." The emergence of the noun betokens a decisive advance in abstraction, systemization, institutionalization. "To state," "to deny," "to accuse," "to justify"—these are verbs predicting something about the subject of the sentence. Once the nouns "statement," "denial," "accusation," "justification," are formed, the activity itself has become the subject, to be focused upon; it is established, "substantivised." Whoever first went beyond "to bear" to "birth," or beyond "to die" (*meth* in Hebrew, *thneisko* in Greek, *morior* in Latin) to "death" (*maweth, thanatos, mors*) made no small contribution to the world of mind, for better or for worse.

Many of these steps in the development of our language—the birth of the verb and the accession of the noun—occurred over rather recent centuries: "to deny" in the fourteenth century, "denial" in the sixteenth; "to state" in the sixteenth, "statement" in the eighteenth. "To suicide"—probably not a legitimate verb in any case—or "to commit suicide" comes in, as we know, rather late, only in the seventeenth century. Daube says that, "In the matter of sui-

cide, impressively, there seems to have been an unbreachable barrier
[and] one can only speculate about the reasons for this slowness."

In the meantime there were Greek and Latin phrases to convey
the fact (from Daube): *haireo thanaton*, to seize death; *lambano
thanaton*, to grasp death; *katalyo bioton*, to break up life; *teleutao
bion*, to end life; *aporregnymi bion*, to break off life; *apallassomai
bion*, to be delivered from life; *apallassein heauton*, to deliver oneself; *ekleipo hoaos*, to leave the light; *hekon eis haidou erchomai*, to
go voluntarily to Hades; *biazesthai heauton*, to do violence to oneself; *pheugo to zen*, to flee living; *anairein heauton*, to carry oneself
off; *katergazesthai heauton*, to get through with oneself; *diachras-
thai heauton*, to consume onself; *analiskomai*, to dispose of oneself;
hekousios apothneisko, to die voluntarily; *kteiein (apoktenein,
katakeinein) heauton*, to kill oneself; *diaphtheirein heauton*, to destroy oneself; *ekpodon poiein heauton*, to get oneself out of the way;
autocheiria, an act with one's own hand; *authentes*, self-acting (au-
thentic); *autocheri sphagei*, by slaughter with his own hand;
biaiothanatos, dying by violence.

There were also a number of Latin phrases: *sibi mortem con-
sciercere*, to procure one's own death; *vim ibi inferre*, to cause violence to oneself; *sui manu cadere*, to fall by one's own hand; and
even a phrase, *vulnero me ut moriar*, to wound oneself in order to
die, which refers to a suicide attempt that did not result in death.

Hidden within Burton's *Anatomy of Melancholy* (1652) is a
baker's dozen phrases that are meant to convey what we today call
suicide. They include: To procure their own death; to free themselves from grievances; to offer violence unto themselves; to fall by
one's own hand; to let himself free with his own hands; to make
away with themselves; to execute themselves; to put an end to themselves; to dispatch themselves; to take death into their own hands; to
precipitate themselves; to die voluntarily; to kill themselves. In all
these phrases from Burton the general meaning seems clear enough:
The individuals had themselves ended their own lives.

Voltaire, in *Candide* (1758), perspicaciously described individuals
who committed suicide as those "who voluntarily put an end to their
misery." It is a description very close to our modern understanding.

A study could be done on the changed views over the centuries toward what we now call "suicide." Indeed, one small study might be done of the Lucretia–Pelagia legend. The essence of that story is of a woman who kills herself either after she has been raped or in order to preserve her chastity. Ovid (43 B.C.–18 A.D.) and Livy (59 B.C.–17 A.D.) wrote on the rape of Lucretia. Lucretia, the wife of Lucius Tarquinius Collatinus, was raped by Sextus Tarquinius, who was a self-invited guest in her house while her husband was away at war. She subsequently informed her father and husband and, having extracted an oath of revenge from them, stabbed herself to death. The ensuing actions drove out the Roman monarchy and established a republic (519 B.C.).

Saint Pelagia (circa 304) was a 15 year old Christian girl who lived in Antioch during the persecution of Christians by Diocletian. When soldiers came to her home to seize her, she eluded them and "in order to avoid outrage," she threw herself to her death from the housetop. She is venerated by Catholics as a maiden martyr (Attwater, 1965).

Chaucer used the same general theme in *The Legend of Good Women* (1386); so did Daniel in *The Complaint of Rosamond* (1592). Shakespeare's lengthy poem, *The Rape of Lucrece* (1594), is graphic with details of the struggle, the heinous act, and the self-imposed death. It is an Elizabethan textbook on the folkways regarding high-caste, self-inflicted death. Here is the death stanza:

> *Even here she sheathed in her harmless breast*
> *A harmful knife, that hence her soul unsheathed:*
> *That blow did bail it from the deep unrest*
> *Of that polluted prison where it breathed:*
> *Her contrite sighs unto the clouds bequeathed*
> *Her winged sprite, and through her wounds did fly*
> *Life's lasting date from cancell'd destiny.*

In our century there is another saint related to this issue of death before dishonor. Saint Maria Coretti was born in Italy near Ancona in 1890 and died near Nettuno in 1902. She was the daughter of a poor peasant family, known for her cheerful unselfishness and religious disposition. When she was 12 she began to be pestered by the overtures of a young man, whom she repulsed. Eventually he attempted to ravish her, threatening to kill her if she resisted. When she did so, he stabbed her numerous times and she died the next day. Maria was canonized in 1950.

The difference between self-killing or self-slaughter (and all the circumlocutions and phrases) on the one hand, and "suicide," on the other, may seem to be a small one, but it is not a trivial distinction. It is a significant, albeit subtle difference, reflecting a major shift in man's relationship to himself and to his God—and to his disavowal of gods—and of his role in his own ultimate fate. It is as old as history that a man could destroy himself by ruining his reputation and his career, or take his own life; but it was a seventeenth century insight and invention that a man could forever terminate his not-so-immortal existence and do more than inimical things to himself. He could—dispensing with the notion of soul and hereafter—for the first time, "commit suicide."

It follows, as a subtlety, that of all those today who take their own lives, only those who do not believe in a hereafter,—in short, only those who believe that this life is the only life—commit suicide. All the others are playing Pascal's "Bet Situation" (betting on the existence of God) and, while undoubtedly doing lethal harm unto themselves, are banking on a (hopefully benign) transmigration of their immortal souls to another life.

Here, at the outset of our joint suicidological journey, I shall cite my previous definition of suicide (from the 1973 edition of the *Encyclopaedia Britannica*). It is not the definition we shall rest with, but it will suffice for a start: *Suicide is the human act of self-inflicted, self-intentioned cessation.* It is a pithy definition with several inherent puzzlements that require clarification.

One might make a quick tour of twentieth century definitions of suicide, fudging temporally just a little bit and beginning with Durkheim (1897). Durkheim's definition:

We may then say conclusively: The term suicide is applied to all cases of death resulting directly or indirectly from a positive or negative act of the victim himself which he knows will produce this result. (*Nous disons donc définitivement: On appelle suicide tout cas de mort qui resulte directement ou indirectement d'un acte positif ou negatif, accompli par la victime elle-même savait devoir produire ce resultat.*)

An exigesis, paring, and dissection of this definition took Jack Douglas (1967) almost 400 pages to accomplish. Others, students of Durkheim and neo-Durkheimians—including Halbwachs (1930), Achille-Delmas (1932), Deshaies (1947), Baechler (1975/1979) and Maris (1981)—have all wrestled with the topic of the definition of suicide without anyone (to be straightforward about it) pinning the idea to the conceptual mat long enough for a suicidological referee to call a clear win.

In the United States there is a current spate of definitions of suicide from the philosophical point of view. This activity stems from a deeper interest in a whole series of ethical problems relating to suicide (Battin, 1982; Battin & Mayo, 1980; Battin & Maris, 1983). Much of the focus on the ethical issues in suicide reflects changes and developments in the last quarter century in organ transplants, attitudes toward assisted death of the ill (organizations like EXIT and Hemlock), and the swirling debates about active and passive euthanasia. There are many new currents in the thanatological wind.

In this present setting we can omit the elaborate discussions which typically accompany these definitions of a suicide by contemporary philosophically minded writers and simply present some examples (Mayo, 1983). R. G. Frey (1980) believes that a suicide is a death which occurs intentionally as a result of a person's "knowingly and willingly placing himself in perilous circumstances." This includes standing in front of a train, wandering out into a blizzard, manipulating another into killing one, and heroic and altruistic acts such as a soldier throwing himself on a live grenade.

Tom Beauchamp (1978) wants to include under suicide both heroic acts of self-sacrifice as well as self-willed deaths that involve the refusal of potentially life-saving medical treatment. His complex definition of suicide is this:

An act is suicide if a person intentionally brings about his or her own death in circumstances where others do not coerce him or her to action, except in those cases where death is caused by conditions not specifically arranged by the agent for the purpose of bringing about his or her own death.

Peter Windt (1980), in the spirit of Wittgenstein (believing that the best one can do with certain complicated concepts is to indicate a list of criteria for that concept's application) argues that suicide is a death that is "reflexive," that is, a person must either kill himself or get himself killed or let himself be killed. In addition, suicide must be a reflexive death in which the deceased caused the death by his actions or behavior; wanted, desired, or wished for the death; intended, chose, decided, or willed to die; knew that death would result from his behavior; and was responsible for his death.

Glenn Graber (1981) focuses on the sense in which a suicide "intends" his own death and asserts:

Suicide is defined as doing something that results in one's death in the way that was planned, either from the intention of ending one's life or the intention to bring about some other state of affairs (such as relief from pain) that one thinks it certain or highly probably can be achieved only by means of death.

This definition would exclude, according to Graber, a spy who resists divulging information, knowing that such resistance will mean death, but where death is not really desired at all—neither as an end in itself nor as a means to an end.

In their own setting these philosophical definitions are explicated in a scholarly way but they suffer from intellectual overkill. An excellent discussion of the problem of definition was made by Jack Douglas (1967). He outlines the fundamental dimensions of meanings that are required in the formal definition of suicide. He indicates these dimensions as follows:

1. The *initiation* of an act that leads to the death of the initiator.

2. The willing of an *act* that leads to the death of the willer.

3. The willing of self-destruction.

4 The loss of will.

5. The *motivation to be dead* (*or to die*) which leads to the initiation of an act that leads to the death of the initiator.

6. The *knowledge* of the actor that actions he initiates tend to produce the objective state of death.

I shall return later to the topic of definition of suicide. It is central to any efforts toward a comprehensive discussion of therapy and response. That is why it should be done operationally, sensibly, and, as I see it, preferably from a clinical point of view.

In additional to the word "suicide," other closely related words need similar clarification. They are discussed below.

ATTEMPTED SUICIDE

In general it was believed that two "populations" (those who commit suicide and those who attempt suicide) are essentially separate, made up of different individuals (Stengel, 1964/1974). In a sense the words "attempt suicide" are a contradiction in terms. Strictly speaking, a suicide attempt should refer only to those who sought to commit suicide and fortuitously survived. Over a 10 year period, the overlap of the percentage of individuals who commit suicide with those who *previously* attempted suicide is 40%, whereas the overlap of those who attempt suicide and those who *subsequently* commit it is about 5% (Maris, 1981). To attempt suicide with less than total lethality might be called "quasi-suicide" except that this term has the unfortunate connotation that such persons are malingerers or are simply seeking attention, and thus do not merit our full professional and sympathetic response. Any event which uses a suicidal modality is a genuine psychological crisis, even though it might not, under strict semantic rules, be called a "suicidal" event.

Attempted suicide should be used only for those events in which there has been a failure of a conscious effort to end the life. Those events are attempted suicides. All others—self-mutilations, excessive dosage of drugs, and other events of this ilk—are, properly speaking, "quasi-suicidal attempts" or probably, most accurately, "non-suicidal attempts." The English speak of *parasuicide* to describe these events. I shall use this term.

Richard Fox, an English psychiatrist and suicidologist, writes (1976):

> The fact that deliberately self-injuring behavior has increased strikingly since WW II underlines the claims by Stengel (1964) that suicides and attempted suicides are different groups ... Overdosing is the overwhelmingly predominant method of self-injury in Britain and is also the method permitting discovery in time and a second chance, Stengel's "gamble with death." In the writer's view, the majority represent semi-suicidal cries for help; conscious or unconscious manipulations; unplanned, impulsive acts (the motive for which even the victim is sometimes unable to explain later); or just the wish to "opt out" for a while, for example, the overstressed young housewife whose children are out of hand and whose husband is unhelpful. Less common cases are the confused elderly on multiple medications, the malingerer who claims to have overdosed in order to escape into the hospital, and the person who has not overdosed but appears drowsy and sedated and so is wrongly thought to have done so. *There are clear virtues to the use of terms other than "attempted suicide" for cases that are not. Parasuicide is the term most canvassed in Europe and researchers such as Kreitman (1969) now use no other.*

In a comparable fashion, I would hold that the words "attempted murder" should be limited to those events where homicidal death was intended, but where something went awry or the intended victim lived. Shooting at someone with the intention to miss in order only to scare him or to "shake him up" is an untoward act, but it is not attempted murder. We have words like first degree murder, second degree murder and manslaughter to reflect nuances of intention to commit homicide. In suicide, the current levels are committed suicide, attempted suicide, and threatened suicide, where attempts and threats, in fact, range from zero lethality to full lethality. One can attempt to feign, attempt to attempt, attempt to commit—and all of these events must come under the same term. A similar situation exists with threats.

On this account alone we should do two things:

1   Limit the term "suicide" to acts of committed suicide (or efforts or attempts to be dead by suicide). This means that the discussion in this book of suicide is not a discussion of attempted suicide as ordinarily understood. For me, only those individuals who have "committed suicide" *and* fortuitously survived (see my accounts of the two young women—one of whom immolated herself, the other jumped from a high balcony—in *Voices of Death* [1980/1982]) can legitimately be called "attempted suicide." An individual who holds a fully loaded gun to his temple and pulls the trigger but the gun does not fire, can legitimately be said to have attempted suicide—or to have committed suicide and fortuitously survived. All other events (which involve "suicidal" modalities) where the end goal is not cessation (total and irreversible death) should more accurately be called, not attempted suicides, but "quasi-suicidal efforts." A quasi-suicidal effort is not a pseudo-suicidal event; rather, it represents a genuine psychological crisis and a focused effort to resolve some intense (usually dyadic) difficulty, and it should be treated with compassion and understanding. It should not, for this account, be confused with a suicide attempt.

I believe we need a separate term of self-inflicted sub-lethal acts. Instead of saying "attempted suicide," as we now ordinarily use it for non-lethal acts, we ought to say, more accurately and following the British, that an individual who has done a non-lethal, self-inflicted, injurious, suicide-like act has committed *parasuicide*.

In the 1960s the noble Erwin Stengel, a noted psychiatrist, wrote a monograph entitled *Suicide and Attempted Suicide*. He is not clear exactly to what extent groups of individuals who commit suicide and groups who attempt suicide are different populations. What is obviously clear is that the two *acts* are radically different. It is not different demographic populations with which we must deal; rather, it is different *psychological* populations. In a sense there is no point in talking about populations at all. There is more point in talking about the psychological characteristics of the actor rather than about "people." Suicidal acts are committed by suicidal individuals and parasuicidal acts are committed by parasuicidal individuals. Stengel was right in distinguishing between committed and attempted suicide and asserting that they are essentially separate events. He did not, however, go far enough in explicating the different psychological characteristics of individuals who are the principal actors in these two different dramas.

2.   We should also evaluate each "suicidal" event on a continuum (say, from 1 to 9) of *lethality*. The term "suicide," "committed suicide," or "attempted suicide" should be reserved only for those events in which the lethality is reasonably judged to be high—eight or nine. This may depend on the method used (shooting, jumping, hanging, immolating), or where cutting or barbiturates are the method used, on the risk to rescue ratio (Weisman, 1974). A suicide attempt is an event where the risk of death is extremely high and the probability of rescue or intervention is extremely low. Shooting a gun into oneself or jumping off a high place present few theoretical problems for this paradigm; the difficulties occur mostly in relation to barbiturates. The rule is: It's not what you do, it's the way that you do it. A psychological autopsy (or even a close look at the details of the scenario of the act) will usually disclose whether the effort was (a) on the life of the subject, or (b) one in which there was some usurpation of the word "suicide" in an instance in which a lethal outcome was not clearly in the mind of the chief protagonist.

SUBINTENTIONED DEATH AND INDIRECT SUICIDE

No thoughtful person can look about the world and fail to notice inimical and covertly self-destructive behaviors in others—and even in himself. We often wish that we could somehow effect changes in the living patterns of our loved ones and our friends, especially those behaviors which seem obviously to nibble at the length and the quality of their lives. These behaviors include excessive smoking, drug ingestion, taking risks, disregard of the canons of ordinate prudence and common sense, and those other "stupidities" of life that seem to unnecessarily demean or truncate life, or even to put life at risk. And when such persons die—whether "accidentally" or "having gotten themselves murdered" or died "unnecessarily early" of natural causes—we muse (even though their death certificates may read Accident, Homicide, or Natural) that they themselves played some psychological role in effecting both the date and manner of their own deaths. The notion of subintentioned deaths (Shneidman, 1973, 1981) was meant to describe these deaths—perhaps a *majority* of all deaths in which the decedent has played a covert, partial, latent, unconscious role in hastening his own death. What is implied here is a three fold classification of all deaths: intentioned suicides, unintentioned (many natural, accidental, and homicidal) deaths and subintentioned (many natural and some accidental and homicidal) deaths. This tripartite classification is offered in addition to the traditional four-part classification of the modes of death—what I have acronymically called the NASH categories of death: natural, accidental, suicidal, and homicidal. *Deaths of Man* (1973/1983) contains a history of the death certificate and of the development of the NASH categories, especially since the time of John Graunt and his observations of the London bills of mortality in 1662.

Karl Menninger, in his enormously impactful book *Man Against Himself* (1938), wrote persuasively about different kinds of unconsciously touched deaths which he called chronic, focal, and organic suicides (including such behaviors as aestheticism, addiction, and polysurgery). More recently Norman Farberow (1980) edited a book on "indirect suicide" which encompasses such topics as drug abuse, alcohol abuse, obesity, drunk driving, and high-risk sports. My own view is that all of these deleterious outcomes are more meaningfully called *subintentioned deaths* than one or another kind of suicide. If we use the word suicidal in the metaphoric (almost poetic) sense of anything which jeopardizes health or well-being, we tend to rob the word of its more powerful and potentially more accurate meanings. We cannot gainsay the important semantic and psychological difference between an emphysemic person who continues to smoke and expires in a hospital bed having been a more-or-less intractable patient, and an individual in relatively good physical health who writes a note and shoots a bullet through his head. All this is to say that this book is about suicide, conscientiously defined. We shall not put out of our mind the vastly larger area of subintentioned deaths, but that is not the topic of our present efforts.

C

Classifications and Approaches

In the professional literature on suicide the most frequently quoted classification of suicide is that of Emile Durkheim from *Le Suicide*. The durability of this schemata is something which itself merits a special study in the sociology of knowledge. Considering that it was published in 1897 (although not generally available in English until 1951); considering further that Durkheim's primary interest was not specifically the topic of suicide but rather the explication of his then-new sociological method (he might have done his study equally well, say, on alcoholism or prostitution); and considering that his classification of types of suicides has relatively little applicability or power for the active clinician who sees self-destructive people—considering all these, its vitality is surprising. It is a classification scheme that is used and reused so often in textbooks and the technical literature that sometimes there seem to be almost no alternatives.

Le Suicide established a model for sociological investigations of suicide. There have been many subsequent studies of this genre. The monographs and books by Cavan on suicide in Chicago (1928), of Schmid on suicide in Seattle (1928) and Minneapolis (1939), of Sainsbury of suicide in London (1955), of Shneidman and Farberow in Los Angeles (1961) and of Dublin and Bunzel (1933), and of Henry and Short (1954) on suicide in the United

States, all fall within the sociological tradition. They each take a plot of ground, a city, or a country and figuratively or literally reproduce its map several times to show its socially shady (and topographically shaded) areas and their differential relationships to suicide rates.

According to Durkheim, suicide is the result of society's strength or weakness of control over the individual. He posited four basic types of suicide, each a result of man's relationship to his society. In one type, the *altruistic* suicide is literally required by society. Here, the customs or rules of the group demand suicide under certain circumstances. Hara-kiri (in feudal Japan) and suttee (in pre-colonial India) are examples of altruistic suicides. In such instances the person seemed almost boxed in by the culture. Under those circumstances, self-inflicted death was honorable; continuing to live would be ignominious. Society dictated their action and, as individuals, they were not strong enough to defy custom.

Most suicides in the United States would be called *egoistic* by Durkheim. Contrary to the circumstances of an altruistic suicide, egoistic suicides occur when an individual's ties to his community are too few or too tenuous. In this case, demands to live do not reach him. Thus, proportionately, more individuals, especially men who are on their own, compared with men who are married or who are church members, kill themselves.

Durkheim's third type of suicide is called *anomic*—from the word *anomie* which Durkheim may have developed himself—to describe that special kind of aloneness or estrangement that occurs when the accustomed relationship between an individual and his society is precipitously disrupted or shattered. The shocking, immediate loss of a job, of a close friend, or of a fortune is thought sufficient to expedite anomic suicides; or, conversely, poor men surprised by the disruption of a sudden wealth have also been shocked into anomic suicide.

A fourth type, *fatalistic* suicide, is suicide deriving from excessive regulation of the individual, where the individual has no personal freedom and no hope, as in the suicide of slaves, "with futures piteously blocked and passions violently choked by oppressive discipline," "very young husband, (or) the married woman who is childless." Admittedly, this type of suicide is rare.

If we move to 1967, Douglas, in his analysis of definitions of suicide, lists six fundamental dimensions of meanings. The key words are *initiation* of the act); the *act* (that leads to death); the *willing* (of self-destruction); the *loss* (of will); the *motivation* (to be dead); and the *knowledge* (of the death potential of the act).

In 1968, I suggested that all (committed) suicides be viewed as being of one of three types: egotic, dyadic, or ageneratic.

Egotic suicides are those in which the self-imposed death is the result, primarily, of an *intra-psychic* debate, disputation, struggle-in-the-mind, or dialogue within one's self, in the "congress of the mind." The impact of one's immediate environment, the presence of friends or loved ones, the existence, "out there" of group ties or sanctions all become secondary, distant perceptual "ground" as compared with the reality and urgency of the internal psychic debate. The dialogue is within the personality; it is a conflict of aspects of the self, within the ego. Such deaths can be seen as egocide or ego destruction; they are annihilations of the "self," of the personality, of the ego. At the time it happens, the individual is primarily "self-contained" and responds to the "voices" (not in the sense of hallucinatory voices) within him. This is what one sees in the extremely narrowed focus of attention, self-denigrating depression, and other situations where the suicide occurs without regard for anyone else including loved ones and significant others. Egotic suicides are essentially *psychological* in their nature.

Dyadic suicides are those in which the death relates primarily to the deep unfulfilled needs and wishes pertaining to the significant other—the partner in the important current dyad in the victim's life. These suicides are primarily *social* in their nature. Although suicide is always the act of a person and, in this sense, stems from within his mind, the dyadic suicide is essentially an interpersonal event. The cry to the heavens refers to the frustration, hate, anger, disappointment, shame, rage, guilt, impotence, and rejection, in relation to the other, to him or to her—either the real him or her or a symbolic (or even fantasied or fictional) person in life. The key lies in the undoing: "If only he (or she) would . . ." The dyadic suicidal act may reflect the victim's penance, bravado, revenge, plea, histrionics, punishment, gift, withdrawal, identification, disaffiliation, or whatever—but its arena is primarily interpersonal and its understanding (and thus its meaning) cannot occur outside the dyadic relationship.

Ageneratic suicides are those in which the self-inflicted death relates primarily to the individual's "falling out" of the procession of generations; his losing (or abrogating) his sense of membership in the march of generations and, in this sense, in the human race itself. This type of suicide relates to the Shakespearean notions of ages or eras within a human life span, and a period within a life in which an individual senses, at one level of consciousness or another, his "belonging" to a whole line of generations; fathers and grandfathers and great-grandfathers before him, and children and grandchildren and great-grandchildren after him.

This sense of belonging and place in the scheme of things, especially in the march of generations, is not only an aspect of middle and old age, but it is a comfort and characteristic of psychological maturity, at whatever age. To have no sense of serial belonging or to be an "isolate" is truly a lonely and comfortless position, for then one may, in that perspective, truly have little to live for. This kind of hermit is estranged not only from his contemporaries but, much more importantly, he is alienated from his ancestors and his descendants, from his inheritance and his bequests. He is without a sense of the majestic flow of the generations: He is ageneratic. Ageneratic suicides are primarily *sociological* in nature, relating as they do to familial, cultural, national, or group ties.

I must add that I now see things somewhat differently, as will be evident in this book. I now prefer to collapse these three rather clumsy categories to one—the egotic—and explicate the dimensions of that category.

In Jean Baechler's book *Suicides* (1979), he propounds four kinds of suicidal acts; or, to put it in his terms, suicidal acts among which four typical meanings (to the chief protagonist) can be distinguished. They are: escapist, aggressive, oblative, and ludic suicides.

An *escapist* suicide is one of flight or escape from a situation sensed by the subject to be intolerable. This can be because of a combination of felt emotions (e.g., shame, guilt, fear, worthlessness) or attendant to the loss of a central element of the individual's personality or way of life. There are two subtypes: flight and grief. The key word is "intolerable." To my mind, all suicides are of this type.

Aggressive suicides are of four subtypes: crime (involving another in one's death), vengeance (to create remorse or opprobrium), blackmail, and appeal ("informing one's friends and family that the subject is in danger"). I puzzle how these differ from the need to escape intolerable inner pain.

Oblative suicides, those of sacrifice or transfiguration are, says Baechler, "practically unknown in daily life." They relate vaguely to higher values or infinitely desired states. The topics of seppuku and the immolation of Buddhist monks would be subsumed under this category.

The fourth category is *ludic* suicides, which refer to proving oneself through the ordeal or the game. Baechler cites Roger Caillois' *Man, Play and Games* (1961) and one immediately thinks also of Johan Huizinga's *Homo Ludens: A Study of the Play Element in Culture* (1938). The relationship of play (carnivals, orgies, holidays, "unpluggings") to death and self-destruction is a fascinating topic on its own, whether or not it provides a reasonable separate taxonomic category for suicide.

Writing from what he calls a modified Kantian point of view, Thomas E. Hill, Jr. (1983), recognizing that, "Real life is admittedly more complex than any of our philosophic categories . . ." focuses attention on four specially defined types of suicide, as follows:

1. *Impulsive suicide* . . . is prompted by a temporarily intense, yet passing desire or emotion out of keeping with the more permanent character, preferences and emotional state of the agent. We need not suppose that he is "driven" or "blinded" or momentarily insane, but his act is not the sort that coheres with what he most wants and values over time. In calmer, more deliberate moments, he would wish that he would not respond as he did. . .

2. *Apathetic suicide.* Sometimes a suicide might result not so much from intense desire or emotion as from apathy. The problem is not overwhelming passion, but the absence of passion, lack of interest in what might be done or experienced in a continued life. One can imagine, for example, an extremely depressed person who simply does not care about the future . . . not intense shame, anger, fear, etc., but rather emptiness. . .

3. *Self-abasing suicide* . . . results from a sense of worthlessness or unworthiness, which expresses itself not in apathy, but rather in a desire to manifest self–contempt, to reject oneself, to 'put oneself down'. . . . One's life is seen as having a negative value . . . contemptible like a despised insect one wants to swat or turn away from in disgust. . .

4. *Hedonistic calculated suicide* . . . that is decided upon as a result of a certain sort of cost/benefit calculation. seeing that others will be unaffected by his decision (our simplifying hypothesis), the hedonistic calculator regards his choice as determined by his best estimate of the balance of pleasure and pain he expects to receive under each option.

In the same issue of the journal that contains Hill's article, the editor, Ronald Maris, states (1983):

Hill's typology of impulsive, apathetic, self-abusing, and hedonistic suicides, which deviate from some ideal rather than from others' interests or values or effects on others, is very far removed from real life self-destructive situations. I must confess that such classical Kantian typologies always leave me a little cold. Where is the relevance of such typologies to actual suicidal circumstances in which one has to decide to commit suicide or not? . . . Although it may not have been his objective, Hill's suicidal types do not correspond very well with actual suicides I have known.

Currently (in 1984), under the joint sponsorship of the American Medical Association and the American Psychiatric Association, there is an on–going study of 110 physician deaths by suicide and 110 matched non–suicidal physician deaths. One would hope that their extensive questionnaire—over 130 questions in a 58 page booklet—would reflect the current state of the art. The key question in that book, on the last page, reads as follows:

How do you classify this suicide?

1. Rational (to escape pain, etc.)
2. Reaction (following loss)
3. Vengeful (to punish someone else)
4. Manipulative (to thwart others' plans)
5. Psychotic (to fulfill a delusion)
6. Accidental: (reconsidered too late)

It is easy to see some holes in that one.

I submit that all these classifications, taken singly or together, have either an arbitrary, esoteric, or ad hoc quality to them. They do not seem impressively definitive. I know for a fact that the best known of them is of practically no use in the clinic, where the task is saving lives, where conceptualizations really count. In my several years at the Los Angeles Suicide Prevention Center—where I happily resided from its beginnings in the early 1950s until I left for NIMH in 1966—I never once heard my colleagues at the Center or the County Coroner, Dr. Theodore Curphey, refer to a suicidal death as altruistic, egoistic, or anomic, or in terms of any of the other classifications cited just above. True, none of these people was trained as a professional sociologist or philosopher, but every day we witness people not trained as psychoanalysts employing psychoanalytic language, sometimes quite effectively. None of the classifications of suicide that I know of has an urgent usefulness.

From all this I tentatively conclude that it may well be, if we are theoretically serious about suicide, that we do best not to concentrate on classification. That is precisely what I have suggested to myself: To eschew the attempt at taxonomy, and to do this for a very compelling reason. My belief, to use an anachronistic example, is that Linnaeus' perfect arrangement of all of Darwin's creatures is not an appropriate goal for a contemporary suicidologist. It is like trying to impose a biological screen on a variety of existential events. A suicidologist is essentially a personologist. The accuracies of other fields of science, like physics or chemistry, are not consistent with what we know today about the activities, conscious and unconscious, of the human mind. The human person is, of course, our legitimate subject matter. There is no point in achieving accuracy if one sacrifices relevance in the process. I am interested, as a clinical suicidologist and thanatologist, in what is useful and makes sense, not in what has specious accuracy simply for the sake of accuracy.

As we work our collective way toward a meaningful definition of suicide we need to touch briefly upon various contemporary *approaches* to the assessment, understanding, and treatment of suicidal phenomena. In a sense, a review of these approaches will tell us, operationally, what suicide *is* by informing us of the various vantage points from which it is currently regarded. This survey of contemporary approaches to suicide is all the more appropriate in that, by way of a preview, we can state that our definition of suicide will seek to reflect not only the multidisciplinary components of its current study, but also the multiple ingredients of its very nature.

1. *Theological.* Neither the Old nor the New Testament directly forbids suicide. In the Western World, the pervasive moral ideas about suicide are Christian, dating from the fourth century A.D., enunciated by St. Augustine (354–430) for essentially non–religious reasons. Historically, the excessive martyrdom of the early Christians frightened the church elders sufficiently for them to seek to introduce a serious deterrent. Augustine did this by relating suicide to sin. We now know that Augustine was not against suicide on chiefly theological grounds. He was primarily against the decimation of Christians by suicide and, even more narrowly, against the suicide by Christians only for reasons of martyrdom (or religious zealotry, fired by the hope of immediate martyred entrance into heaven). Sui-

cide by reason of physical or emotional suffering, old age, altruism toward others, personal honor, illness, and the like—in short, the very reasons with which 99.9% of the suicides committed nowadays are associated—were not the target of Augustine's writings (Battin, 1982).

But that is not the way it went historically. By 693 the Council of Toledo had proclaimed that an individual who attempted suicide was to be excommunicated from the Church. This view was elaborated by Saint Thomas Aquinas (1225–1274) who emphasized that suicide was a mortal sin in that it usurped God's power over man's life and death. By that time the notion of suicide as sin had taken firm hold and for hundreds of years the idea played, and continues to play, an important part in Western man's view of self-destruction.

That Augustine's condemnations of suicide rested largely on tactical reasons—to keep up the numbers of his own group—has been largely forgotten. The Christian injunctions against suicide are seen historically as resting on a respect for life (especially the life of the soul in the hereafter) and as being a more humane reaction to the way in which life was regarded by, say, the Romans. But even those motivations by the Church seem to have gone awry in that the effects were excessive and counterproductive, and resulted in degrading, defaming, and persecuting individuals who had attempted suicide, committed suicide, or were survivors whom the Church had originally claimed to succor. It is sobering to contemplate that for hundreds of years what had appeared to be God's word about suicide, had begun as a fifth century political–tactical ploy further distorted by a twist in logic condemning those it was originally meant to protect.

2. *Philosophical.* Philosopher Jacques Choron (1972) outlined the position of the major Western philosophers in relation to death and suicide. In general, the philosophers of suicide never meant their written speculations to be prescriptions for action but simply to reflect their own inner intellectual debates. The following are some philosophers who have touched upon the topic of suicide: Pythagorus, Plato, Aristotle, Socrates, Seneca, Epictetus, Montaigne,

Descartes, Spinoza, Voltaire, Montesquieu, Rousseau, Hume, Kant, Schopenhauer, Nietzsche, Kierkegaard, Camus.

In classical Rome, during the centuries just before the Christian era, life was held rather cheaply and suicide was viewed either neutrally or even positively. The Roman Stoic Seneca said:

> Living is not good, but living well. The wise man, therefore, lives as well as he should, not as long as he can. . . . He will always think of life in terms of quality not quantity.

The French philosopher Jean-Jacques Rousseau (1712–1778), by emphasizing the natural state of man, transferred the sin (blame) from man to society, stating that man is generally good and innocent and that it is society that makes him bad. David Hume (1711–1776) was one of the first major Western philosophers to discuss suicide in the absence of the concept of sin. His famous essay "On Suicide," was published in 1777 (a year after his death) and was promptly suppressed. It refutes the view that suicide is a crime; it does so by arguing that suicide is not a transgression of our duties to God, to our fellow citizens or to ourselves: ". . . prudence and courage should engage us to rid ourselves at once of existence when it becomes a burden."

The existential philosophers of our own century—Kierkegaard, Jaspers, Camus, Sartre, Heidegger—have made the meaninglessness of life (and the place of suicide) a central topic. Camus begins *The Myth of Sisyphus* by saying that the topic of suicide is the central problem of philosophy.

3. *Demographic.*   The demographic approach relates to various statistics on suicide. The medieval English coroners (the word coroner means the custodian of the Crown's pleas) began to keep "rolls," that is, documents that incorporated death (and birth) records. From the eleventh century on, whether or not the property of a deceased individual was to be kept by the heirs or had to be forfeited to the Crown depended on whether or not the death was judged (by the coroner) to be an act or a felony. Suicide was the latter, a felony against the self (*felo de se*); thus the way in

which a death was certified was of enormous importance to the survivors.

In 1660, John Graunt, a tradesman, published a small book of observations on the London bills of mortality (a listing of all deaths) that was to have great social and medical significance. Graunt devised categories of information—sex, locale, type of death—and made mortality tables. He was the first to demonstrate that regularities could be found in mortality phenomena and that these regularities could be used by the government in making policy.

In 1741, the science of statistics, as it is known today, came into existence with the work of a Prussian clergyman, Johann Sussmilch. He called his efforts "political arithmetic;" it was what we now call vital statistics. From his studies came the laws of large numbers, which permitted long-range planning (i.e., the need for food and supplies based on the size of the population) in Europe as well as in the American colonies. Recently, Cassedy (1969), who wrote about colonial America, said that Sussmilch's "exhaustive analysis of vital data from church registers . . . became the ultimate scientific demonstration of the regularity of God's demographic laws." The traditions about statistics on suicide stem from Graunt and Sussmilch.

Currently, in the United States, the suicide rate is 12.6 per 100,000 people. It ranks as one of the 10 leading causes of adult deaths. Suicide rates gradually rise during adolescence, increase sharply in early adulthood, and parallel advancing age up to the age bracket 75 to 84, when it reaches a rate of 27.9 suicides per 100,000. Male suicides outnumber female suicides at a ratio of two to one. More whites than non-whites commit suicide. Suicide is more prevalent among the single, widowed, separated, and divorced.

The suicide rate in young people, ages 15 to 24, has risen sharply since the 1950s, from 4.2 in 1954 to 10.9 in 1974. The suicide rate for non-whites has also increased significantly. Data indicate that in the 35 years since 1946, the suicide rate of blacks has doubled, a rise attributed to increased opportunities for mobility and the attendant frustrations, role shifts, and social stresses. Since 1960 suicide has increased significantly for women. The ratio of men to women narrowed from 4 to 1 to 2 to 1.

Demographers of suicide in this century include especially Louis I. Dublin on suicide in the United States (1963) and Peter Sainsbury on suicide in London (1955). International statistics have been given by the World Health Organization (1968).

4. *Sociological.* Emile Durkheim's giant book, *Le Suicide* (1897) demonstrated the power of the sociological approach. As a result of his analysis of French data on suicide, Durkheim proposed four kinds of suicides, all of them emphasizing the strength or weakness of the person's relationships or ties to society. "Altruistic" suicides are literally required by society: "Egoistic" suicides occur when the individual has too few ties with his community; "Anomic" suicides are those that occur when the accustomed relationship between an individual and his society is suddenly shattered; and "Fatalistic" suicides derive from excessive regulation.

For years after Durkheim, sociologists have not made major changes in his theory. Henry and Short (1954) added the concept of internal (superego) restraints to that of Durkheim's external restraint, and Gibbs and Martin (1964) sought to operationalize Durkheim's concept of social integration.

In a major break with Durkheim, sociologist Jack Douglas (1967) pointed out that the social meanings of suicide vary greatly and that the more socially integrated a group is, the more effective it may be in disguising suicide. Further, Douglas suggested that social reactions to stigmatizing behaviors can themselves become a part of the etiology of the very actions the group seeks to control.

Maris (1981) believes that a systematic theory of suicide should be composed of at least four broad categories of variables: those concerning the person, the social context, the biological factors, and "temporality," oftentimes involving "suicidal careers."

5. *Psychodynamic.* As Durkheim detailed the sociology of suicide, so Sigmund Freud fathered the psychological explanations of suicide (Friedman, 1967). To him, suicide was essentially within the mind. The major psychoanalytical position on suicide was that it represented unconscious hostility directed toward the introjected (ambivalently viewed) love object. Psychodynamically, suicide was seen as murder in the 180th degree.

Karl Menninger, in his important book, *Man Against Himself* (1938), delineates the psychodynamics of hostility and asserts that the drives in suicide are made up of three items. (a) the wish to kill; (b) the wish to be killed; and (c) the wish to die.

Gregory Zilboorg (1937) refined this psychoanalytical hypothesis and stated that every suicidal case contained not only unconscious hostility but also an unusual lack of capacity to love others. He extended the concern solely from intrapsychic dynamics to include the external world, specifically in the role of a broken home in suicidal proneness.

In an important exegesis of Freud's thoughts on suicide, Robert E. Litman (1967, 1970) traces the development of those thoughts from 1881 to 1939. It is evident from Litman's analysis that there is more to the psychodynamics of suicide than hostility. These factors include several emotional states (i.e., rage, guilt, anxiety, dependency) as well as a great number of specifically predisposing conditions. Feelings of abandonment and particularly of helplessness and hopelessness are important.

A further word about the locus of blame: The early Christians made suicide a personal sin, Rousseau transferred sin from man to society, Hume tried to decriminalize suicide entirely, Durkheim focused on societies' inimical effects on people, and Freud—eschewing both the notions of sin and crime—gave suicide back to man but put the locus of action in man's unconscious mind.

6. *Psychological.* The psychological approach can be distinguished from the psychodynamic approach in that it does not posit a set of dynamics or a universal unconscious scenario but, rather, emphasizes certain general psychological features which seem to be necessary for a lethal suicidal event to occur. Four have been noted (Shneidman, 1976): (1) acute *perturbation*, that is, an increase in the individual's state of general upsetment; (2) heightened *inimicality*, an increase in self-abnegation, self-hate, shame, guilt, self-blame, and overtly in behaviors which are against one's own best interests; (3) a sharp and almost sudden increase of *constriction* of intellectual focus, a tunneling of thought processes, a narrowing of the mind's content, a truncating of the capacity to see viable options which would

ordinarily occur to the mind; and (4) the idea of *cessation*, the insight that it is possible to put an end to suffering by stopping the unbearable flow of consciousness. This last is the igniting element that explodes the mixture of the previous three components. In this context, suicide is understood not as a movement toward death (or cessation) but rather as a flight from intolerable emotion.

7.   *Cognitive.*   Of course, the cognitive and psychodynamic approaches to suicide are not mutually exclusive: Intellect operates within a context of affect and affect most often has some substantive content. Nonetheless, focused attention to the cognitive aspects of suicide can lead to special insights. Apart from the exciting and burgeoning development of cognitive psychology, there is a history of studies, especially of psychotic behaviors from the cognitive point of view. *Language and Thought in Schizophrenia* (1944/1964), edited by Kasanin and containing contributions by Goldstein, Sullivan, Angyal, and von Domarus, is one outstanding example. More recently, the work of Arieti—his *Interpretation of Schizophrenia* (1955/1974) especially—has kept the topic of cognitive aspects of aberrant states in the forefront of discussion.

The concept of dichotomous (either/or) thinking is believed to be an important component in the thinking patterns of suicidal individuals (Shneidman, 1957, 1961, 1981, 1982). In addition dichotomous thinking has been found by Beck to exist in severly depressed persons. Rigidity and lability of thinking in suicidal persons has also been empirically demonstrated by Neuringer and Ringel. Narrow or dichotomous thinking in the suicidal person was reported 100 years ago by Westcott, who observed that the suicidal situation is one in which the person perceives only two odious alternatives of which the least odious was suicide. A variety of terms (e.g., fixity of idea, psychological myopia, gun-barrel vision, constriction, tunneling of perception) has been employed by various authors to describe the style of thinking found in suicide notes.

I have developed a system of logical content analysis of written text including political speeches (e.g., the Kennedy–Nixon "Great Debates"), letters, diaries, and suicide notes. The text is analyzed in terms of 55 cognitive maneuvers and 40 idiosyncracies of reasoning

which, taken together, reflect all the ways that people reason, de-
duce, induce, syllogize, and come to conclusions or "concludify."
From this, a contra-logic is developed that represents the assump-
tions and reasoning styles of an individual that make his idio-logic
appear sensible or reasonable to him. The psycho-logic answers the
question (in terms of mentational psychological traits) of what kind
of a person, psychologically, that individual would have to have been
in order for him to have reasoned as he did. And the pedago-logic
has to do with the ways in which one would instruct or do therapy
with an individual in order to resonate to his particular idio-logical
styles of thinking. There is an extensive and logical analysis of this
method applied to suicide, both manually (Shneidman, 1969) and by
computer (Ogilvie, Stone, and Shneidman, 1976).

8. *Biological, Evolutionary.* Philosopher Stephen Pepper
makes a common-sense point about suicide and evolution (1942, p.
242):

> It is most unlikely that a drive to commit suicide, whether piecemeal
> or all at once, is an instinctive basic drive. For organisms so endowed
> would long ago have eliminated themselves and left the world to
> those inheriting repertories of drives toward self-preservation.

Dr. Henry Murray succinctly says: "Suicide does not have *adaptive*
(survival) value but it does have *adjustive* value for the organism . . .
because it abolishes painful tension" (1953, p. 15; 1980, p. 216).

Suicide has been variously called the most daring, most coura-
geous, most generous way to die (*and* its opposite, the most cow-
ardly way to die), but, a priori, it certainly is not the most adaptive
mode of death in an evolutionary sense. Does suicide serve any evolutionary function?

One might say that suicide is a way of weeding out the unfit, a
self-selected way of thinning out the human herd. It is a way of
death in which the suicide proclaims by his act that he is unfit to be
a member of the human race and, by indirect implication, not fit to
reproduce in it. Suicide is the ultimate contraceptive. When one
speaks in this way, one would seem to limit the discussion of suicide

to individuals of child-bearing or child-initiating age. For males, this would be adolescence through old age—the range of practically all male suicides. For both sexes, suicide in today's world would seem to be unnecessary, at least biologically speaking, in that a hysterectomy or vasectomy would produce the same evolutionary results.

We also need to consider the instances in which older persons (beyond child-bearing age) may commit suicide by removing themselves from the group and thereby indirectly providing more of a limited food supply to the younger and potentially child-bearing members. The oft-told stories of the Eskimos come to mind in this connection, and at a tangent (where the element of childbearing is irrelevent), the saga of Captain Robert Scott in the Antarctic. It may well be, however, that from the biological and evolutionary points of view suicide occurs so infrequently compared with all other modes of death, that these reflections are moot.

This leads us to the next thought: In the sense that neo–Darwinian Richard Dawkins (*The Selfish Gene*, 1976) writes about natural selection, the act of suicide is not inconsistent with evolutionary theory. In one of the key sentences in his book he says: ". . . a predominant quality to be expected in a successful gene is ruthless selfishness" (p. 2). In a similar way, the suicidal individual behaves rather like the selfish gene—essentially concerned with its own individual fate and unconcerned with the welfare of the species. Suicide is an individual act, motivated by the urge to satisfy, or reduce, certain psychological needs. The presence of suicide in our species is, from a biological point of view, similar to the presence of, say, Down's syndrome. The most remarkable fact about Down's syndrome is its relative infrequency. In general, the single best sperm selfishly beats all the inferior (equally selfish?) sperm to the ovum (and the better ova are receptive to sperm); otherwise we might be an even less successful race of mostly Down's syndrome individuals. Similarly, suicide is a selfish event of relatively infrequent occurrence in a race of individuals almost every one of whom, at one time or another, suffers some psychological insults and existential emptiness that might be grounds for committing suicide—but doesn't do so.

9. *Constitutional.* There is a long historical thread of trying to understand man's behavior in terms of his constitution or his inner biological (physiological, biochemical) workings. The ancient Greek physician Galen (130–200 A.D.) posited four humors: sanguine (blood), phlegmatic (phlegm), choleric (yellow bile), and melancholic (black bile). Burton's *Anatomy of Melancholy* (1652) is an explication of melancholy. Early in this century, Ernest Kretchmer (1888–1964) and W. H. Sheldon attempted to link constitutional types to temperament.

10. *Biochemical.* In our own day, with biochemical techniques of increased sophistication, there has been a thrust, particularly by physicians, to put into medical terms different aspects of the human condition, including a substantial effort to reduce the reason for suicide to biochemical depression. While there may be some basis for this, it is far from the whole story. Suicide and depression are not synonymous. Nonetheless, the substantial work of current investigators of depression like George Murphy, Aaron T. Beck, Ari Kiev, and Frederick K. Goodwin merits careful study. The treatment of depression with pharmaceuticals enjoys considerable success.

11. *Legal.* In the United States, only Alabama and Oklahoma consider *committing* suicide a crime, but inasmuch as punishments are too repugnant to be enforced, there is no penalty for breaking this law. In several states, suicide attempts are misdemeanors, although these laws are seldom enforced. Thirty states have no laws against suicide or suicide attempts but every state has laws which specify that it is a felony to aid, advise, or encourage another person to commit suicide. There are essays and books about the legal aspects of suicide by, among others, Helen Silving (1957), Glanville Williams (1957), Thomas Shaffer (1976), and Margaret P. Battin (1982).

12. *Preventional.* Shneidman, Farberow, and Litman (1970) are generally associated with approaching suicide from a preventive perspective. The Suicide Prevention Center in Los Angeles was established in 1958. They concluded from their research there that the vast majority (about 80%) of suicides have a recognizable presuicidal phase. In reconstructing the events preceding a death by means of a

"psychological autopsy" (to help answer "*what* mode of death" and "*why*") they have concluded that suicidal behavior is often a form of communication, a cry for help, with clues, "messages of suffering and anguish and pleas for response" (Farberow & Shneidman, 1961).

13.   *Global, political, supranational.*   Henry A. Murray (1954) said:

> There will be no freedom for any exuberant form of life without freedom from atomic war . . . nothing is of signal importance today save those thoughts and actions which, in some measure, purpose to contribute to the diagnosis and alleviation of the global neurosis which so affects us.

Contemporary national neuroses (amounting to an international insanity) may very well lead to the self-induced death of human life. We live in a death-haunted time (Shneidman, 1973). Overwhelmingly, the most important kind of suicide for everyone to know about and to prevent is the global suicide which threatens us all and which, by the very presence of that threat, poisons our lives. Lifton (1979) appropriately urges on our consciousness the fact that we are in great danger—even if the bombs do not explode—of breaking our psychological connections to our own sense of continuity, generativity, and fantasized immortality. These connections are necessary to sustain our human relationships.

It may well be that the most important meaning—perhaps the only existential meaning—of the studies of suicidal phenomena is that they can serve as illuminating paradigms of human self-destruction on a global level, which, if it comes, will render everything meaningless.

Part
Two

Related Topics

Part
Two

Related Topics

D

Headnote

Obviously the best way to study suicide is to do so directly—by systematically examining anamnestic records, case histories, suicide notes, demographic data, biochemical assays, and so on. But there are, in addition, *indirect* approaches which come to the topic at a tangent. In this part of the book, two such examples will be presented, representing separate topics related to suicide: (1) the larger topic of *death* (in that death is clearly superordinate to suicide, every suicide being a case of death); and (2) the related topic of *sleep* (in the sense that sleep can be a sanctuary—the common goal of suicide—from overbearing psychological pain).

First, the discussion of the Idols of Death, following the pattern of Bacon, even as they apply to our understanding of suicide, may or may not have direct heuristic value. In any event, a more profound understanding of suicide requires some philosophical understanding of death.

Secondly, sleep phenomena can be seen as paradigms of escape, temporary deaths, "unpluggings," and refuge from pain. What is more, empirical studies of sleep phenomena can be done. In relation to suicide and sleep, we are interested in at least two facets of their possible connection: To explore the conceptual relationships between suicide and sleep; and to investigate some of the anomolies (changes, abnormalities, variations, etc.) that occur in sleep attendant to various intensities of suicidal tension.

E

Some Idols
About Death

It is fairly obvious that death and suicide are related, for what is suicide but the setting of one's own time and circumstances of death. More than 20 years ago a set of common-place fables (misconceptions or myths) about suicide was developed (Shneidman & Farberow, 1961). These fables (commonly believed erroneous notions) included the following: That people who talk about suicide don't commit suicide; that suicide happens without any warnings or clues; that suicidal people are fully intent on dying; that once a person is suicidal he is suicidal forever; that sudden improvement following a suicidal crisis always means that the suicidal risk is over; that suicide strikes much more often among the rich or, conversely, that it occurs almost exclusively among the poor; that suicide is inherited or "runs in families;" that all suicidal individuals are mentally ill, and that suicide is always the act of a psychotic person. None of these is true.

On further reflection it is clear that these misconceptions rest on more fundamental *idols* (erroneous ways of looking at nature), specifically, idols about death itself. In order to discuss the idols surrounding death we need first to turn to the writings of Sir Francis Bacon on the general idols which stand in the way of our clear perception and understanding of all (or any) knowledge.

Bacon was a great Elizabethan intellect who was central in facili-
tating the transition from medieval scholasticism to the modern scientific method which combines direct observation and inductive
reasoning. His most celebrated work, *Novum Organum*, published
first in 1620, is considered to have made a major turning point in the
overall evolution of Western thought.

Bacon considered it important to discuss in detail those human
fallacies which act as obstacles to clear observation and to incisive
inductive thinking. He called these obstacles "idola." They are the
"false notions which are now in possession of human understanding." These idols (*idolae*) are erroneous ways of looking at nature. In
the *Novum Organum* Bacon named and discussed their four kinds,
roughly as follows:

1.   Idols of the Tribe (*Idola Tribus*).   These are fallacies that accrue to humanity in general. They include the tendency to support a
preconceived opinion by emphasizing instances which tend to cor-
roborate it and by neglecting or disregarding negative occurrences
which oppose it.

2.   Idols of the Cave (*Idola Specus*).   These are errors peculiar
to the particular mental makeup of each individual. Here, Bacon's
practical suggestion is:

> In general let every student of nature take this as a rule, that what-
> ever his mind seizes and dwells upon with particular satisfaction is to
> be held in suspicion.

3.   Idols of the Market Place (*Idola Fori*).   These are errors aris-
ing in the mind from the influence of *words*, especially words that
are names for such non-existent things as "mind" or "soul."

4   Idols of the Theater (*Idola Theatri*).   These are erroneous
modes of thinking resulting from uncritically accepting whole systems of philosophy or from fallacious methods of demonstrating empirical proof. Bacon certainly implied that not everything that
Aristotle said is true: Sweet Nature herself should be looked at directly. One should—as Aldous Huxley some 200 years later wrote in

a heart-breaking letter attendant to the death of his small daughter—
sit before Nature as a child and let the facts array themselves before
one's unprejudiced eyes.

Of particular interest to us in the present context are the Idols of
the Cave. As Bacon tells us: "The idols of the individual man, for
everyone . . . has a cave or den of his own which refracts and discol-
ors the light of nature." With respect to suicide, each person figuratively builds for himself in relation to the cryptic topics of his life
and death, his own (mis)conception—vault of beliefs, understandings, and orientations: "Idols of the Grave," as I will call them. Further, I would propose four subcategories of these Idols of the Grave,
specifically as they concern: (1) the classification of suicidal phenomena; (2) the relationships between suicidal and death phenomena;
(3) the classification of death phenomena; and (4) the concept of
death itself.

THE IDOL THAT THE PRESENT
CLASSIFICATIONS OF SUICIDAL
PHENOMENA ARE MEANINGFUL

The use of an illustration may be the best introduction to this topic.
A woman of about 30 years of age was seen on the ward of a large
general hospital after she had returned from surgery. She had, a few
hours earlier, shot herself in the head with a .22 caliber revolver, the
result being that she had enucleated an eye and torn away part of
her frontal lobe. Emergency surgical and medical procedures had
been employed. When she was in bed subsequent to surgery, her
head was enveloped in bandages, and the appropriate tubes and
needles were in her. Her chart indicated that she had attempted to
kill herself, her diagnosis being "attempted suicide." It happened
that in the next bed there was another young woman of about the
same age. She had been permitted to occupy the bed for a few hours
to "rest" prior to going home, having come to the hospital that day
because she had cut her left wrist with a razor blade. The wound

required two stitches. She had had, she said, absolutely no lethal
intention, but had definitely wished to jolt her husband into attend-
ing to what she wanted to say to him about his drinking habits. Her
words to him had been, "Look at me, I'm bleeding." She had taken
this course after she had, in conversation with her husband, previously threatened suicide. Her chart, too, indicated a diagnosis of "attempted suicide."

Common sense should tell us that if we obtained scientific data
from these two cases (psychiatric anamnestic data, psychological
test data, blood and urine specimens, etc.) and then grouped these
materials under the single rubric of "attempted suicide," we would
obviously run the risk of masking precisely the differences which
we might wish to explore. Common sense might further tell us that
the first woman could most appropriately be labelled as a case of
"commited suicide" even though she was alive), and the second
woman as "nonsuicidal" (even though she had cut her wrist with a
razor blade). But, aside from the issue of what would be the most
appropriate diagnosis in each case (and hundreds of similar instances), the common heading of "attempted suicide" might definitely limit rather than extend the range of our potential
understanding.

Individuals with clear lethal intention, as well as those with ambivalent or no lethal intention, are currently grouped under the
heading of "attempted suicide": We know that individuals can attempt to attempt, attempt to commit, attempt to be non-suicidal. All
this comes about largely because of oversimplifications as to types of
causes and a confusion between modes and purposes. (The law pun-
ishes the holdup man with the unloaded or toy gun, precisely because the victim must assume that the bandit has, by virtue of his
holding a "gun," covered himself with the semantic mantle of "gun-
man.") One who cries "help" while holding a razor blade is deemed
by society to be suicidal. Although it is true that the act of putting a
shotgun in one's mouth and pulling the trigger with one's toe is almost always related to lethal self-intention, this particular relationship between method and intent does not hold for most other
methods, such as ingesting barbiturates or cutting oneself with a ra-

zor. Intentions may range from deadly ones, cries for help, and psychic indecisions, all the way to clearly formulated nonlethal intention in which a semantic usurpation of a "suicidal" mode has been consciously employed.

It may not be inaccurate to state that in this century there have been two major theoretical approaches to suicide: the sociological and the psychological, identified with the names of Durkheim and Freud, respectively. Durkheim's delineation of four etiological types of suicide is probably the best-known classification. For my part, I have often felt that this famous typology of suicidal behaviors has acted as a brilliantly conceived sociological motorcycle (anomic) with three psychological sidecars (altruistic, egoistic, and fatalistic) performing effectively in textbooks for almost a century, but running low on power in clinics, hospitals, and consultation rooms. This classification epitomizes some of the strengths and shortcomings of any study based almost entirely on social, normative, tabular, nomothetic data. It is probably fair to say, however, that Durkheim was not as interested in suicide per se, as he was in the explication of the power of his general sociological method.

The Freudian psychological formulation of suicide, as hostility directed toward the introjected love object, was more a brilliant inductive encompassment than an empirical, scientific particularization. In this country, the psychoanalytical concept of suicide was given its most far-reaching exposition by Karl Menninger, who, in *Man Against Himself* (1938), not only outlined four types of suicide (chronic, focal, organic, and actual) but also proposed three basic psychological components: the wish to kill, the wish to be killed, and the wish to die.

Neither of these two theoretical approaches to the nature and causes of suicide constitutes the classification most common in everyday clinical use. That distinction belongs to a rather homely, supposedly common-sense division, which in its barest form implies that all humanity can be divided into two groupings, suicidal and nonsuicidal, and then divides the suicidal category into committed, attempted, and threatened. Although the second classification is superior to the suicidal versus nonsuicidal view of life, that it is not theoretically nor practically adequate for understanding and treatment is one of the main tenets of my suicidology.

THE IDOL THAT LIVING AND DYING ARE SEPARATE

Living and dying have too often been seen (erroneously) as distinct, separate, almost dichotomous activities. To correct this view one can enunciate another activity, which might be called the psychodynamics of dying. One of its tenets is that, in cases where an individual is dying over a period of time, which may vary from hours to years in persons who "linger" in terminal illnesses, this interval is a psychologically consistent extension of styles of coping, defending, adjusting, interacting, and other modes of behavior that have characterized that individual during most of his life up to that time.

As we grow older, we grow more like ourselves. This can also be taken to mean that during the dying period, the individual displays behaviors and attitudes which contain great fealty to his lifelong orientations and beliefs. Draper says (1944): "Each man dies in a notably personal way." Suicidal and/or dying behaviors do not exist in vacuo, but are an integral part of the life-style of the individual.

It is important for a potential helper to avoid seeing a dichotomy between the "living" and the "dying." Most people who are seriously ill with a life-threatening disease (unless they are in extended coma) are very much alive, often exquisitely attuned to the symphony of emotions within themselves and the band of feelings of those around them. To tell a person that he or she has cancer may change the person's inner mental life irretrievably, but it does not lobotomize that person into a psychologically nonfunctioning human being; on the contrary, it may stimulate that person to consider a variety of concerns and reactions.

Nor is there any natural law—as those who talk about a certain number of set stages of dying would seem to assert—that an individual has to achieve a state of psychoanalytical grace or any other kind of closure before death sets its seal. The cold fact is that most people die too soon or too late, with loose threads and fragments of life's agenda uncompleted.

My own notion of the psychology of dying is that each individual tends to die pretty much as he or she has lived and especially as he or she has previously reacted in comparable periods of threat, stress, failure, challenge, shock, and loss during the life. In this context I can paraphrase the nineteenth century German biologist Haeckel's famous dictum and say that, in a sense, *oncology recapitulates ontogeny*; by which I mean, roughly speaking, the course of an individual's life while he or she is dying over time, say of cancer, duplicates or mirrors or parallels the course of the life during its previous "dark periods." That is, one dies as one has lived in the terrible moments of one's life.

To anticipate how a person will behave as he or she dies, we look at neither the plateaus nor the highlights of the life, but we search, as an eminent cancer doctor has recently put it, "in the hollow of the waves." Dying is stressful; thus it makes sense to look at earlier episodes in one's life that would appear to be comparable or parallel or psychologically similar. There are certain deep consistencies in all human beings. An individual lives characteristically as he or she has lived in the past; and dying is living. There are no set phases. People live differently and people die differently—much as they have lived during other episodes in their lives that were, to them, presages of their final dying period. My assertion is that the psychological history of the individual while he has cancer mirrors or reflects that same person's psychological history, in comparable periods throughout his lifetime, from early years on.

A recent article by Hinton (1975) reports a study of 60 terminally ill cancer patients. The study inquired into the relationship of each patient's personality and state of mind before and during the illness. The results indicated that we need to know the individual's previous patterns of handling life's demands *in detail*—the dozens of ways in which an individual has been strong, long-suffering, aggressive, weak, passive, fearful, and all the rest.

Hinton's findings, although tentative, are thought provoking:

Facing problems: This is the quality of previous character described by the husband or wife to indicate that the patient was one who coped effectively with life's demands rather than avoiding issues. It does appear to influence the most during the terminal illness. The uniform trend was for those who had previously coped well to be less depressed, anxious or irritable and to show less social withdrawal. This was one of the more consistent significant findings in the whole study. . . . Past difficulties in coping also increased the likelihood of current depression and anxiety . . . there is support for the frequent impression that a patient's previous manner of living influences the way he dies.

All this suggests that if one could know a great deal about the other person (over the span of the entire life) then one could make accurate statements about future behavior that would not be simply prediction in the ordinary sense, but would be more like reasoned extrapolations from the individual's past patterns of behavior. While death may occur as a totally unexpected event (like being assassinated or killed in an accident), suicide, *in theory*, should never come as a total surprise *if* one knew enough about the intimate inner life over the entire course of the individual's psychological history. That history *is* the individual, and individuals are rarely—by definition, never—radically inconsistent with themselves. It is not only that they have loyalty or fealty to themselves; it is that they are stuck with their own armamentarium of coping behaviors.

THE IDOL THAT THE TRADITIONAL CLASSIFICATION OF DEATH PHENOMENA IS CLEAR

The International Classifications of the Causes of Death lists 137 *causes* such as pneumonia, meningitis, malignant neoplasms, myocardial infarctions. In contrast, there are only four commonly recognized *modes* of death: natural, accidental, suicidal, and homicidal—the NASH categories of the modes of death. In some cases, cause of death is used synonymously to indicate the *natural* mode of death. Thus, the standard U.S. Public Health Service Certificate of Death has a space to enter the cause of death (implying the mode as natural) and, in addition, provides a space to indicate the accidental, suicidal, or homicidal modes. It is implied that these four modes of death constitute the final ordering into which each of us must be classified. The psychological fact is that some of us do not fit easily into one of these four crypts.

The main shortcoming of the common classification of the NASH modes is that, in its over simplification and failure to take into account certain necessary dimensions, it often poses serious problems in classifying deaths meaningfully. The basic ambiguities can be seen most clearly by focusing on the distinctions between natural (intrasomatic) and accidental (extrasomatic) deaths. On the face of it, the argument can be advanced that most deaths, especially in the younger years, are unnatural. Perhaps only in the cases of death of old age might the termination of life legitimately be called natural. Let us examine the substance of some of these confusions.

If an individual (who wishes to continue living) has his skull invaded by a lethal object, his death is called accidental; if another individual (who also wishes to continue living) is invaded by a lethal virus, his death is called natural. An individual who torments an animal into killing him is said to have died an accidental death, whereas an individual who torments a drunken companion into killing him is called a homicidal victim. An individual who has an artery burst in his brain is said to have died from a cerebral-vascular accident, whereas it might make good sense to call it a cerebral-vascular natural death. What has been confusing in this traditional approach is that the individual has been viewed as a kind of biological *object* (rather than as a psychological, social, biological *organism*) and as a consequence, the role of the individual in his own demise has been omitted. My profered solution to these puzzlements is to suggest that all deaths, in *addition* to their NASH designation, also be identified as intentioned, subintentioned (where an individual plays an unconscious or latent role in effecting his natural, accidental, or homicidal death) or unintentioned. This classification puts man back into his own dying by recognizing that there are psychological components in most dying scenarios.

THE IDOL THAT THE CONCEPT "DEATH" IS ITSELF OPERATIONALLY SOUND

We come now to what for some may be the most radical and iconoclastic aspect of this presentation so far; specifically, the suggestion that a major portion of the concept of "death" is operationally meaningless and ought therefore to be eschewed. Let the reader ask the question of the author: "Do you mean to say that you wish to discuss suicidal phenomena without the concept of death?" The author's answer is in the affirmative, based, I believe, on compelling reasons. Essentially, these reasons are epistemological; that is, they have to do with the process of knowing and the question of what it is that we can know. Our main source of quotable strength is the physicist Percy W. Bridgman. Essentially his concept is that death is not experienceable, that if one could experience it, one would not be dead. One can experience *another's* dying and *another's* death and his own dying—although he can never be sure—but no man can experience his own death.

In his book *The Intelligent Individual and Society*, Bridgman (1938) states his view as follows:

There are certain kinks in our thinking which are of such universal occurrence as to constitute essential limitations. Thus the urge to think of my own death as some form of my experience is almost irresistible. However, it requires only to be said for me to admit that my own death cannot be a form of experience for if I could still experience, then by definition, it would not be death. Operationally my own death is a fundamentally different thing from the death of another in the same way that my own feelings mean something fundamentally different from the feelings of another. The death of another I can experience; there are certain methods of recognizing death and certain properties of death that affect my actions in the case of others. Again it need not bother us to discover that the concept of death in another is not sharp, and situations arise in practice where it is difficult to say whether the organism is dead or not, particularly if one sticks to the demands that "death" must be such a thing that when the organism is once dead it cannot live again. This demand rests on mystical feelings, and there is no reason why the demand should be honored in framing the definition of death. . . . My own death is such a different thing that it might well have a different word, and perhaps eventually will. I am always alive.

This pragmatic view of death—in the strict philosophical sense of pragmatism—is stated most succinctly in a side remark about death by the father of pragmatism, Charles Sanders Peirce, who in discussing metaphysics said (1955):

We start then, with nothing, pure zero. But this is not the nothing of negation. For *not* means *other than*, and *other* is merely a synonym of the ordinal numeral *second*. As such it implies a first; while the present pure zero is prior to every first. The nothing of negation is the nothing of death, which comes *second to*, or after, everything.

Two further thoughts on death as an experience: Not only, as we have seen, is death misconceived as an experience, but (1) it is further misconceived as a bitter or calamitous experience. It may very well be that for the survivors, but they are the witnesses to an outcome, not the participants to a process in which there is no viable survivor; and (2) it is still further misconceived as an *act*, as though dying were something that one had to perform. On the contrary, dying can be a supreme passivity, rather than the supreme act or activity. One does, of course, participate in one's own dying and can select to act in this way or that, but, in essence, it will be done for you. Dying is one thing that no one has to "do." Live long enough—or just live—and it will happen, try to the contrary as you will.

We should recognize that our notions of suicide are, at *any* time in history, shaped in part by our notions of "death." That is why it was deemed necessary to explore some of the Idols of the Dead to look at the pervasive confusions attendant to this obfuscatory word.

F

Sleep and Self-Destruction

For those who work continuously with suicide it seems only natural to ask some questions about sleep. Are there, for certain individuals, some instructive parallels between overt self-destructive behaviors and changes in ordinary states of consciousness, especially sleep?

The kinship between death and sleep is in our folk language. There are many metaphors which tie the two together. A perusal of Bartlett's *Familiar Quotations* leads one to see that the relationships, even in metaphor, are complicated and tangled. At least four kinds of relationships can be distinguished. (1) Sleep is seen as the replenisher of life. A famous quotation in this connection is from *Macbeth:* "Sleep that knits up the ravell'd sleave of care,/The death of each day's life, sore labour's bath,/Balm of hurt minds, great nature's second course,/Chief nourisher in life's feast." (2) Sleep is also seen as "unplugging" from life, as in the quotation from Spenser: "Rest, the gift of Gods, sweetly sliding into the eyes of man, doth drown in the forgetfulness of sleep, the careful travails of the painful day." (3) Sleep is called the brother of death. A quotation from Joseph Conrad (one might also quote Tennyson, Shelley, Hesiod, or Homer) will suffice: "The men, the women, the children; the old with the young; the decrepit with the lusty—all equal before sleep, death's brother." (4) Sleep is substituted for suicide, as in e.e. cummings' statement:

"Rightly or wrongly, however, I prefer spiritual insomnia to psychic suicide."

The familial relationship between sleep and death is not too clear. If they are siblings, sleep must then be viewed as the cryptic brother of death, the closeness of the relationship depending upon how inimical to life is the intention of the sleeper.

We know that our current conceptualizations of both death and suicide are packed with counterproductive confusions. Even the *word* "death" is filled with obfuscations. I have proposed that we operationalize death by defining it in terms of consciousness, in which case we call it "cessation."

In this scheme, *cessation* is defined as the final stopping of the potentiality of any (further) conscious experience. It is the last introspective millisecond in life. It is what Melville (in *Pierre*, Book XII, Part iii) called "The last scene of the last act of man's play." It is the final curtain, with no encores.

In order to understand the role of cessation, three additional concepts of termination, interruption, and continuation seem to be required. These terms can be defined as follows:

Termination is the stopping of the physiological functions of the body, specifically the stopping of the exchange of gases between the organism and his environment. Although termination carries with it cessation, it is, of course, possible (in an individual with a crushed skull, for example) for cessation to occur for that individual hours or days prior to the occurrence of his termination.

Interruption is defined as the stopping of consciousness with the actuality, and usually the expectation, of further conscious experiences. It is, to use two contradictory terms, a kind of "temporary cessation." Again from Melville (*Mardi*, 1849, chap 143): "When I sleep . . . I live while consciousness is not mine, while to all appearances I am a clod."

Continuation (James, 1890) is the experiencing, in the absence of interruption, the stream of temporally contiguous conscious events. Our psychological lives are thus made up of a series of

alternating continuation and interruption states; the end, the
nothingness, the naughtment, the conclusion of the conscious life
is cessation.

In terms of our definitions above, sleep is an excellent example of
an interruption state. Other interruption states include being under
an anaesthetic, in an alcoholic stupor, in a diabetic coma, epileptic
seizure, fainting spell, and so on. It is interesting to note that the
opening sentence in the first edition of Kleitman's book *Sleep and
Wakefulness* (1938/1963) is:

Sleep is commonly looked upon as a periodic temporary cessation, or
interruption, of the waking state which is the prevalent mode of existence for the healthy human adult.

Our task now is to generate psychological and sociological similarities between sleep phenomena (viewed as *interruption* phenomena)
and death or suicide phenomena (viewed as *cessation* phenomena),
attempting to show how various interruption states—for which data
are relatively easy to obtain—might be related as conceptual analo-
gies or paradigms (or even metaphors) to various cessation behaviors.
An outline of various alterations of consciousness can be envis-
aged. Its two main rubrics would be (I) Discontinuation and (II)
Alerted Continuation. Under the first, one would find (A) Final discontinuations (cessation) that have such various labels as naughtment, demise, termination, death, and suicide; and (B) Periodic,
Intermittent, Temporary discontinuations of consciousness (inter-
ruptions) as with sleep, unconsciousness, anaesthetized states, stupor, coma, fainting, and seizures. The second main category of
Alerted Continuation is one in which consciousness continues unin-
terruptedly from moment to moment, but in a way which is qualita-
tively different from that individual's modal (or "normal") way of
moving consciously through life. These would include such sub-cate-
gories as inimical behaviors, unpluggings, escapades, insomnias,
psychoses, intoxication, drugged states, hypnosis, anoxias, and such
feigned alterations as malingering, spying, or feigning death.

A number of theoretical similarities between sleep and suicidal death can be imagined. We know that death can have various personal meanings to different people (i.e., as punishment, as separation, as reunion, as a lover) and that suicide can have six different meanings to a half-dozen individuals each of whom shoots out his brains. It is also so that sleep has different meanings to different people at different times: as a replenishment, a nice long nap, a bothersome interruption of one's activities, a chance to dream, an escape from pain, a temporary death, an escape from the world, a pleasant way to pass the time, a reunion with loved ones, and so on.

Some phenomenological similarities between sleep and death include the following: aspects of "defining the self" in both death and sleep; the presence of coded messages in both sleep and dying behaviors; the possibility of viewing both sleep and death as a resource; and aspects which threaten the sense of competence in death and sleep, especially in relation to insomnia.

Some similarities between sleep and death can be seen immediately by focusing on data from studies of sleep deprivation, insomnia, electrocoma treatment, seizures, anaesthesia, and the processes of dying patients. It is easy to view individuals who have been deprived of sleep as experiencing not sleep deprivation but *enforced* (as opposed to elective or casual) continuation; individuals deprived of consciousness (through ECT, seizures, etc.) as undergoing enforced interruption; and individuals who were dying or threatened with death (by homicide, terminal disease, etc.) as reacting to the imminence of enforced cessation.

The ugly topic of enforced continuation—keeping a person awake, depriving him of the opportunity for sleep (interruption)—is well known as a brutal interrogation method in police states. Behavioral changes attendant to sleep deprivation include fatigue, instability, misperceptions, disorientation, feelings of persecution, and visual and tactile hallucinations. These changes become very evident after about 100 hours of total sleep deprivation. Many a self-incriminating false confession has been signed under such dire circumstances.

Both sleep and suicide can be seen as metaphenomena, that is, as secondary reactions to more substantive occurrences. Sleep, for example, can be seen as a resonating (or secondary) reaction to what might be called "unvigilance." And surely some suicidal occurrences can be seen as metaphenomena. My own current view of many suicidal acts is that they can be seen to represent metacrises. On the one hand, we hear reported almost every "reason" for suicide (i.e., ill health, being jilted, loss of fortune, pregnancy, loss of job, school grades,—some certainly more persuasive than others), and on the other hand, we hear of the circumstances where "we simply can't imagine why he did it." It may well be that the substantive reasons, whatever they are, are almost never sufficient cause. What seems to happen in some cases is that the individual becomes disturbed (over ill health, loss of work, etc.) and then develops a panic reaction (a metacrisis) to his perception that he is disturbed. He becomes agitated over the fact that he is anxious. At the time of the greatest resonating perturbation the content which sparked the original disturbances may not be at all uppermost in his mind. Suicide may represent a reaction to an overwhelming crisis which is itself a reaction to another substantively bound crisis—a panic reaction to the individual's feeling that things are simply getting out of control. Erikson (1950) provided us with a timeless quotation which clarifies our notion of the metacrisis.

> This is the truth behind Franklin D. Roosevelt's simple yet magic statement that we have nothing to fear but fear itself, a statement which for the sake of our argument must be paraphrased to read: We have nothing to fear but anxiety. For it is not the fear of a danger (which we might be well able to meet with judicious action), but the fear of the associated states of aimless anxiety which drive us into irrational action, irrational flight—or, indeed, irrational denial of danger.

It may well be that suicide is often a metacritical act, representing a reverberating crisis, with its own (essentially content-free) autonomy; a need to do something and to do it quickly, thoughtlessly, recklessly, in order to discharge the pressure of the psychological pain.

About 25 years ago, some social scientists wrote about yet another topic: the sociology of sleep (Aubert & White, 1959; Naegele, 1961). What is interesting to us in our current context is that a number of the attributes which they cited as sociological characteristics of sleep can equally be applied almost directly to death, dying, and suicidal behaviors. Among the sociocultural similarities between death (including suicide) and sleep, the following are of special interest:

1. Modal times and locations for death (suicide) and sleep.
2. Taboos and sanctions in relation to death (suicide) and sleep.
3. Artifacts and rituals and aspects of communion rites.
4. Obvious elements of social disengagement.
5. The presence of deviant patterns.
6. "Norms of secrecy."
7. Coded messages.

There is obviously much to be done in the sociology of suicide apart from the demographic investigations and correlations with socioeconomic data.

A suicidal man, 50 years old, college-educated, wrote the following memorandum to me about his sleep.

To me at least, I have no significant attitude (or set of attitudes) toward the concept of SLEEP–PLUS–BED–PLUS–PRIVACY–PLUS–DARKNESS–PLUS etc., etc. (Mainly of course just SLEEP–PLUS–BED.) Our language does not at the moment supply us with a portmanteau to cover this concept. Categories such as "escape from the work-a-day world" or "temporary death" do not supply the meaning I have in mind. If I speak of SLEEP as a *refuge*, which is the nearest one-word description of my attitude that I have come up with to date, I am not reifying SLEEP, but I come close to reifying the concept of SLEEP–PLUS–BED, and perhaps properly so, since BED at least is a *res*, and is a very important part of the concept. I look forward to sleep both as a period of oblivion and as a time for dreaming. I am quite serious when I say that to me

SLEEP–PLUS–BED is a *wonderfully pleasant way to pass the time* (particularly during periods of depression), and that this is its main attraction to me ... more so than *refuge,* or *return to the womb,* or *the protected place,* or *the private place,* although I give you all these labels as additional truths.

Occasionally one finds a suicide note—that is *not* part of the sleep study—that openly speaks of the yearnings for both cessation (death) and for interruption (sleep). Below is a copy of such a note. This note was written by a 72 year old Caucasian divorced woman, who committed suicide with an overdose of barbiturate. The note is addressed to her attorneys. (All names have been changed.) I have added a few comments that bear on the concept of cessation (death, including death by suicide), interruption (including sleep), altered continuation (including mollifying the pain of the world by drugs), partial continuation (of truncated living), and continuation of life itself.

Suicide Note	Comments
Dear Bill and Bob: Since Thursday, I have been in such extreme pain that no amount of medication will bring it under control.	Relates to focally altered continuation state.
If I could only sleep. I honestly think that only complete sedation would stop it. But what doctor would agree to such a treatment? This they are willing to do only in terminal cases.	Yearning for interruption and for cessation.
I have thought about this a great deal. There are so many reasons why I regret this action, especially since my daughter passed away.	Relates to her "internal debate." Relates to an "ending" in her life.

Suicide Note	Comments
I had such hopes of doing all the creative things that nature seemed to bless me with. I used to say what a wonderful life I would have when I retired. That, when I got tired of writing, I could play the piano; and then I had my paint brushes ready and waiting for me. I have enjoyed a small degree of success in my painting.	Relates to modal continuation behavior.
Now with this added problem of glaucoma, and a bad right arm, I can no longer paint. I was never meant to be idle. I have always had a drive to do more and better things no matter what form it took.	Partial continuation—discontinuation state credo statement.
I think this action hurts me most because of my friends, Betty Brown and family. Of course no one in the family would ever let my Aunt Susan know the real reason. She knows that I have had two heart attacks, let her believe that was the reason.	Instructional; concern with others.
Perhaps if I were willing to live on strong pain killers, I might be able to get by on drugs, but who wants to live in a fog?	Addicts and alcoholics do live in a fog (an altered continuation state).
I would like to ask a favor. My legal name is Jones. I did not have it changed at the time of my divorce. Would you thus have the death certificate and grave marker made out in the name of Mrs. Mary M. Jones. I want to be remembered this way. There are some papers in my safety deposit box proving that I am one and the	Concern with post-self.

Suicide Note	Comments
one and the same, so there should be no complaint with Social Security, etc. And please do not let my dear neighbors next door know the truth.	
Surely there must be a justifiable Mercy death. In sorrow and deep regret, Mary	Relates to the way she wishes to live and die; and to how she wishes to be remembered (her post-self).

Sleep has a special "time-out" quality and plays a unique role in human life in that it is an interruption usually used constructively to restore and to replenish (elevative), often used to escape or simply to exist (temporative), but, in its very nature, very rarely used to destroy or denigrate one's own existence (reductive).

Thus sleep itself is rarely self-destructive, "death's brother." The subjects in our sleep study seemed to view it rather differently, as the silent therapist of disturbance, gyroscopically moving with the individual's perturbation, balancing it, leveling it, and all the while reflecting the ups and downs in the total life. Troubled sleep is part of troubled wakefulness. This is particularly true—and tragically true in the case of suicide—if by "sleep" we also include our thinking and feeling in both the pre-sleep and post-sleep intervals, especially the attitudes and feelings, the desperations and hopelessness upon lying down and awakening to an unabatedly dismal consciousness.

Part
Three

Basic Texts

G

Headnote

It is an unarguable advantage to come to the topic of suicide refreshed by concepts of non-suicidological giants. Certain fructifying books, singly or together, can, in my opinion, serve as a strong springboard for new ideas and insights relating to suicidal phenomena.

But this comment addresses the question of "Why books?" rather than "Why certain books?" specifically the three books discussed below. The personal answer to that question is that each of them is a favorite of mine and has been an important part of my own intellectual development. Together they have, as I hope the reader will see before the end of this book, directly and indirectly stimulated my own thinking about suicide, shaped it, and influenced its content and its tone.

Part of whatever merit this book might have derives from its resting on new foundations that support twentieth century wisdoms and its being based on the writings of three serious contemporary thinkers: A philosopher, a systems theorist, and a personologist. None of them was primarily concerned with suicidal topics, but each of them, as I hope to show, wrote about the human condition in ways that have important implications for the understanding of suicide. Each of the following three chapters is devoted to the key work of these three major intellects of our time.

The reader should keep in mind that I have included these books not only because of their personal meanings for me (although that might be sufficient reason) but primarily because of their potential for the better understanding of the phenomena of suicide. Each one of these books gives a separate view of the topic; taken together, they can provide a fresh vision.

It is easy to be over enthusiastic about one's favorite books and trumpet them as seminal works. That is, however, exactly what I aim to do with three volumes that have had a special impact on three areas of my own intellectual development. The first book helped resolve the basic metaphysical questions and the puzzle of how to simplify and understand various competing philosophical orientations; the second book addressed the topic of the fundamental consistencies among the various living systems and how systems "work;" and the final book addressed and helped to resolve what has been for me the most interesting of all questions—the basic question of psychology—specifically the nature of personality, how it is formed, and the ways in which human beings function. These three questions have dominated my adult intellectual life, and the three books have provided the necessary keystones for my understanding. The three books, in order, are Stephen Pepper's *World Hypotheses* (1942), James G. Miller's *Living Systems* (1978), and Henry A. Murray's *Explorations in Personality* (1938). These three books, which supplement, support, and enhance each other, represent an unsurpassed compendium of topmost insight and wisdom.

As I see it there are three main questions about suicide or, perhaps more accurately, there are three main dimensions in terms of which the critical questions about suicide can be asked: the philosophic, the psychological, and the systematic.

It seems too obvious for words that each individual suicide is, in part, a philosophical or existential event. It is so when one examines it from the outside, and it is so when one thinks about the meaning, purpose, or worthwhileness of one's own life. We do not need to quote well-known contemporary philosophers (i.e., the opening sentence of Albert Camus' *The Myth of Sisyphus* (1940) which runs: "There is but one serious philosophic problem and that is suicide," or Ludwig Wittgenstein's *Notebooks, 1914–1917:* "If suicide is allowed then everything is allowed. If anything is not allowed, then suicide is not allowed") in order to feel that there is an important philosophical component in suicide.

Stephen Pepper's *World Hypotheses* permits anyone to place the writings of any philosopher into a clear-cut schema of six categories really only four adequate categories and to make sense of any cosmology or epistemology that any patient might espouse, either directly or by implication. It is the first of the three books that make up this section. It forms a necessary background for any reader to grasp my understanding of suicide.

In my view of American psychology, I would place among the half-dozen most important books (with William James' *Principles of Psychology* [1890]), Henry A. Murray's *Explorations in Personality*. It is probably *the* most important book—works of fiction aside—in my own career. It is for me, as it has been for many others, a humming beehive of nourishing ideas. If I may be permitted a seemingly outlandish statement: For me, *Explorations* is Freud *and more.*

When *Explorations in Personality* first appeared in 1938, *The Quarterly Review of Biology* said that it was: "... the most original, thorough–going, and systematic attempt at a consistently scientific appraisal and understanding of human personality that has ever been made ... a contribution belonging in the absolutely first rank of significance." *Explorations in Personality* is the second of the three books that make up this Part. It forms an indispensable background for my view of suicide.

The third book satisfies (in Murray's terms) my need for order. It puts almost everything—*and I mean everything*—in a proper place. It is a book that explicates systems theory: James C. Miller's *Living Systems*. Are there paradigmatic similarities between "self-destruction" in cells and organs (at the lower end) and self-induced dissolution of groups and nations (e.g., ancient Rome) and super-national groups (e.g., the League of Nations), at the upper end, to suicide in human beings? And, taking human beings only—which is the entire focus of this book—what are the common functions or activities or processes that one can find in each (every) suicidal event? One can see immediately that systems theory latently contains an enormous and hitherto untapped potential for providing new insights into human self-destruction.

This Part, then, contains some comments about the main illuminating works by a trio of wise men and other shepherds of the mind. I derive a special pleasure from sharing them with those readers for whom these works may be new. My suggestion—plea—to each reader who has not already done so, is to have the special experience of perusing the original works.

So now I shall discuss them, without apology and with special pleasure.

H

Cosmology

PEPPER'S *WORLD HYPOTHESES*

Stephen Pepper was Mills Professor of Intellectual and Moral Philosophy and Civil Polity at the University of California at Berkeley. He wrote his book, *World Hypotheses*, to fulfill his consuming personal desire to know the truth in matters of importance to men—as near as one could get at truth in our time. He proceeded to do this by developing a new method, rather than by adopting an old creed. His method was an instrument of thought that could get at truth.

World Hypotheses was published in 1942. It has been reprinted nine times, most recently in 1980. It has only 348 pages.

WORLD HYPOTHESES

Pepper intends that his work supply a complete survey of metaphysics; *all* of truth. He does this by first demonstrating the logical shallowness of two untenable points of view about truth—the position of the utter skeptic and that of the dogmatist. He distinguishes three kinds of dogmatists: Those who appeal to infallible authority, to self-evident principles, and to indubitable fact. He wishes to deal with hypotheses. With a certain quality of hypotheses, specifically the major hypotheses of (or about) the world. (Not surprisingly, he calls these World Hypotheses). Each of these few world theories can be identified and understood in terms of its own special "root metaphor." There are six World Hypotheses (and Root Metaphors). Two of them, the Anamistic and the Mystic, are inadequate as world views of truth: The first is inadequately precise and the second has inadequate scope. This leaves four adequate World Hypotheses. They (and their Root Metaphors) are:

1. *Formism* is associated with realism or Platonic idealism and with Plato, Aristotle, the scholastics, neoscholastics, neorealists, and modern Cambridge realists; it is related to Apollonianism and Confucianism ("nothing in excess"), Christianity ("sympathetic concern for others") and Stoicism ("manly self–control"), and is linked to the Root Metaphor of *similarity*.

2. *Mechanism* is associated with materialism, realism, Democritus, Lucretius, Galileo, Descartes, Hobbes, Locke, Berkeley, Hume, and Reichenbach, and is linked to the Root Metaphor of a *machine*.

3. *Contextualism* is associated with pragmatism, Peirce, James, Bergson, and Dewey, is related to Mohammedanism ("group activity, group enjoyment"), Prometheanism ("man the eternal maker and remaker"), and is linked to the Root Metaphor of the *historic event*.

4. *Organicism* is associated with absolute idealism, objective idealism, Schelling, Hegel, Bradley, Bosanquet, and Royce; it is related to Charles M. Morris's Maitreyan way ("dynamic integration of diversity"), and is linked to the Root Metaphor of *integration*.

These four ways of "looking at things" (which emphasize issues rather than men) encompass *all* of metaphysics. The virtue of the root metaphor method is that it puts metaphysics on a purely factual basis and pushes philosophic issues back to the interpretation of evidence. They are *ways* of looking at the world (philosophically). By extension, they are ways of looking at man (e.g., a suicidal man), at acts (e.g., a suicidal act), or at definitions (e.g., the definition of suicide). One important implication is that there is more than *one* way to conceptualize or to define suicidal phemenona.

In the end, Pepper urges a balance of all four adequate World Hypotheses. His book provides a powerfully rich intellectual experience, laden with implications for thought and action. Quite simply, it is a book which changes men's lives.

CONTEXTUALISM

It would be an overwhelming task for me to attempt to apply all four of the adequate World Hypotheses to the topic of suicide. Instead, I can both illuminate something of the power of Pepper's work and ride with my own intellectual preference by choosing the one that is the most congenial to my own ways of thinking and seems to be the most relevant to suicide. That World Hypothesis is Contextualism.

In a sense, Contextualism is the most psychological of the World Hypotheses. Historically, it is connected with the metaphysics of Charles Sanders Peirce, of William James (who I consider to be the greatest of all American psychologists) and of John Dewey. Compared with the other three World Hypotheses, Contextualism seems to have the most contemporary feel to it—if that is a philosophic advantage.

A further reason, I have made Contextualism central to this book is that Contextualism focuses on the *act* (i.e., the deed, the event, the occurrence) and thus provides, in my opinion, the best World Hypothesis in terms of which suicide—which is essentially an *act*—can be understood.

But, I am quick to add, the importance of other World Hypotheses, especially Organicism, cannot be minimized. We cannot do without it in any comprehensive cognitive system. It is the World View which stresses integration and organic wholes. Without Organicism we could not speak of an integrated Systems Theory, which is at the heart of Miller's work and of Murray's work, and, by extension, the *sine qua non* of every one of man's truly original enterprises.

Now, we let Pepper speak for himself. The topic is Contextualism (Chapter X of *World Hypotheses*):

> *The contextualistic root metaphor....* The best term out of common sense to suggest the point of origin of contextualism is probably the *historic event*. And this we shall accordingly call the root metaphor of this theory.
>
> By historic event, however, the contextualist does not mean primarily a past event, one that is, so to speak, dead and has to be exhumed. He means the event alive in its present. What we ordinarily mean by history, he says, is an attempt to *re-present* events, to make them in some way alive again. The real historic event, the event in its actuality, is when it is going on *now*, the dynamic dramatic active event. We may call it an "act," if we like, and if we take care of our use of the term. But it is not an act conceived as alone or cut off that we mean; it is an act in and with its setting, an act in its context.
>
> To give instances of this root metaphor in our language with the minimum risk of misunderstanding, we should use only verbs. It is doing, and enduring, and enjoying: making a boat, running a race, laughing at a joke, persuading an assembly, unraveling a mystery, solving a problem, removing an obstacle, exploring a country, communicating with a friend, creating a poem, re-creating a poem.° These acts or events are all intrinsically complex, composed of interconnected activities with continuously changing patterns. They are like incidents in the plot of a novel or drama. They are literally the incidents of life.
>
> The contextualist finds that everything in the world consists of such incidents. When we catch the idea, it seems very obvious.† For this

°And, one might add: "committing a suicide." Certainly, solving a problem and removing an obstacle are, as we shall see, related to committing suicide.
†Here it is perfectly appropriate to cite a wondrous line by a great Contextualist, William James: "Individuality is founded in feeling; and the recesses of feeling, the

reason, it is sometimes easy to confuse the historic event of contextualism with common sense fact, and some contextualists have encouraged the confusion. But there are lots of things in common sense
that are not events. Common sense is full of animistic, formistic, and
mechanistic substances. But contextualism holds tight to the changing present event. This event itself, once we note it, is obvious
enough, but the tightness of the contextualists' hold upon it is not
usual. It is this hold that makes contextualism a distinctive philosophic attitude and a world theory. For the tightness of this grip is
obtained through the set of categories derivative from the historic
event as a root metaphor. . . .

Disorder is a categorical feature of contextualism, and so radically so
that it must not even exclude order. That is, the categories must be so
framed as not to exclude from the world any degree of order it may
be found to have, nor to deny that this order may have come out of
disorder and may return into disorder again—order being defined in
any way you please, *so long as it does not deny the possibility of
disorder or another order in nature also.* This italicized restriction is
the forcible one in contextualism, and amounts to the assertion that
change is categorical and not derivative in any degree at all.

Change in this radical sense is denied by all other world theories. If
such radical change is not a feature of the world, if there are un-
changeable structures in nature like the forms of formism or the
space–time structure of mechanism, then contextualism is false. Contextualism is constantly threatened with evidences for permanent
structures in nature. It is constantly on the verge of falling back upon
underlying mechanistic structures, or of resolving into the overarching implicit integrations of organicism. Its recourse in these emergen-
cies is always to hurry back to the given event, and to emphasize the
change and novelty that is immediately felt there, so that sometimes
it seems to be headed for an utter skepticism. But it avoids this im-

---

darker, blinder strata of character, are the only places in the world in which we can
catch real fact *in the making,* and directly perceive how events *happen* and how
[psychological] work is actually *done*" (Italics added; James, 1902, p. 501).

passe by vigorously asserting the reality of the structure of the given event, the historic event as it actually goes on. The whole universe, it asserts, is such as this event is, whatever this is. . . .

Contextualism is accordingly sometimes said to have a horizontal cosmology in contrast to other views, which have a vertical cosmology. There is not top nor bottom to the contextualistic world. In formism or mechanism or organicism one has only to analyze in certain specified ways and one is bound, so it is believed, ultimately to get to the bottom of things or to the top of things. Contextualism justifies no such faith. There is no cosmological mode of analysis that guarantees the whole truth or an arrival at the ultimate nature of things. On the other hand, one does not need to hunt for a distant cosmological truth, since every present event gives it as fully as it can be given. All one has to do to get at the sort of thing the world is, is to realize, intuit, get the quality of whatever happens to be going on. The quality of blowing your nose is just as cosmic and ultimate as Newton's writing down his gravitational formula. The fact that his formula is much more useful to many more people doesn't make it any more real.

The commission of suicide is a real and legitimate event for extended contextual analysis. One need not be formistic or mechanistic or organicistic (and certainly not creedish and moralistic and pompous) about it.

PEPPER'S OTHER WRITINGS IN WHICH SUICIDE IS DISCUSSED

Although suicide is mentioned nowhere in *World Hypotheses*, Pepper did write specifically about suicide in two of his works. Let us turn to them.

In his 1970 book, *The Sources of Value*, he discusses psychological drives and proposes a psychological theory in which the *repression* of drives plays a pivotal (and nefarious) role (pp. 241–242). According to Pepper, the goal of psychotherapy is to "bring the repressed mediating judgments back into the voluntary conscious control of the agent. . . . Psychiatric practice has steadily confirmed this conclusion. For repeatedly it has been observed that after a repression has been removed, the agent ceases to have his suicidal impulses. . . . The agent wants to act as he does only because he is inhibited from knowing the grounds of his [repressed] impulses, which he recognizes as the fartherest from his desires as soon as these grounds are uncovered."

The villain is not the drives within a person. That is not what propels him to suicide; rather it is the repression of these drives that causes psychological mischief. One major implication of this is that mental health is gained through insight and that one should, whenever possible, eschew repression. Pepper advocates the judicious use of psychotherapy. Here is what he says (1970, pp. 515–516):

A suicidal neurotic impulse represents an increase in frustration, not a decrease. If suicide is attempted it will simply add more conflict, count as an error, and increase the exasperation. Besides, recent study of these acts indicates that they all are blindly and mistakenly trying desperately to reduce the frustrations motivating them. Suicide attempts are regular appetitive and apprehensive acts seeking satisfaction, but, because of the repressed segments, meeting inexplicable frustrations. In short, an empirical description of a suicidal impulse shows that it is a mistake in terms of the ends the impulse is seeking to satisfy. The repressed system acknowledges in its very structure the legislation over it of the integrative system of the personality. As we say in common speech, a neurotic does not *really* want to commit suicide. He really wants something quite different. Just as we would say of a thirsty man in a desert trudging toward a mirage: "He doesn't really want the mirage; he wants water." This, I believe, is the proper and fully adequate empirical answer.

Turning now to Pepper's essay specifically on suicide, called "Can a Philosophy Make One Philosophical?" I have a personal note to communicate. I believe that I was instrumental in his writing this essay. In 1962, as Co-director of the Los Angeles Suicide Prevention

Center, I invited Professor Pepper to be a Fellow at the Center and in 1967 I edited *Essays in Self-Destruction* written by Fellows especially for that volume. Thus he was stimulated to write an essay about suicide and elected to deal with the question of rational and irrational suicide and the role of a philosophy—as opposed to a creed—in preventing suicide. I shall avail myself of the double opportunity to quote from Professor Pepper's essay, including some statements in which he refers directly to some of my own work. Here are some selections from his chapter in *Essays in Self-Destruction*:

> I want to commit myself to a certain hypothesis at this point, one with which some psychologists will not agree but which has been gaining steadily in acceptance and which I think will eventually be proved correct. This is that the dynamics of human action is one thing and the intellectual channeling of it another—the hypothesis that there are no, or very few, dynamics or drives intrinsic to thought. All the dynamics (or nearly all) come from drives and (in the wide sense) the emotional side of personality.
>
> This hypothesis, if correct, is important for our present subject. It sets certain limits to rational guidance. It means that we cannot assume that correct reasoning from a set of true concepts will always be effective in leading a man to act reasonably. It means that a philosophy will not necessarily make a man philosophical. It does not by any means imply, however, that philosophy cannot be efficacious. It implies only that there are limits to its efficaciousness which have nothing to do with its truth or adequacy. This conclusion may pertain directly to the general topic of our volume, which is self-destruction.
>
> I do not propose to argue for the above hypothesis in this paper. That would be an essay in itself. I only want from now on to show its bearing on the problem of suicide for those who accept it.
>
> To begin with, I think it leads to a distinction between what could be called rational and irrational grounds for suicide. This suggests that all suicides need not be regarded as irrational. Incidentally, the wide

acceptance of the view that all suicides are owing to depression or other emotional conditions beyond the rational control of the victim is strong evidence for the hypothesis I am advocating. But in suggesting the possibility of rational suicides, I am opposing the opposite extreme of granting no efficacy to the conceptual channelling. A rational suicide would be one that is based on a dynamic demand for sound logical and evidential grounds for actions or for an equivalent in rationally accepted institutionalized authority. . . .

Here is where a man's philosophy of life relates to the problem of suicide. How much influence does a man's philosophy of life have upon the releasing or the restraining of suicidal impulses? We are assuming that a set of concepts cannot of itself instigate dynamic impulses. However, if a person is caught in a serious predicament loaded with conflicting impulses of fear, love, hate, loyalty, and respect for obligations, law, and other such, the dynamics of these impulses could charge a philosophy of life in which this person has gained confidence and effectively guide him to a decision. The philosophy of life would function in this instance just as the rules of scientific procedures guide a scientist to his results. The decision would be rational even if it were for an act of suicidal self-sacrifice or at the risk of death. And the philosophy of life would clearly be responsible for that decision. There is just one important qualification: the decision could not be regarded as *entirely* rational if the philosophy of life that led to this decision was not itself as rational or reasonable as possible. This means, according to our earlier discussion, that the philosophy must be as adequate as any available to the person confronted with the problem. . . .

I think we must grant that any act of self-destruction is rational if it is voluntary and deliberate and wholly determined by factual conflicts of a situation that was considered with the guidance of a philosophy of life. It would be rational whether the guiding philosophy was the man's own choice or creation or one that he had acquired through acculturation. However, the degree of rationality of the act would depend on the degree of rationality of the philosophy which was guiding the person's deliberations.

What then would be irrational suicide? These would be cases for which efforts for prevention are obviously in order. These would seem to be cases based on serious emotional disturbance, in which rational guidance is cut off, or largely cut off, by the intensity of the emotional conflicts. In most such cases, I suspect that the emotional impulses are beyond the person's voluntary control, being in the region of the inhibitions of the unconscious. Here whatever reasoning there is takes the form of rational-unconscious, and a person's perceptions of the reality of the situation are either blanked out or interpreted to fit his emotional projections instead of used to test his hypotheses and imaginations. To the person, it seems that the only way out is suicide; whereas to a psychologically trained outsider it is evident that the problems are of the person's own making because of his lack of insight into his own motivations and twists of interpretation. By careful professional help such persons may gain insight into the nature of their impulses and acquire a correct awareness of the reality of their situation and thereby gain a capacity for rational intellectual guidance for their actions. The therapist may often have to do much more. He may have to give them the support that they may have been lacking until they are able to stand on their own feet. He may even have to build up a stable inner core of integrated character (ego strength as it is often called) with which the person can then build on further and function effectively in his environment. . . .

Shneidman recently conducted an informative series of conferences with suicide-prone subjects and inquired about their philosophies of life. He asked each of them in a disarmingly informal manner the following questions: (1) What is your philosophy of life? (2) What is the purpose of life? (3) Is that a real tree (or chair, and so forth)? (4) What are the tests of reality or of truth? (5) What is your idea of causation, chance, decision?

In all he interviewed six subjects at the Suicide Prevention Center. The first question seemed to mystify or be misunderstood by most of these subjects. One man (the most disorganized of the group) replied, "Passive indifference. I don't seem to care about anything." But to the second question he answered, "Health in the normal way, happiness, good, accomplishments." Pressed further he stated that he was a "strictly dogmatic Catholic," expected to see people after death in "heaven, hell, or what. If I find happiness, I don't know what form it will take."

About the tree, his belief that it was real was based on its "form, shape." His belief in the hereafter was based, however, on "intellectual conviction and faith."

Luck, he said, played no part in his life; but as for being "preordained," he did not believe in it at all. Asked about cause and effect, he replied, "Vague in my own mind what you mean." He was sure he had no right to commit suicide.

This sort of vagueness about a philosophy of life, perception, tests of truth, and cause and effect ran through the answers of all these subjects except one. She was an agnostic.

Her answers, went like this: As to her philosophy of life, she was Unitarian, although raised Methodist. "Never believed in God, but always sort of wished I could." As for afterlife, "Nothing." As for purpose of life, it was "human relationships, to love and be loved." Taken more broadly, "Life is purposeless. It just happened." To Shneidman's inferring, "You are an adventitious circumstance of biological roulette," her reply was, "Yeah, I think it was just a question of which sperm got to the ovum first. An awful lot of ova there who didn't get any sperm at all, but I think it was strictly chance." Referring to the birth of her child she said, "I was delighted with him." And to the question of whether she thought of him as arbitrary, "I don't feel any lack about the fact that this is biological." About immortality, her reply was, "Improbable." About the reality of the tree, "Accepted," but "No explanation of the origin of the world." She found no difficulty with the notion of infinity in connection with space and time for the world.

Her comments on suicide were vivid: "I think suicide is one of the greatest things to keep you going. If you knew you couldn't die, I think the world would be unbearable . . . I think it's great . . . I think it's a completely moral justifiable thing that nobody need do, but if you are miserable yourself and you're not doing anybody any good, I think it's great." On Shneidman's asking if her suicide would not put her "skeleton in the grandchildren's psychological closet," she recognized that "this kind of scar will be very bad."

Asked if she felt her life was entirely within her hands, she replied yes. Pressed further about whether this would be so if she were in a depressed state, she admitted that "you perceive only those things you care to perceive. But I think it's my right." Shneidman then asked, "What about the decision itself? Granted that you have the right." Her answer: "The decision, will I be able to make an intellectual decision about an emotional thing? Probably not. I think it will be an emotional decision, not an intellectual one."

This woman in these last few words just about summarizes the conclusions of the present paper. She has a rather well developed naturalistic philosophy of life, which does, as Hume convincingly shows in his essay "On Suicide," grant to a man on the basis of a naturalistic, individualistic ethics a right to end his life if he finds such an act is one that will maximize the satisfactions of all concerned. "A man who retires from life," he wrote, "does no harm to society: He only ceases to do good. . . . I am not obliged to do a small good to society at the expense of a great harm to myself." The woman whose comments we have just quoted is simply stating the same thesis, that under certain justifiable conditions an act of suicide is rationally justified if it conforms to an adequate philosophy and is performed after careful rational deliberation. However, she also sees that in a state of depression a person is most likely to act irrationally, and suicide under such motivation is not rationally justified. The decision then is "not an intellectual one."

Along with his concern with unrepressing the repressed, Pepper trumpets out his belief in the positive values provided by an adequate world philosophy as a guide for life. He says: "An explicit philosophy is a guide greatly superior to a purely institutionalized ideology or creed. For even when not inadequate, the latter is rigid and dogmatic, whereas the former may be flexible and open to revision." (1967, p. 127).

There is, also, not unexpectedly a caveat. Pepper reminds us that in order to be able effectively to use a world philosophy in one's life one has to possess a relatively well-integrated personality (free of over–powering unconscious conflicts) in the first place. This limitation may make a useful philosophy unavailable for just those many who need it most.

AN EXAMPLE OF CONTEXTUALISM: "THE BET" (ON THE HEREAFTER) AS EXEMPLIFIED IN PASCAL'S SEVENTEENTH–CENTURY *PENSEES* AND JOHN FOWLES'S TWENTIETH–CENTURY *ARISTOS.*

In this section we shall discuss two views of one act. The act that we are talking about is the act of being worried about death (i.e., being concerned with the "what," if anything, happens to us after the dying is over), or, as Pepper might have said, the act of "worrying over a death." That act is what the two people whom we shall quote— Blaise Pascal and John Fowles — are really discussing. Further, the fact that our concern is about an act, an occurrence, an historical event is precisely what makes our discussion a contextual one.

For an example, I have chosen to contrast two discussions of the "same" philosophic point, three centuries apart. Specifically, Pascal's discussion of the Bet Situation (betting on whether or not there is a God and a hereafter) and a discussion of this same point by the contemporary novelist, John Fowles. I shall also add some observations of my own. But first, some background material.

Blaise Pascal (1623–1662) is a complexity. In his interests he is either a disparate creature or an amazingly integrated man. He is a scientist–religionist who, before he died at age 39, measured atmospheric pressure, formulated a law of pneumatics, made signal contributions to mathematics, *and* wrote a set of letters and a set of 923 pithy thoughts (*pensèes*) on the evidences of religion—specifically, the intellectual and emotional reasons for a belief in God and in Christianity—not to mention his acknowledged contributions, by virtue of the clarity and vigor of his style, to the French language itself.

Keep in mind the *context* of Pascal's writing. It is a seventeenth–century apologia of spirituality. He is a dual genius of his time, standing between a waning religion and an emerging science, and contributing notably to both of them—but unable to synthesize them or to understand one in terms of the other. They are *separate* threads in his life, albeit both brilliantly illuminated by him. On his religious side, he wrote with a passionate conviction of the importance of the suffering of Christ. His main purpose was to prove that one can find peace by coming to God only through the sufferings attendant to the fallen state of man, made palpable through Jesus Christ, the Redeemer.

Pascal now sounds curiously quaint, almost medieval and anachronistic to modern ears. His countryman Voltaire, born at the end of that same century (in 1694) was a quite different writer (of essays, plays, witticisms), a man much less concerned with the next world and much more a man of the world—this world. In the time between Pascal and Voltaire, the intellectual center on the equator of the Western world had turned, so that the very context of the times was different, and, of course, it has continued to turn, as John Fowles will show us.

Here we shall focus first on Pascal's *Pensèes*—his thoughts, specifically about God, Christianity, and the saving of one's soul. In these writings, he discusses the "wager" (*le pari*), the "Bet Situation." This discussion is in Pensèe No. 233. In order to give the reader something of the flavor of its context, I have reproduced several other of Pascal's pensèes.

205

When I consider the short duration of my life, swallowed up in the eternity before and after, the little space which I fill, and even can see, engulfed in the infinite immensity of spaces of which I am ignorant, and which know me not, I am frightened, and am astonished at being here rather than there; for there is no reason why here rather than there, why now rather than then. Who has put me here? By whose order and direction have this place and time been allotted to me?

206
The eternal silence of these infinite spaces frightens me.

207
How many kingdoms know us not!

208
Why is my knowledge limited? Why my stature? Why my life to one hundred years rather than to a thousand? What reason has nature had for giving me such, and for choosing this number rather than another in the infinity of those from which there is no more reason to choose one than another, trying nothing else.

209
Art thou less a slave by being loved and favoured by thy master? Thou art indeed well off, slave. Thy master favours thee; he will soon beat thee.

210
The last act is tragic, however happy all the rest of the play is; at the last a little earth is thrown upon our head and that is the end for ever.

211
We are fools to depend upon the society of our fellow-men. Wretched as we are, powerless as we are, they will not aid us; we shall die alone. We should therefore act as if we were alone, and in that case should we build fine houses, etc. We should seek the truth without hesitation; and, if we refuse it, we show that we value the esteem of men more than the search for truth.

233

. . . We know that there is an infinite, and are ignorant of its nature. As we know it to be false that numbers are finite, it is therefore true that there is an infinity in number. But we do not know what it is. It is false that it is even, it is false that it is odd; for the addition of a unit can make no change in its nature. Yet it is a number, and every number is odd or even (this is certainly true of every finite number). So we may well know that there is a God without knowing what He is. Is there not one substantial truth, seeing there are so many things which are not the truth itself?

We know then the existence and nature of the finite, because we also are finite and have extension. We know the existence of the infinite, and are ignorant of its nature, because it has extension like us, but not limits like us. But we know neither the existence nor the nature of God, because He has neither extension nor limits.

But by faith we know His existence; in glory we shall know His nature. Now, I have already shown that we may well know the existence of a thing, without knowing its nature.

Let us now speak according to natural lights.

If there is a God, He is infinitely incomprehensible, since, having neither parts nor limits, He has no affinity to us. We are then incapable of knowing either what He is or if He is. This being so, who will dare to undertake the decision of the question? Not we, who have no affinity to Him.

Who then will blame Christians for not being able to give a reason for their belief, since they profess a religion for which they cannot give a reason? They declare, in expounding it to the world, that it is a foolishness, *stultitiam*; and then you complain that they do not prove it! If they proved it, they would not keep their word; it is in lacking proofs, that they are not lacking in sense. "Yes, but although this excuses those who offer it as such, and takes away from them the blame of putting it forward without reason, it does not excuse those who receive it." Let us then examine this point, and say, "God is, or He is not." But to which side shall we incline? Reason can decide nothing here. There is an infinite chaos which separated us. A game is being played at the extremity of this infinite distance where heads or tails will turn up. What will you wager? According to reason, you can do neither the one thing nor the other; according to reason, you can defend neither of the propositions.

Do not then reprove for error those who have made a choice; for you know nothing about it. "No, but I blame them for having made, not this choice, but a choice; for again both he who chooses heads and he who chooses tails are equally at fault, they are both in the wrong. The true course is not to wager at all."

Yes; but you must wager. It is not optional. You are embarked. Which will you choose then? Let us see. Since you must choose, let us see which interests you least. You have two things to lose, the true and the good; and two things to stake, your reason and your will, your knowledge and your happiness; and your nature has two things to shun, error and misery. Your reason is no more shocked in choosing one rather than the other, since you must of necessity choose. This is one point settled. But your happiness? Let us weigh the gain and the loss in wagering that God is. Let us estimate these chances. If you gain, you gain all; if you lose, you lose nothing. Wager, then, without hesitation that He is.—"That is very fine. Yes, I must wager; but I may perhaps wager too much."—Let us see. Since there is an equal risk of gain and of loss, if you had only to gain two lives, instead of one, you might still wager. But if there were three lives to gain, you would have to play (since you are under the necessity of playing), and you would be imprudent, when you are forced to play, not to chance your life to gain three at a game where there is an equal risk of loss and gain. But there is an eternity of life and happiness. And this being so, if there were an infinity of chances, of which one only would be for you, you would still be right in wagering one to win two, and you would act stupidly, being obliged to play, by refusing to stake one life against three at a game in which out of an infinity of chances there is one for you, if there were an infinity of an infinitely happy life to gain. But there is here an infinity of an infinitely happy life to gain, a chance of gain against a finite number of chances of loss, and what you stake is finite. It is all divided; wherever the infinite is and there is not an infinity of chances of loss against that of gain, there is no time to hesitate, you must give all. And thus, when one is forced to play, he must renounce reason to preserve his life, rather than risk it for infinite gain, as likely to happen as the loss of nothingness.

For it is no use to say it is uncertain if we will gain, and it is certain that we risk, and that the infinite distance between the *certainty* of what is staked and the *uncertainty* of what will be gained, equals the finite good which is certainly staked against the uncertain infinite. It is not so, as every player stakes a certainty to gain an uncertainty, and yet he stakes a finite certainty to gain a finite uncertainty, without transgressing against reason. There is not an infinite distance between the certainty staked and the uncertainty of the gain; that is untrue. In truth, there is an infinity between the certainty of gain and the certainty of loss. But the uncertainty of gain is proportioned to the certainty of the stake according to the proportion of the chances of gain and loss. Hence it comes that, if there are as many risks on one side as on the other, the course is to play even; and then the certainty of the stake is equal to the uncertainty of the gain, so far is it from fact that there is an infinite distance between them. And so our proposition is of infinite force, when there is the finite to stake in a game where there are equal risks of gain and of loss, and the infinite to gain. This is demonstrable; and if men are capable of any truths, this is one.

Here are some further Pascal pensèes:

344
Instinct and reason, marks of two natures.

345
Reason commands us far more imperiously than a master; for in disobeying the one we are unfortunate, and in disobeying the other we are fools.

346

Thought constitutes the greatness of man

347

Man is but a reed, the most feeble thing in nature; but he is a thinking reed. The entire universe need not arm itself to crush him. A
vapour, a drop of water suffices to kill him. But, if the universe were
to crush him, man would still be more noble than that which killed
him, because he knows that he dies and the advantage which the
universe has over him; the universe knows nothing of this.

All our dignity consists, then, in thought. By it we must elevate ourselves, and not by space and time which we cannot fill. Let us endeav-
our, then, to think well; this is the principle of morality.

348

A thinking reed.—It is not from space that I must seek my dignity,
but from the government of my thought. I shall have no more if I
possess worlds. By space the universe encompasses and swallows me
up like an atom; by thought I comprehend the world.

Three centuries later, the mind of John Fowles—which, in 1964,
had yet to produce *The Magus, The French Lieutentant's Woman,
The Ebony Tower,* or *Daniel Martin*—turned also to thoughts of
death in his own set of *pensèes*, which he called *The Aristos* (which
means "the best for a given situation"). Of course, he had read Pascal and had mused upon him and then, willy nilly, when he wrote
about him he reflected twentieth century views of that "same"
topic. In his Aphorism 3, he addresses the selfsame anxiety that stimulated Pascal's thoughts about death: We do not know what lies beyond it. There is that Bet Situation. But the ambience of the
gambling casino of life has changed; and Fowles gives us—in Apho-
risms 11 and 12—a bold and assertive twentieth–century pronounce-
ment (1964/1975, pp. 29–30).
     Fowles has brought Pascal (and the Bet Situation) into the twenti-
eth century. He (legitimately) denies facts about men's beliefs that

were the very cornerstones for Pascal, reflecting, as he did, the *zeitgeist* of his day and displayed in the contrast between these two sets of *pensèes*. We believe that Pascal is quaint and, for us, anachronistic. Were Pascal unchanged, transmitted to the present, he would be shocked at what has happened to his "indubitable facts." Here, from *The Aristos*, are some of Fowles' modern *pensèes*:

1.   Why do we think this is not the best of all possible worlds for mankind? Why are we unhappy in it?

2.   What follow are the great dissatisfactions. I maintain that they are all essential to our happiness since they provide the soil from which it grows.

DEATH

3.   We hate death for two reasons. It ends life prematurely; and we do not know what lies beyond it.

4.   A very large majority of educated mankind now doubts the existence of an afterlife. It is clear that the only scientific attitude is that of agnosticism: we simply do not know. We are in the Bet Situation.

5.   The Bet Situation is one in which we cannot have certainty about some future event; and yet in which it is vital that we come to a decision about its nature. This situation faces us at the beginning of a horse race, when we want to know the name of the winner. . . .

6.   To Pascal, who first made this analogy with the bet, the answer was clear; one must put one's money on the Christian belief that a recompensatory afterlife exists. If it is not true, he argued, then one has lost nothing but one's stake. If it is true, one has gained all.

7.   Now even an atheist contemporary with Pascal might have agreed that nothing but good could ensue, in an unjust society where the majority conveniently believed in hellfire, from supporting the idea, false or true, of an afterlife. But today the concept of hellfire has been discarded by the theologians, let alone the rest of us. Hell could be just only in a world where all were equally persuaded that it exists; just only in a world that allowed a total freedom of will—and there-

fore a total biographical and biological similarity—to every man and woman in it. . . .

8.   The idea of an afterlife has persistently haunted man because inequality has persistently tyrannized him. It is only to the poor, the sick, the unfortunate underdogs of history, that the idea appeals; it has appealed to all honest men's sense of justice, and very often at the same time as the use of the idea to maintain an unequal *status quo* in society has revolted them. Somewhere, this belief proposes, there is a system of absolute justice and a day of absolute judgment by and on which we are all to be rewarded according to our desserts.

9.   But the true longing of humanity is not for an afterlife; it is for the establishment of a justice here and now that will make an afterlife unnecessary. This myth was a compensatory fantasy, a psychological safety-valve for the frustrations of existential reality.

10.   We are ourselves to establish justice in our world: and the more we allow the belief in an afterlife to dwindle away, and yet still do so little to correct the flagrant inequalities of our world, then the more danger we run.

11.   Our world has a badly designed engine. By using the oil of this myth it did not for many centuries heat up. But now the oil level is dropping ominously low. For this reason, it is not enough to remain agnostic. We *must* bet on the other horse; we have one life, and it is ended by a total extinction of consciousness as well as body.

12.   What matters is not our personal damnation or salvation in the world to come, but that of our fellow men in the world that is."

Fowles' thoughts on Death and on Pascal's Bet Situation stimulate some thoughts in me, hopefully in the spirit of Popper's skepticism. I do not believe that we are in a Bet Situation at all. It seems more accurate to say that we are in a Choice Situation. We don't have to *bet*. We certainly do not have to bet on (the welfare of) our souls, inasmuch as the question of the existence of the soul is itself a matter of skepticism. There is a vast difference between making a wager in a horse race (not a life and death matter) and deciding under great pressure to stay with an apparently sinking ship or to take to the life raft.

For us, Pascal was betting out of fear. And he is also wrong for us when he says that even if it turns out that there are no gods—how could one ever tell?—nothing is lost. A great deal can be lost. Self-respect may be lost.

Pascal misleads us when he asserts that if we make the Bet and it turns out that there is no God and no afterlife "then one has lost nothing but one's stake." A major point is missed: The stake is not just nothing. The stake is self-pride, independence, one's essential humanness, the freedom from abnegation and kow–towing (bending, genuflecting, kneeling, groveling, and prostrating oneself to what?). One gains freedom from superstition. The stake is considerable to a really proud and independent person who eschews slavery and entrapment of any sort. To lose that is to lose quite a bit. It cannot be called "nothing."

If one wants to bet, it makes as much sense, in the context of skepticism, to bet that there is no deity and no afterlife, especially if the bet serves to enhance one's own sense of self–regard. Consider: If one has to bet and is correct (that there is nothing "up there" or nothing "beyond" then one has gained self–respect while alive—that's all there is—and there is nothing after death to lose. If one is in error (and there really is a God and a hereafter) then one, by betting against it, has fortified oneself with an added self–respect and will be better able to meet the vicissitudes of afterlife.

It is important to note the contextual element in all of this: the differences between the sixteenth and the twentieth centuries. Pascal is out of date for us. Inasmuch as the concept of hellfire has been discarded by most educated people today, if one is dead wrong on this issue there will be plenty of company in the nether regions of that after-space. The main problem might not be the heat, but the overcrowding.

In any event, it is extremely unlikely that the dogmatists, standing as they do on the untenable ground of "infallible authority speaking self-evident facts" are right. The various dogmatic positions in the world today cancel each other out, and none of them (for this and other reasons) seems sound. One example will suffice: Should one believe the American Fundamentalists on the New Testament or the Ayatollah Khomeini on the Koran? They are equally shrill and dogmatic about the "inerrancy" of their texts; and that, common sense and philosophic reflection tell us, is precisely why, although each may be a political force to be reckoned with, neither espouses a cognitive position that any serious or critical mind can entertain.

The *contextual* point to note is that the discussion by Pascal, embedded in the beliefs of the seventeenth century, and by Fowles (and by me), reflecting the beliefs of the twentieth century, of what appears to be the same topic, reflect rather different views of it. Can you imagine how a discussion of this topic three centuries hence, in the latter part of the twenty–third century might sound? As one appreciates these differences, one then sees the enormous importance of temporal contextualism. And, of course, at any moment of time, there are always spatial and social and interpersonal and intrapsychic contextualisms as well.

A juxtaposition of Pascal and Fowles on the same issue, the Bet Situation, is of course, also a comparison between a seventeenth century Western mind and a twentieth century Western mind. The fact that man's notions about death and dying (and suicide) have undergone changes should not surprise us. (The basic lesson of Philippe Aries's 1981 monumental volume, *The Hour of Our Death*—a 1000 year survey of wills, testaments, letters, diaries, poems, paintings, effigies, and town plans indicating the location of burial grounds—is that attitudes and emotions toward death and dying, and the practices attendant to them, like other human events, have a wide range of constantly changing cultural patterns.) The results of our Pascal–Fowles comparison reinforces the notion that in the twentieth century suicide is seen (and has become) less and less as a maneuver *toward* a goal (heaven, reunion with God and with loved ones, attaining the peace of death, etc.) but rather more and more as a movement *away from* (an egression or escape from) some unacceptable or intolerable psychologically defined inner–felt anguish. For Pascal, death had to entail suffering (like Christ's death), and the goal of dying was to attain immortality through a Christ–like death. Suicide (from St. Augustine on) was interdicted and, for good Christians, was outside the pale of permissible acts. On the other hand, for many of us today (with Fowles as one spokesman), the quality of the *process* of dying—and not any pseudo-reality of a reified death— is, when we think about the topic, the main focus of our concern; suicide, when it does occur, is the understandable (but not necessarily welcomed) effort to forge a solution to a difficult problem, part of which is always the distressing presence of psychological pain.

I

Personology

MURRAY'S *EXPLORATIONS IN PERSONALITY*

For Henry A. Murray—biochemist, embryologist, surgeon, psychoanalyst, psychologist—the proper study of psychology is the human personality. "Man is today's great problem. What can we know about him and how can it be said in words that have clear meaning?" (1938, p. 3). All else is propaedeutic or ancillary. Ordinary common sense tells us that the study of man's personality has to include his thoughts and wishes and feelings and creations, as well as his behaviors when he is alone and when he is with others. Murray calls the study of personality "personology." Any systematic scheme about human personality (e.g., Freud's) can be called a personology.

Admittedly, I have an idiosyncratic view of Murray. For example, I think that the four most important things to know about him are that he has been a surgeon, that he was an embryologist, that he is a foremost Melville scholar, and that he was born wealthy. Successively, these four biographical facts relate, in my mind, to four outstanding characteristics of his thought, his approach, his work. They are: (1) His concern with precision and clarity; his penchant for *dissection* of ideas and his concern with classification and taxonomy; his detailed and careful concern with the real nature of things—reflections of the surgeon in him. (2) His concern with *time*, with process, with development, with *long*-term, longitudinal study (of a relatively few individuals); with serials, durances, micro- and macro-temporal units; his concern with the temporal elaboration of ideas; his statement that "The history of the individual is the individual"—all reflections of the embryologist in him. (The surgeon and the embryologist taken together are the physician in him, that aspect of him which is caring, compassionate, nurturing, concerned, and help-giving.) (3) His concern with philosophic, aesthetic and moral issues, especially the basic, core, hard, no-nonsense philosophic, aesthetic, and moral issues; his infinite preference for depth and elegance in thought and speech—all reflections of his profound understanding of and love for the genius works of Herman Melville. (4) His breathtaking creativity, originality, independence of thought; his intellectual autonomy; even his relative intellectual isolation; his princely manner—all reflections of his status as an independent person.

MURRAY'S EXPLORATIONS IN PERSONALITY

Murray's great whale of a book is called *Explorations in Personality* (1938). Murray's personology is a liberated and expanded psychoanalytically oriented approach to the study of personality and, like psychoanalysis, it is both a (separate) *theory* and a (special) *method* attempting, through the study of lives, to discover the basic facts about personality.

What are the special features of Murray's personology? His Personological System studies the whole organism, its internal states, its whole life history ("The history of the organism is the organism"), its environment (and the environment's *press* on the organism), its drives and needs, its behavioral trends, its unity thema (the "threads" of behavior that run through the life history), the functions and processes of its regnant (governing) brain ("No brain, no personality"), its inner thoughts (introspective awareness), its creative and proactive (in addition to its reactive) thrusts, its conscious and unconscious regnant processes, and more—as they interact and form a living human organism reacting and proacting in its physical and social environment. Murray is a centralist and wants to study—alive, dead, fictional, mythological—individuals, not to focus on behavioral bits and parts of fragmented traits ("the unimportant fragments of personality"). As to method: Murray's Personological System conducts personality studies serially over long durations of time (macrotemporal), in a multidisciplinary way (using a "Diagnostic Council" of experts assessing the same few individuals intensively from a variety of views and levels). All this has been done by Murray with conspicious originality and then written about by him in a Melvillean style quite unlike that of any psychologist now alive.

Because one of the main functions of personality is to reduce inner tension (some of the other main functions being self-expression and the reduction of conflicts by scheduling and by social conformity) and because the reduction of tension often revolves around the satisfaction of inner demands, the motivational aspects of psychological life and the concept of *needs* is a central focus of Murray's personology. Needs and hypothetical processes are necessary to account for observed behavior (action patterns) that reflect introspectively reportable inner tensions. A need, therefore, reflects both an inner experience of the mind and some directed (vectorial) magnitude in the brain.

In order to avoid the taint of anthropomorphism, Murray prefers to use the letter "n" to the word "need." He names and explicates some 30 psychological needs. Here—in an un-Murray-like fashion—is a list: n abasement, n achievement, n acquisition, n affiliation, n aggression, n autonomy, n blameavoidance, n counteraction, n conservance, n contrarience, n construction, n defendance, n deference, n dominance, n exhibition, n exposition, n harmavoidance, n infavoidance, n inviolacy, n nurturance, n order, n play, n recognition, n rejection, n retention, n sentience, n sex, n similance, n succorance, and n understanding. I shall discuss a half-dozen of these needs in a little more detail in the section on suicidal persons below.

THE ROOT METAPHORS IN
MURRAY'S PERSONOLOGY

Like any major psychological theorist, Murray presents a certain view of psychology, specifically that the proper subject matter for psychology is human personality and that the appropriate approach to this subject matter is a comprehensive (holistic, global, multidisciplinary) one that takes into account everything that ought to be accounted for. Murray is talking about a science of personality, which he calls personology. That science has a certain philosophy or methodological point of view. In order to understand the content and concepts of Murray's Personology, one must first understand its "philosophy."

The basic trade-off, it seems to me, in the study of anything as obviously complicated as human personality is between exact *precision* (of items of information which may or may not have too much practical bearing) and maximum *relevance* (of items of information that bear on the issues of interest but that may not have the desired level of preciseness). Many of the elegant parts of astronomy and physics and chemistry have that dual attraction of being both relevant and precise. In psychology, because of its very subject matter (mostly the products of the human mind) grasping both these goals simultaneously is certainly difficult, perhaps impossible to do. Much of the twentieth century American university-based psychology reflects a choice—most often, an overzealous one—for precision (in the model of nineteenth century physics, mostly) over relevance. Too often, the most interesting babies (of the mind) have been thrown out of the bathtub of academic psychology because they were not sufficiently statistically clean. The result is that we have often been left with the cleaner (there is nothing wrong with that) but the duller, often only distantly related, offspring. If a science of personality is not related to the important issues of its subject matter, then it cannot be too useful—no matter how (speciously) precise it seems to be.

This is not the place to recount a history of psychology or how, in Pepper's terms, the root metaphors of Formism and Mechanism have dominated and constricted the efforts of academic psychology. If Murray's work seems especially exciting and different it may be not only on account of its greater potential relevance to the problems of man in today's world, but also because it reflects the broader philosophic root metaphors of Contextualism and Organicism.

MURRAY'S WRITINGS ON SUICIDE

Tucked among Murray's writings there are occasional references to suicide. In one place he states: "Suicide does not have *adaptive* (survival) value but it does have *adjustive* value for the organism. Suicide is *functional* because it abolishes painful tension." One of the main functions of personality is to reduce tension. In this view, suicide is (only) an extension of normal personality functioning, albeit in an extreme circumstance.

As with Professor Pepper, I had the happy opportunity to play a catalytic role in stimulating Dr. Murray to write an essay on suicide. Inasmuch as the great American author, Herman Melville, has been the constant object of study by Murray throughout all his long adult life, it is no surprise that he chose to write an essay combining the topics of suicide and Melville. It is entitled "Dead to the World: The Passions of Herman Melville." It was written for a Special Lecture sponsored jointly, in 1963, by the University of Southern California and the Los Angeles Suicide Prevention Center. The central topic would seem to be varieties of deaths, including: ". . . temporary or permanent cessation of a part of psychic life—the cessation of affect (feeling almost dead), for example—or the cessation of an orientation of conscious life—the cessation of social life (dead to the outer world) or of spiritual life (dead to the inner world), for example—or . . . of different degrees and of change of degrees of life— near-cessation (as good as dead) or a trend toward cessation (diminution)."

Then, speaking of suicide and suicide-like events (pp. 499–500, 502): "Their intention was no more than an urgently felt necessity to stop unbearable anguish, that is, to obtain relief by interrupting . . .

the stream of suffering. . . . For what is suicide in most instances but an action to interrupt or put an end to intolerable affects? But do we know all we need to know about the nature of intolerable affects?"

A study from the Los Angeles Suicide Prevention Center (SPC) reported that suicides were characterized by: "(1) more crying spells, (2) more fist fights and violent episodes, (3) more severe depressions, and (4) more periods of withdrawal and mutism. Furthermore (5) they escaped from the hospital more often."

Murray takes these rather pedestrian points and transforms them into psychodynamic art, translating them to deeper layers of psychological understanding—much as Melville (in the fall from the yardarm in *White–Jacket*, for example) transmuted his straightforward source material into mystic art.

Here are Murray's five suicidal (and sub-suicidal) categories (pp. 503–516):

1. Pitiful forlorness, deprivation, distress, and grief (. . . as the nearest equivalent of the SPC's crying spells and maybe of one form of the SPC's depression).

2. Extrapunitiveness (blaming others), anger, hate, and physical aggressiveness (. . . nearest equivalent to the SPC's fist fights and violent episodes).

3. Intrapunitiveness, remorse, guilt, depression, bad conscience, and need for punishment (. . . nearest equivalent to the SPC's depression).

4. Affectlessness (one variety of "dead to the world," . . . nearest equivalent to the SPC's withdrawal and mutism).

5. Egression and desertion (. . . nearest equivalent to the SPC's leaving the hospital).

These are some of the main categories of affective states relating to suicide and substitutes for suicide; to death and to partial deaths of the social (outer) and psychic (inner) self. To summarize, these states can be listed as: distress (perturbation), anger (more perturbation), guilt, affectlessness (constriction), and egression (stopping the flow of unbearable emotion by leaving the scene or stopping one's conscious awareness of it). Taken together, that seems as cogent a psychological understanding of suicide as any.

And here is how, psychodynamically, Murray explains the suicidal and part-suicidal threads and inclinations in Melville's life (1967, p. 27; 1980, p. 516):

> The thread of fateful continuity that runs through the whole procession of negative states and emotions which we have been surveying in Melville's craving for the responsive, undivided, utter love of somebody whom he loves with his whole heart. Since this vision of affectional mutuality—the golden haven on the attainment of which his felicity depends—was never actualized for long enough to unify his being (because of internal and external impediments), what I have had to exhibit to you in this paper consists of hardly anything but a variety of reactions to the frustration of this craving in different situations, dating from childhood when love was fixated on his mother: piteous forlornness, desolation, grief—rage, fantasies of suicidal homicide, suicidal depression, egression as a substitute for suicide, egression as an intentional social suicide, and eventually, after several cycles of these grievous dispositions, a burned-out crater, dead inside as well as outside.

EXAMPLES OF POSSIBLE APPLICATIONS TO SUICIDAL PERSONS

We know that one of the hearts of Murray's personology is a focus on the motivational aspects of life—what Murray has labelled man's psychological *needs*. It makes fully as much sense to me to label, if label we must, suicidal incidents in terms of the psychological needs they were meant to redress as to label them in terms of Durkheim's anomic, egoistic, fatalistic, and altruistic suicides or Baechler's aggressive, escapist, oblative, and ludic suicides. I would, inasmuch as most suicides represent combinations of various needs, propose that we identify each suicidal act in terms of the two (and occasionally three) needs which seem to have been operative in the commission of that act. There is never a suicide without some keen need. The fulfillment or resolution of some need(s) answers the question of the *why* of any suicide. There are many pointless deaths, but never a needless suicide.

Here are some illustrative vignettes from *Voices of Death* (Shneidman, 1980, pp. 48–55) using Murray's terminology, of how suicides might be identified in terms of the psychological needs which they seem to seek to satisfy.

Dr. Paul Kammerer (1880–1926)

Some suicides seem to be related particularly to a sense of shame, "loss of face," disgrace or a sense of dereliction of duty. Prideful people especially seem vulnerable to these emotions. An example is the suicide of Dr. Paul Kammerer, an eminent Viennese biologist. His experiments with Alytes, the midwife toad (called that because the male toad wraps the fertilized eggs around his legs and carries them until they are hatched), attempted to prove the inheritance of certain acquired characteristics, specifically friction (or nuptial) pads on the front paws of the male toad, which helped him hold the female during mating. He had done 15 years of very careful work, breeding and observing these toads, when it was discovered that injections of India ink had been made into the paws of the demonstration specimens, thus producing false results. Although it is not known whether he, or a laboratory assistant attempting to be helpful, did the forging, Kammerer was a ruined man.

In the woods near Vienna, in 1926, six weeks after he was accused, Kammerer shot himself through the head. Here is a translation of the suicide note found beside his body:

Letter to whosoever finds it:

Dr. Paul Kammerer begs not to be brought to his home so that his family might be spared the sight. It would be the simplest and cheapest way to use the body in a dissecting laboratory of a university. This would also be most agreeable to me since, in this way, I would render science at least a small service. Perhaps my esteemed colleagues will discover in my brain a trace of the qualities they found absent in the expressions of my intellectual activities while I was alive. Whatever happens to the corpse—burial, cremation or dissection—its owner belonged to no religious denomination and wishes to be spared any kind of religious ceremony which would probably be refused to him in any event. This is not animosity against any individual priest who is as human as the rest of us and often a good and noble person.

There are several interesting details in this lugubrious document. The sense of shame, repentance, and restitution are evident. His attitude toward himself as already a corpse is striking, but his inability to see himself as dead—Freud had written that no one can truly imagine his own death, but always remained a spectator—is seen in the contradiction that he does not care what happens to the corpse, but that he (the living man? the corpse? and if the corpse, what difference does it make?) wishes to be spared a religious ceremony. There is a sense of counteraction: he rejects others before they reject him, as in his phrase ". . . which would probably be refused to him in any event."

What is *not* in the note are statements of affection and wishes for forgiveness from his family, warmth, and love. The note is largely a set of instructions to the person who finds his body, to the pathologist who dissects his brain, and to the priest who may or may not be good enough to conduct a tender ceremony. Finally, one can also infer that on an unconscious level, he views himself as a kind of priest of science who is as human as anyone and is really a good and noble person.

It seems to make most sense to view Kammerer's suicidal act as an overwhelming concatenation, in a disturbed individual, of several emotional surges in addition to the overarching shame: anxiety, anger, depression, hopelessness, guilt, rejection.

How shall we—using Murray's needs—label this suicide? I propose that we call it *Infavoidance–Defendance* suicide. Murray's definitions of these needs are:

n *Infavoidance*: To avoid pain, physical injury, illness and death. To escape from a dangerous situation. To take precautionary measures.

n *Defendance*: To defend the self against assault, criticism and blame. To conceal or justify a misdeed, failure or humiliation. To vindicate the ego.

Taken together, an Infavoidance–Defendance suicide implies that the purposes of that suicide are to avoid (continued shame), to defend (one's reputation against further assault), and to preserve and protect (one's self against further trauma in a future that is paradoxically destroyed by the suicide itself).

Admittedly, this kind of labelling in terms of needs may initially have an unfamiliar (and even peculiar) ring, but, on consideration, it is no more clumsy (and not a whit less meaningful) than to call a suicidal act Anomic or Oblative.

Fanny Godwin (1794–1816)

The sense of total rejection, in a personality that already deprecates itself, is often a root cause of self–destruction. In the following tragedy the cast of characters is as complicated as it is well known. Fanny Imlay, later Fanny Imlay Godwin, had a seemingly star-crossed life from the moment she was conceived. Her genealogy is a bit complicated but repays careful tracing. She was born in 1794, the illegitimate daughter of Mary Wollstonecraft, who was a famous feminist (the author of *The Rights of Women*) and of an American Revolutionary War captain named Imlay. Her mother then married William Godwin, a famous pamphleteer and political philosopher and novelist (who wrote *Caleb Williams*). A few days after giving birth to her half-sister (Mary Wollstonecraft Godwin, later the author of *Frankenstein*), who became the second wife of the poet Percy Bysshe Shelley, her mother died. Thus Fanny was Shelley's half-sister-in-law—and in love with him. All her short life she was the odd one: illegitimate, half-orphaned, excluded from the excitement of her half-sister's life, unnoticed or rejected by the beautiful Shelley, unemployed because of her famous but unsavory relatives, and living with the legacy of her own mother's suicide attempt when she was a young woman. In 1816, at age 22, Fanny Godwin poisoned herself in an inn at an English seaside resort. This is her suicide note:

> I have long determined that the best thing I could do was to put an end to the existence of a being whose birth was unfortunate and whose life has only been a series of pains to those persons who have hurt their health in endeavoring to promote her welfare. Perhaps to hear of my death may give you pain, but you will soon have the blessing of forgetting that such a creature ever existed.

The key words in this painful note are "being" and "creature." She is not a woman or a person or a human; she is just a biological thing that never should have been born. This is a note filled with nothingness; an overpowering sense of void and worthlessness. And to her mind, without love to fill that void, she might as well be dead.

In 1817, the year after Fanny's suicide, Shelley wrote a poem entitled "On Fanny Godwin."

> *Her voice did quiver as we parted,*
> *Yet knew I not the heart was broken*
> *From which it came, and I departed*
> *Heeding not the words then spoken.*
> *Misery—O Misery,*
> *This world is all too wide for thee.*

What to call this death? First the definitions:

n Abasement: To submit passively to external force. To escape injury, blame, criticism, punishment. To surrender. To become resigned to fate. To admit inferiority, error, wrongdoing, or defeat. To confess and atone. To blame, belittle, or mutilate the self. To seek and enjoy pain, punishment, illness, and misfortune.

n Succorance: To have one's needs gratified by the sympathetic aid of an allied person. To be nursed, supported, sustained, surrounded, protected, loved, advised, guided, indulged, forgiven, consoled. To remain close to a devoted protector. To always have a supporter.

I suggest we call Fanny Godwin's death an *Abasement–Succorance* suicide. Her abasement and self-abnegation seem apparent; her "gift" (that she gives to Shelley with her suicide) is her deep affiliation; and her crying need (coupled, no doubt with yearnings and fantasies) is for succorance. Quite a different psychological scene from that of Dr. Kammerer.

Elton Hammond (1786–1819)

Some few suicide notes are written as creeds. They are essays about suicide itself, specifically about a man's moral and legal right to take his own life if he so chooses. The most famous piece of "credo" suicidal writing is not contained in a suicide note but in the essay "On Suicide" by the eighteenth–century Scottish philosopher David Hume. So controversial was it considered that it was not published until a year after his death.

In his essay, Hume—who died a natural death (apparently of cancer) at age 65—sought to decriminalize suicide. In current terms, he might say that where the victim is oneself, it is an act within a consenting adult, and thus there is, in either the legal or the moral sense, no victim. Hume asserted that suicide is no crime; that there is no culprit; and, certainly, there is no sin.

Elton Hammond was an English eccentric who committed suicide at age 33 in 1819. Hammond was on the fringe of the literary life of eighteenth century England. He was somewhat peculiar, perhaps even insane. (He once announced to his sister that he was going to be greater than Jesus Christ.) But the main point here is not Hammond's mental health, but the clear way in which, in his suicide note, he stated a man's right to ownership of himself. It is an anti-clerical, anti-authoritarian credo.

It is probable that a man like Hammond would have known of Hume's essay. The similarities in thought and language between the two documents strongly suggest this possibility. But Hammond goes one better: He is not only writing about his beliefs about suicide, he is putting his life where his mind is.

Here is Hammond's suicide note:

TO THE CORONER AND THE GENTLEMEN WHO WILL SIT
ON MY BODY

Norwood, 31st Decr. 1819.

Gentlemen,

To the charge of self-murder I plead not guilty. For there is not guilt in what I have done. Self-murder is a contradiction in terms. If the King who retires from his throne is guilty of high treason; if the man who takes money out of his own coffers and spends it is a thief; if he who burns his own hayrick is guilty of arson; or he who scourges himself of assault and battery, then he who throws up his own life may be guilty of murder,—if not, not.

If anything is a man's own, it is surely his life. Far, however, be it from me to say that a man may do as he pleases with his own. Of all that he has he is a steward. Kingdoms, money, harvests, are held in trust, and so, but I think less strictly, is life itself. Life is rather the stewardship than the talent. The King who resigns his crown to one less fit to rule is guilty, though not of high treason; . . . the suicide who could have performed the duties of his station is perhaps guilty, though not of murder, not of felony. They are all guilty of neglect of duty, and all, except the suicide, of breach of trust. But I cannot perform the duties of my station. He who wastes his life in idleness is guilty of a breach of trust; he who puts an end to it resigns his trust,—a trust that was forced upon him,—a trust which I never accepted, and probably never would have accepted. Is this felony? I smile at the ridiculous supposition. How we came by the foolish law which considers suicide as felony I don't know; I find no warrant for it in Philosophy or Scripture.

I would rather be thrown naked into a hole in the road than that you should act against your consciences. But if you wish to acquit me, I cannot see your calling my death accidental or the effect of insanity, would be less criminal than a jury's finding a £10 Bank-of-England note worth thirty-nine shillings, or premeditated slaying in a duel simple manslaughter, both of which have been done. But should you think this is too bold a course, it is less bold to find me guilty of *felo de se* when I am not guilty at all, as there is no guilt in what I have done? I disdain to take advantage of my situation as culprit to mislead your understandings, but if you, in your consciences, think premeditated suicide no felony, will you, upon your oaths, convict me of felony? Let me suggest the following verdict, as combining liberal truth with justice:—"Died by his own hand, but not feloniously." If I have offended God, it is for God, not you, to enquire. . . . I am free to-day, and avail myself of my liberty. I cannot be a good man, and prefer death to being a bad one—as bad as I have been and as others are.

I take my leave of you and of my country condemning you all, yet with true honest love. . . . God bless you all!

Elton

As a footnote to this suicide document, it is sad to relate that the coroner's jury did not accede to Hammond's request; they rendered a verdict of suicide by virtue of insanity—exactly what Hammond did not wish. (This was done, in part, because Hammond's friend Henry Crabb Robinson did not turn over Hammond's letter to the jury, hoping, perhaps, to save his reputation.)

I shall call Hammond's death an Autonomy–Achievement suicide. Here are Murray's definitions of these needs:

n Autonomy: To get free, shake off restraint, break out of confinement. To resist coercion and restriction. To avoid or quit activities prescribed by domineering authorities. To be independent and free to act according to impulse. To be unattached, to defy convention.

n Achievement: To accomplish something difficult. To master, manipulate, or organize physical objects, human beings, or ideas. To do this as independently as possible. To overcome obstacles and attain a high standard. To excel oneself. To increase self-regard by the successful exercise of talent.

Ordinarily it would seem unlikely to identify any suicide with the need for achievement, but in Hammond's death—an act which we can legitimately call a "Credo suicide"—it is not difficult for us to understand his suicide as an intellectual protest, a philosophic essay in action, and as a conceptual achievement.

J

Systems Theory

MILLER'S *LIVING SYSTEMS*

Within the last 50 years, there has been an important advance in theoretical thinking based on the insight that there is a viable alternative to the mechanistic theories that have permeated physics, biology, psychology, and the social sciences. This alternative, called *general systems theory*, emphasizes the interconnectedness of parts within cell, organism, or collectivity, and the uniqueness of the whole. In her recent book on human behavior, *Thinking Creatively* (1984), Leona Tyler—leaning heavily on the work of Bertalanffy—lists nine characteristics found in all living systems:

1. Living systems are *open* rather than closed and have inputs, throughputs and outputs that process matter and energy, on the one hand, and information, on the other.

2. For a time such a system *counteracts entropy*, the universal tendency of matter to move toward a dispersed, inert state.

3. Systems show *complexity*, or differentiation of parts.

4. They contain basic *blueprints* that control their functioning—DNA for individuals, charters or bylaws for large groups.

5. They are made up of *macromolecules* and may include nonliving components.

6. They contain *subsystems*, the most critical of which is the decider.

7. They carry on processes through their own subsystems but may make use of nonliving materials outside their boundaries.

8. Subsystems are *integrated* into the system as a whole, which manifest *purposes* and *goals*.

9. Every system requires a *particular environment* for its functioning.

And Tyler adds:

10. Fundamental to systems thinking is the idea of *hierarchy* or systems within systems, organizations within organizations. In the human life, molecules are organized into cells, cells into organs, organs into the individual person, persons into groups, groups into organizations, organizations into societies. System theorists are seeking to elaborate principles that apply to all levels.

Ludwig von Bertalanffy is among the several major system theorists. His book, *General Systems Theory* (1969), is considered to be a landmark work. Other concepts and names associated with systems theory are the homeostatic physiology of Walter B. Cannon, the Gestalt psychology of Wolfgang Köhler and Kurt Koffka; the organismic neurology of Kurt Goldstein; the cybernetics of Norbert Wiener; the game theory of John von Neumann; the mathematical theory of communication (called information theory) of Claude Shannon and Warner Weaver; the social system theory of Talcott Parsons; the biomathematical general systems work of Anatol Rapoport; and the living systems of James Grier Miller.

Miller's 1978 book, *Living Systems*, is a big book; over 1100 closely reasoned, double-columned pages of small print, an encyclopaedia of twentieth-century physical, biological, and social science organized in a masterful fashion in terms of a brilliantly conceived scheme. More than an encyclopaedia, it is an empirically testable (confirmable or disconfirmable) scientific theory.

Miller states (p. 1):

> The general living systems theory which this book presents is a conceptual system concerned primarily with concrete systems which exist in space–time. Complex structures which carry out living processes I believe can be identified at seven hierarchical levels—cell, organ, organism, group, organization, society, and supranational system. My central thesis is that systems at all these levels are open systems composed of subsystems which process inputs, throughputs, and outputs of various forms of matter, energy, and information. I identify 19 critical subsystems whose processes are essential for life, some of which process matter or energy, some of which process information, and some of which process all three. Together they make up a living system. . . .
>
> Systems at each of the seven levels have the same 19 critical subsystems. The structure and processes of a given subsystem are more complex at a more advanced level than at the less advanced ones. This is explained by what I call the evolutionary principle of 'shred–out,' a sort of division of labor. . . . If at any single point in the entire evolutionary sequence any one of the 19 subsystems' processes had ceased, the system would not have endured. This explains why the same 19 subsystems are found at each level from cell to supra–system. And it explains why it is possible to discover, observe, and measure cross–level formal identities. . . .

The 19 critical subsystems of a living system include those which process matter–energy (the Ingestor, the Distributor, Converter, Producer, Matter–Energy Storage, Extruder, Motor, and Supporter); those subsystems which process information (the Input transducer, Internal transducer, Channel decoder, Net Decoder, Associator, Memory, Decider, Encoder, and Output transducer); and two subsystems that process both matter–energy and information (Reproducer and Boundary).

Into this framework, Miller places 173 hypotheses which he discusses in detail.

EXAMPLES OF POSSIBLE
APPLICATIONS OF LIVING SYSTEMS
HYPOTHESES TO SUICIDE

From the suicidological point of view, it seems to me that the main challenge (and the greatest potential) for living systems theory is—after having identified instances of literal or paradigmatic self-destruction in cells and organs and human collectivities—to formulate some generalization about self-destruction in all levels of living systems that are true and relevant for self-destruction *in man*. Perhaps our cells and our organs, our groups and our organizations, even—*especially*—in their self-destructive activities, can give us fresh insights into ourselves.

First example

Miller's Hypothesis 3.3.7.2-14 (p. 101) states:

A system which survives generally decides to employ the least costly adjustment to a threat or strain produced by a stress first, and increasingly most costly ones later.

Miller gives the following explication of this hypothesis (pp. 113–114):

This hypothesis is one manifestation of the principle of least effort. Systems tend to maximize gains and minimize costs. . . .

Cell. A hungry amoeba, for example, will eat food that is nearby first and later swim to more distant food.

Organism, matter–energy processing. If a continuously increasing amount of acid is injected into a dog's veins, a number of adjustment processes will protect the stability of the blood acidity from this stress. The first adjustment to reach its maximal effectiveness will probably be overbreathing, which produces alkalosis to compensate for the acidosis. Excretion of more chloride in the urine than usual (as ammonium chloride) and the 'chloride shift' in tissue fluids are other adjustments which aid in counteracting the stress; these adjustments probably achieve their maximal effects later than overbreathing does. Those organisms which can survive longest under stress may well be the ones which first employ the adjustments that use the most easily replaceable inputs (e.g., the nitrogen in ammonium chloride).

Organism, information processing. A normal person's adjustment processes against informational stresses, like his physiological adjustment processes, may ordinarily be mobilized in order of their costs, just as a good chess player sacrifices pawns before bishops and bishops before the queen. When people are unable to solve a problem or achieve a goal, for example, they may lower their levels of aspiration and try something simpler. This is relatively inexpensive. If this does not make them content, they may rationalize their behavior. . . . Repression, said by many psychiatrists to be a yet more costly adjustment, may be the next way of handling the stress if they are forced to continue working toward the goal. That is, their "attention may wander to other things," but the unresolved strain would still remain within them, which some have said can cause costly psychosomatic symptoms. Finally, to avoid the frustration of having an unresolved problem constantly obtrude on them, they may reject or refuse to attend to the entire informational input and a psychotic state may result, which would cut them off from close human contact and in other ways be extremely costly to them.

Organization. An army, in order to repel an attack, may first sacrifice a squad, then companies or regiments, and if still unsuccessful, finally throw into battle large mobile reserves like divisions.

For me, this cross-level hypothesis of Miller's—and his discussion of it—have obvious and interesting implications for *suicide*. This hypothesis implies a rank ordering of the processes of adjustment, including the employment of those processes ordinarily called "mechanisms of defense." It implies that a suicide is a *serial* phenomenon; that is, that the act of overt suicide is only the last (and not the first) maneuver in a sequence of more and more "costly" adjustment (albeit suicidal) processes. This further implies that we should be able to discern the prodromes of adjustment processes (that occur preliminary to the overt suicidal act). We would find these clues in the detailed (behavioral and introspective) history of that individual.

Further, this line of thought has direct implications for our understanding of the psychological constriction (narrowing of consciousness, tunneling of perception) that one typically sees in the suicidal state. We can now understand this constriction more clearly as being not *in* the overt suicidal act but existing *prior* to the suicidal state and in itself constituting a separate *suicidal* act. That is to say: The perturbation, inimicality, and constriction that are routinely and commonly noticed in relation to suicide may have been misconceptualized. The subtle distinction now is that they are not so much a part of *that* suicidal scene as they may represent a separate, previous (albeit masked) suicide attempt, a *sub*-suicide—which by its nature and through its consequences leads to the final fatal effort. From all this, we can venture to say that suicide is not the alternative to murder or based primarily on hostility (as is believed in this century), but is the consequence of constriction, which, itself, in an earlier turn-of-events, was the adaptive reaction to certain inner-felt psychic pain.

Second example

Hypothesis 5.2-7 (p. 106) states:

> When a barrier stands between a system under strain and a goal which can relieve that strain, the system ordinarily uses the adjustment process of removing the barrier, circumventing it, or otherwise mastering it. If these efforts fail, less adaptive adjustments may be tried, including (a) Attacking the barrier by energetic or informational transmissions, (b) displacing aggression to another innocent but more vulnerable nearby system, (c) reverting to primitive, nonadap-

tive behavior, (d) adopting rigid, nonadaptive behavior, and (e) escaping from the situation.

In Miller's discussion of the System Processes of Organism,° under the general heading of "Pathology" (5.5) he says:

> Diseases of organisms, like pathologies of systems at other levels, can be caused by lacks or excesses of either matter–energy or information inputs which are too great for the available adjustment processes to handle; inputs of inappropriate forms of matter–energy; inputs of maladaptive genetic information in the template; and abnormalities in either matter–energy or informational internal processes.

Then, under the category "Abnormalities in internal information processes," in a sustained reference to Karl Menninger's *The Vital Balance,* Miller says the following (p. 479):

> According to Menninger normal adjustments to ordinary stresses and the resultant strain includes such information processes as general irritability, feelings of tension, overtalkativeness, often repeated laughter, frequent losses of temper, restlessness, sleepless worrying at night, and fantasies about solutions to various real problems. Beyond these, in responses to stresses and strains of greater magnitude, more costly and more pathological adjustments are resorted to. They are pathological if more expensive adjustment processes are employed when less costly ones would suffice. Two hypotheses seem consistent with the view just stated: Hypothesis 3.3.7.2-14, which states that a system which survives generally decides to use first the least costly adjustment to a threat or strain produced by a stress and increasingly more costly ones later; also Hypothesis 5.2-7, which states that when a barrier stands between a system under strain and a goal which can relieve that strain, the system ordinarily uses the adjustment process

---

°A great deal of basic research exists in relation to this hypothesis. These studies are cited in Miller's book (pp. 106, 118, 479, 512, 592).

of removing the barrier, circumventing it, or otherwise mastering it [and] if those efforts fail, less adaptive adjustment may be tried. . . .

Beyond the normal adjustment processes, Menninger identifies the following five degrees of internal information processing pathology: (i) 'Nervousness,' a slight impairment of smooth adaptive control. (ii) Neurotic hysterical, obsessional, or anxiety symptoms, including character disorders. (iii) Directed aggression and violence, including some forms of 'self defense' or warfare which are condoned in many social contexts as well as chronic repetitions of mild aggression and explosive outbursts of serious violent and social unacceptable aggressions, such as murder, associated with pathological lack of self-control. (iv) Psychotic states of extreme disorganization, regression, and repudiation of the reality of inputs from the environment. And (v) extreme disorganization of control with malignant anxiety and depression, often resulting in death, frequently by suicide. . . .

In Hypothesis 5.2-7, one of the ways that a living system may respond to a barrier, having failed to remove or circumvent it, is escape.* It seems reasonable to suggest that the various ways in which cells, organs, organisms, groups, and organizations *egress*, the very act of egression—leaving the field, wandering off, moving away,†—has important implications for understanding *suicidal* behavior. With this interpretation, one tenable view of human suicide is that it is an effort to *stop* the flow of (inner-felt) unbearable

---

*Miller (in Chapter 5 of *Living Systems*) discusses eight adjustment processes (responses) to information overloading that apply to either meaningful or random materials. They are: chunking (that applies only to meaningful material), omitting, making errors, queuing, abstracting, filtering, employing multiple channels, and—the most extreme (i.e., most costly)—escaping.
†It is important to note the difference between a matter—energy escape (like walking out of a room or escaping from a prison) and the stopping of certain information input overloads, which is an internal information process. Miller uses "escape" to mean the latter. I believe—as I try to apply these ideas to suicide—that I mean both: Suicide is a (metaphoric) way of walking away from a situation or from life, (a busting out of the "prison" of this existence) and suicide is also a stopping of the process of an inner-felt overload of negative affective "information."

anguish or intolerable emotion by *escaping* from or taking leave of the mind that mediates it. All efforts to commit (lethal) suicide are efforts to stop the flow of the mind. What we ordinarily call the causes of suicide can now be seen as the "barriers" which could not be removed or circumvented. One can prevent suicide by making it unnecessary; one need only remove the stressful barriers. (Obviously, suicide prevention has to go outside the consultation office.) Barriers to what? In general, in suicide the barriers are those aspects of the life which stand, as it were, between the individual and a desired amount of sufficient *happiness*. The converse of happiness is pain, or misery, or physical or mental suffering. And when these are overbearing, they become the aspects of life that the suicidal person is seeking to escape.

In spite of these tiny glimpses of possible new insights into suicide, the critical challenge for systems theory still remains to be met: To find a sufficient number of persuasive (true and relevant) examples of self-destruction at the level of the human cell and organ and, again, at the level of human collectivities, and civilizations,* all of which could be duplicated in the self-destructive behaviors of the human organism. What insights and what handles on prevention that might give! A priori, the possibilities of accomplishing this task are there.

---

*Edward Gibbon's *The Decline and Fall of the Roman Empire* is essentially a story of self-destruction. Gibbon makes a persuasive case (in the famous Chapters XV and XVI) that greater than the "comparative harmlessness of the barbarians, and greater than the deleterious effects of Christianity"—perturbation and rigidity—"was the destructive action of the domestic quarrels (internal conflict) of the Romans themselves in finally effecting the fall of the Empire." Gibbon writes (Chapter LXXI): "In comparing the *days* of foreign, with the *ages* of domestic, hostility, we must pronounce that the latter have been far more ruinous to the city; and in our opinion is confirmed by the evidence of Petrach. 'Behold,' says the laureate, 'the relics of Rome, the image of her pristine greatness! neither time nor the barbarian can boast the merit of this stupendous destruction: it was perpetuated by her own citizens, by the most illustrious of her sons; and your ancestors have done with the battering-ram, what the Punic hero could not accomplish with the sword.' "—the *self*-destruction of the Roman Empire.

Part Four

Common Characteristics of Suicide

K

Headnote

The key question about suicide and the best approach to understanding suicide may indeed be isomorphic, one and the same. That question and the approach that it embodies is: What are the common overtly discernible and sensibly inferred characteristics of suicidal acts? I have developed 10 characteristics, postdictively, of individuals who have committed suicide and, paradictively, of individuals who are about to commit suicide. These 10 common characteristics are grouped under six different aspects of suicide. These are the situational, conative, affective, cognitive, relational, and serial aspects of suicide. These common characteristics of suicide are the bones and guts of this book.

The 10 commonalities answer the key question: What are the interesting, relevant common dimensions of committed suicide? They are what suicide is. They tell us what suicide is like on the inside, and what is sensible about it to the person who does it at the moment of its doing. I view these characteristics as reflecting a view of suicide influenced (if not illuminated) by the study of personology, systems theory, and a common–sense cosmological scheme.

Inasmuch as I emphasize the common characteristics of suicide, a few words about "common" may be useful. Each suicide is an idiosyncratic event. In suicide, overall, there are no universals, absolutes, or "alls." The best that one can reasonably hope to discuss are the most frequent ("common") characteristics that accrue to most committed suicides and to make this discussion in as reasonable and as ordinary a language as possible.

The issue of precision versus relevance touches even definition. Recognizing that suicidology (or psychology or psychiatry) does not have the veridical value of the laws of physiology or physics, I do not feel pressured to formulate a definition of suicide that might account for every imaginable esoteric, recondite or arcane occurrence of self-destruction. I am reminded of the flawed definition of Maurice Halbwachs (1930, p. 479):

> By suicide one means every case of death that results from an act undertaken by the victim himself with the intention, or the view to killing himself, *and which is not a sacrifice.''* (Italics in original.)

> (*On appelle suicide tout ças de mort qui resulte d'un acte acompli par la victime elle-même avec l'intention ou en vue se tuer,* et qui n'est pas un sacrifice.)

Why not a sacrifice?

Rather, I aim for a practical definition, guided by wisdom and common sense, that applies sensibly to *almost* every conceivable situation of self-destruction, whether done characterologically (macrotemporally) by a Cesare Pavese (1935–1950 [1961]); thoughtfully (mesotemporally) on principle, by a Socrates; dyadically (mesotemporally) by a John Doe with cancer who arranges his own death; or reflexively (microtemporally), born out of the situation-of-the-moment and the esprit de corps, by a soldier in combat who throws himself, in the presence of his comrades, on an enemy grenade. Each of these instances, I would maintain, can be meaningfully conceptualized—and in *some* cases could have been usefully treated—in terms of the 10 commonalities of suicide.

L

Situational
Aspects
of Suicide

In the popular mind (as reflected, say, in newspaper accounts), the causes of suicide are almost entirely identified with what serious suicidologists would call the precipitating events. These refer to such occurrences as suffering ill health, being jilted, losing one's fortune, being humiliated or shamed, and so forth. Environment is all. The stimulus is the fact wherein we catch the reason for the act.

Of course there are situational aspects in every suicidal act. Let me quote from Henry A. Murray on this matter in general (Murray, 1938, pp. 39–40):

> Since, at every moment, an organism is within an environment which largely determines its behavior, and since the environment changes—sometimes with radical abruptness—the conduct of an individual cannot be formulated without a characterization of each confronting situation, physical and social. It is important to define the environment, since two organisms may behave differently only because they are, by chance, encountering differing conditions. It is considered that two organisms are dissimilar if they give the same response but only to

different situations as well as if they give different responses to the same situation. Also, different inner states of the same organism can be inferred when responses to similar external situations are different. Finally, the assimilations and integrations that occur in an organism are determined to a large extent by the nature of its closely previous, as well as by its more distantly previous environments. In other words, what an organism knows or believes is, in some measure, a product of formerly encountered situations. Thus, much of what is now *inside* the organism was once *outside*. For these reasons, the organism and its milieu must be considered together, a single creature–environment interaction being a convenient short unit for psychology.

There are two common characteristics of suicide that may be thought of as being primarily *situational*. They are:

[I]   *The common* stimulus *in suicide is unendurable psychological* pain

Pain is what the suicidal person is seeking to escape. In any close analysis, suicide is best understood as a combined movement toward cessation of consciousness and as a movement away from intolerable emotion, unendurable pain, unacceptable anguish. Indeed, the wish or need to effect a cessation of consciousness is because of the pain. No one commits suicide out of joy; no suicide is born out of exultation. The enemy to life is pain and when pain does not come from one's soma then the threat to life is from those who cause the pain or the pain of emotion within one's mind. It is psychological pain of which we are speaking; metapain; the pain of feeling pain. As we shall see, the main clinical rule is: Reduce the level of suffering, often just a little bit, and the individual will choose to live.

The "common stimulus" can be read in systems theory terms as the "common information input" and, of course, is not precisely the pain itself but rather the desire to relieve the pain. Yet it is the pain—the naked psychological pain of ache or hurt—which is one of the several essential, but not sufficient, conditions of every suicidal act.

We speak of unbearable pain, unendurable anguish, intolerable emotion. One must ask: Are these in opposition to pain which is bearable, anguish which is endurable, emotion which is tolerable? Or is it not the case that the individual defines for himself what is possible or impossible and that the individual's definition or view of things is then the key factor? And further: In suicide there is the external situation (e.g., a concentration camp is real) and the internal situation, yet the external situation is defined by the individual as possible or impossible. To some extent, humans can define the situation and re-evaluate their needs.

It is methodologically not fair to define a situation post hoc (i.e., to state that the pain must have been unbearable *because* the individual committed suicide). In general, we can assert that an unbearable pain is a great pain about which the individual makes a qualitative judgment: This far and no farther. It is a level of pain exceeding a threshold that is unique to that individual. It is a judgment that touches on life itself. Is life worth living? It relates to Viktor Frankl's post-concentration camp writings (1963) on the *terrifying* meaning of life.

There is, in addition, some tangible evidence on this issue which may serve as the necessary evidence for establishing the operational meaning of "unbearable." These significant bits of evidence come to us from those rare individuals who have done a clearly lethal thing (such as shooting themselves in the head, immolating themselves, jumping from a high place) and have fortuitously survived. *Their* recitations of what was going on in their minds, their stories of unbearable pain and the inner-felt necessity to do *something* to stop the flow of unendurable anguish, give us the necessary epistemological grounds for making our assertions.

[II]   *The common* stressor *in suicide is frustrated psychological* needs

Suicide is best understood not so much as an unreasonable act—every suicide seems logical to the individual who commits it, given that person's major premise, style of syllogizing, and constricted focus—as it is a reaction to frustrated psychological needs. A suicide is committed because of thwarted or unfulfilled needs. Suicides are born, negatively, out of needs. In this sense one may say aphoristically: There are many pointless deaths but never a needless suicide.

Psychological needs are the very color and texture of our inner life. The systems theorist Ludwig von Bertalanffy (1969) emphasizes that self-destruction is intimately connected with man's symbolic and psychological world:

> The man who kills himself because his life or career or business has gone wrong, does not do so because of the fact that his biological existence and survival are threatened, but rather because of his quasi-needs, that is, his needs on the symbolic level are frustrated.

In order to understand suicide in this kind of context, we are required to ask a much broader question, which, I believe, is the key: What purposes do most human acts, in general, intend to accomplish? The best non-detailed answer to that question is that, in general, human acts are intended to satisfy a variety of human *needs*. In relation to suicide, there is no compelling *a priori* reason why a typology (or classification or taxonomy) of suicidal acts might not *parallel* a classification of *general* human needs. Indeed, such a classification of needs now exists. It can be found in Murray's *Explorations in Personality* (1938). These needs, as they stand, provide a possible useful taxonomy of suicidal behaviors.

Most suicides probably represent *combinations* of various needs, so that any particular case of suicide might be subsumed under two or three different categories. An example would be a person who commits suicide by means of Russian roulette (by firing a bullet through his head with a one-out-of-six chance of death), largely because of some scandal in which that person's honor and reputation have been impugned. Such an act would seem to have at least two components: The need, firstly, to avoid criticism, humiliation, shame, or blame, together with the need somehow to vindicate oneself or, to put it in a word, *Defendance*; and, secondly, because in this case the technique of committing suicide is too dramatic to be disregarded—the need, in these dire straits, to play with one's life, to gamble with fate, to take excessive risks, to leave life itself up to chance or, to put it in a word, *Play*. (I shall use the word "Ludic" here instead of "play" simply because the topic is too lugubrious to use this word with its more frivolous connotations.) Thus in this case, we might label that death as a Defendance–Ludic suicide.

The clinical rule is: Address the frustrated needs and the suicide will not occur. In general, the goal of psychotherapy is to decrease the patient's psychological discomfort. One way to operationalize this task is to focus on the thwarted needs.

M

Conative Aspects of Suicide

Traditionally, there were thought to be six "departments" of mental life. The sixfold classification is an old one, and the six types of activities have conventionally been termed: sensing, perceiving, thinking, feeling, *willing*, and doing. Willing and striving—the volitional aspects of mental life—are called conation. It is obvious that there are conative aspects to suicide. That is clear to common sense and immediately implied when we say that suicide is an "intentioned" act of self-destruction. One view of the suicidal world is as will and purpose. (The philosophically oriented reader may think of Schopenhauer's *The World as Will and Idea*, [1819], but that is more of a clang association than one that has direct relevance to this present context.)

In suicide there must be some willing, some formed purpose, some conceptualized goal, some striving in relation to some conflict. I envisage two common characteristics of suicide that form the *conative* aspects of suicide. (I shall continue numbering these characteristics sequentially from the beginning.)

[III] *The common* purpose *of suicide is to seek a solution*

First of all, suicide is not a random act. It is never done pointlessly or without purpose. It is a way out of a problem, dilemma, bind, challenge, difficulty, crisis, or unbearable situation. It has an inexorable logic and impetus of its own. It is the answer—seemingly the only available answer—to a real puzzler: How to get out of this? What to do? Its purpose is to solve a problem, to seek a solution to a problem that is generating intense suffering.

The Greek word *aristos* means the best possible solution in a given situation. The half dozen or more individuals whom I have talked to, who, in one way or another, had committed suicide and fortuitously survived have all said something like this: It was the *only* thing I could do. It was the best way out of that terrible situation. It was *the* answer to the problem I had to solve. I couldn't see it any other way.

In this sense each suicide is an *aristos*. Every suicide has as its purpose the seeking of a solution to some perceived problem. To understand what a suicide is about, one has to know the problem that it was intended to solve. It is important to view each suicidal act as an urgently felt effort to answer a question, to resolve an issue, to solve a problem.

[IV] *The common* goal *of suicide is* cessation *of consciousness*

In a curious and paradoxical way, suicide is both a moving toward and a moving away from something; the something that it is moving toward, the common practical goal of suicide, is the stopping of the painful flow of consciousness. Suicide is best understood not so much as a moving toward the idea of a reified death, as it is in terms of the idea (in the mind of the chief protagonist) of "cessation" (the complete stopping of one's consciousness of unendurable pain)—specifically when cessation is seen by the suffering individual as a solution, indeed the perfect solution, of life's painful and pressing problems. The moment that the idea of the possibility of stopping consciousness (popularly called "death") occurs to the anguished mind as the answer or the way out in the presence of the three essential ingredients of suicide (unusual constriction, elevated perturbation, and high lethality), then the igniting spark has been struck and the active suicidal scenario has begun.

The core ambivalence in suicide reflects the conflict between survival and unbearable stress. This core ambivalence can also be conceptualized as a conflict between incompatible goal states and their purposive desire, but the first view seems to reflect the basic conflict in a desperate life-and-death debate.

In response to the hostile and unfeeling question that, if a person wants to kill himself why not let him? one can answer that, if that same person wants to live, why not throw in one's energies on the side of life? I now believe that it makes more sense not to visualize this as a struggle between, say, two figurative angels or instincts (the angel of death and the angel of life) but rather to discuss this all-too-human conflict in concrete and effective terms, and to answer that question, "Why not let him?" by asking the practical counter question: "Why not reduce the level of his unbearable stress?" In effect, why not be a good person and *do* some things—often quite simple, inexpensive things like talking to some people, making some arrangements, contacting some agencies, manipulating some intransigents—in the suicidal person's behalf. What the suicidal person requires is only the efforts of a benign person, a decent citizen, a righteous champion, an effective ombudsman, a good Samaritan.

N

Affective Aspects of Suicide

Common lore would have us believe that suicide is almost entirely an affective (i.e., emotional) event. The fact that we know that there are many components in a suicidal act need not blind us to the importance of the emotional elements in the act without limiting our vision to them alone.

The discussion of affective states in this section will not be in terms of the usual litany of emotions (shame, guilt, rage, etc.). I shall try, instead, to focus rather simply on two common affective characteristics of suicide.

[V] *The common* emotion *in suicide is* hopelessness–helplessness

At the beginning of life the common emotion is probably randomized general excitement. In the suicidal state it is a pervasive feeling of hopelessness–helplessness. I believe that this formulation permits us somewhat gracefully to withdraw from the (sibling) rivalry among the various emotions, each with the proponents to assess that *it is* the central one of them all. Historically—in the twentieth century, that is—hostility was the eldest brother. Stekel said so in the 1910 meeting of the Psychoanalytic Society in Vienna: No one kills himself except as he fantasized the death of another. And then, in a somewhat more ornate phrase: Suicide is essentially hostility directed toward the (ambivalently viewed) introjected love object. One would plunge a knife into one's chest in order to expunge or kill the internalized homonculus of the loved–hated person within.

Today suicidologists know that there are such other deep basic emotions as shame, guilt, and frustrated dependency. The early psychoanalytic formulations are seen as brilliant hypotheses, more pyrotechnical than universal.

Underlying all of these—and others that might be mentioned—is that emotion of impotence, the feeling of hopelessness–helplessness. There is nothing that I can do (except to commit suicide) and there is no one who can help me (with the pain that I am suffering).

Coupled with this sense of hopelessness–helplessness is a penchant for precipitous capitulation, a tendency to surrender suddenly to all levels of adversity, a proclivity to "throw in the towel" the moment that one falls behind or suffers a set-back. A recent suicide note—written by a 34 year old single male—begins:

> I was diagnosed diabetic a few days ago. . . . They have just retested me but after going to the library and reading about the problem I know I do have the symptoms. At least I hope I'm right. Even if I'm borderline the regime is very stringent, measuring amounts of food and calories at every meal, keeping stress down Ha ha. . . . The kind of lifestyle I have set up for myself makes me lonely but this really does it. Oh, the final ticket is you have to measure amount of sugar in blood or urine at every meal and if its over (amt of sugar) that means you are doing damage to your body. . . . Life has been difficult enough but this has done it. When you read this—unless I've botched up—which judging from my view of life would be consistent—if I'm lucky I should be dead. I've shot myself in my bedroom closet. . . . When I last called you telling you of my disease I just felt a kind of business response (which I realize I didn't communicate enough how

badly I felt). But I debated about calling you before I did this but felt
no one really cared . . . Take care of yourself.

Closely related to hopelessness–helplessness is the overpowering
feeling of loneliness. To be alone in the world may be an existential
truth, but to *feel* alone in the universe can be a totally unnerving
experience. At U.C.L.A. Anne Peplau (1983) has studied and written
about loneliness. She has studied not suicidal people but lonely people—the non-mixers, the isolates, those without psychological and social skills that would permit them to find acquaintances or to make
friends. It is obvious that people are lonely for different reasons and
in different ways. There is emotional loneliness that rests on the important need to have a compatible, close, one-to-one relationship.
There is social loneliness, feeling disconnected, not tied in with
groups or sub-groups. And there is the loneliness of lacking strong
emotional ties; the loneliness of the passionless life, a condition of
affectlessness (Leites, 1953).

Professor Kenneth Colby, in his U.C.L.A. computerized course in
Programmed Information for Dealing with Depression and Suicide
(1984), states:

> In addition to hopelessness, people thinking of suicide often feel a
> terrible loneliness. That may shut one off from unfeeling others and
> one becomes numb, impervious to solace. Life, now grim as well as
> drab, loses its value and one determines to abandon it. Death seems
> the perfect release from troubles. . . Confusion will be ended and
> calm and control will finally be achieved.

That monumental twentieth century intellect Bertrand Russell
thought about loneliness. He wrote of it in the most personal public
place possible, his *Autobiography* (1067). The dramatic opening
lines are:

> Three passions, simple but overwhelmingly strong have governed my
> life: the longing for love, the search for knowledge, and unbearable
> pity for the suffering of mankind. These passions, like great winds,

have blown me hither and thither, in a wayward course, over a deep ocean of anguish, reaching to the very verge of despair. I have sought love ... because it relieves loneliness—that terrible loneliness in which one shivering consciousness looks over the rim of the world into the cold unfathomable lifeless abyss...

Russell speaks of loneliness again in the *Autobiography* when he describes his strange and deep relationship with Joseph Conrad.

The two things that seem most to occupy Conrad's imagination are loneliness and the fear of what is strange.... I have wondered at times how much of this man's loneliness Conrad felt among the English and had suppressed by a stern effort of will.

Here we have both personal loneliness and social loneliness in two great men. As a relevant aside, we now know that Conrad committed suicide and fortuitously survived when he was in his 20s. He shot a bullet through his chest. He told everyone, even his wife, that the front and back wounds were received in a duel, but correspondence written in 1879 from Conrad's uncle to a friend tells the true story. "The bullet goes *durch und durch* near his heart without damaging any vital organ" (Berman, 1977, pp. 30–31).

Dante's *Commedia* describes nine poetically described descending circles in the Inferno to the ultimate devilish pit. In the real hell of life, the levels of misery seem endless. With the possible exception of the Nazi extermination camps, something worse than one's present awful state can usually be imagined. And it is that "something worse" that we fear. That is the common fear—more pain, more degradation, more tension, more shame, more guilt, more terror, more hopelessness, more insanity; something far worse, like having to survive and face the next day. To the extent that suicide is an act to solve a problem, the common fear that drives it is the fear that the situation will deteriorate, become much worse, get out of hand, exacerbate beyond the point of any control. Better dead than mad. We have heard from the past generation of youth (and from humanistic psychologists) of ultimate moments, peak experiences, total actual-

izations, complete emotional states; but life is much more realistically understood in terms, not of superlatives, but of comparatives.
What we fear is something worse than what we have. Oftentimes,
persons literally on the ledge of committing suicide would be willing
to live if things—life—were only a little bit better, a just noticeable
difference, slightly more tolerable. The common fear is that the inferno is bottomless and that we have to draw the line on internal
suffering *somewhere*. Every suicide makes this statement: This far
and no farther—even though he would have been willing to live on
the brink.

[VI]   *The common* internal attitude *toward suicide is* ambivalence

One does not ordinarily think of Freud as a giant in the history of
logic but, in a way, he made as enormous an impact in extending our
understanding of our cognitive maneuvers as perhaps Bacon, Mill, or
Russell. Western logic is, in a word, Aristotelian. Aristotle's logic is
dichotomous; more accurately, it is binary: valid or invalid, true or
false, logical or illogical.

Freud brought to our attention a psychological truth that tran-
scends the Aristotelian conception of the neatness of logic. Something can be *both* A and non-A. We can both like and dislike the
same person; we can both love and hate a parent, a spouse, a child.
It is an Aristotelian question to say, "Make up your mind!" The answer is that we are of two minds, at least. We can now assert that
the prototypical suicidal state is one in which an individual cuts his
throat and cries for help at the same time, and is genuine in both of
these acts. This non-Aristotelian accommodation to the psychological realities of mental life is called ambivalence. It is the common
internal attitude toward suicide: To feel that one has to do it and,
simultaneously, to yearn (and even to plan) for rescue and
intervention.

O

Cognitive
Aspects
of Suicide

Figuratively speaking and from the point of view of logic, the suicidal individual hangs himself from his major premise and makes an erroneous deductive leap into oblivion. In the reasoning that accompanies every suicidal act there is a latent syllogism. Reason is as much a part of suicide as emotion is. Just as emotions may feel "necessary" at the moment of their expression, so illogical conclusions may seem "sensible" when they occupy and sway the mind.

The cognitive aspects of suicide include the individual's idiosyncratic styles of reasoning and his cognitive maneuvers (his *ways* of coming to conclusions) as well as his beliefs (his verbalized and unverbalized view of the world or cosmology, the content and tenacity of his religious beliefs, and his unspoken metaphors and hypotheses about causality—what is generally called his "philosophy of life"). Every adolescent and adult—each person in the world—has some intellectual attitudes about "what the world is like" and "what life is all about," and, in addition, has some ways of making his mentational way through the the labyrinth that is "out there" and, perhaps, beyond.

I have attempted to touch upon and illustrate some of these cognitive issues, as well as other issues, in Part Five. In that part there is a case history in which the reader may find illustrations of the cognitive aspects of suicide that are briefly discussed in this section.

There is no single suicidal logic; however, there are features of logical styles and ways of mentating that facilitate (even predispose) suicidal behavior. I call these kinds of reasoning catalogical because they are destructive; they are destructive not only in the sense that they abrogate the rules for logical and semantic clarity, but they also destroy the logician who thinks them.

Elsewhere, in order to illustrate a method of analyzing logical styles which I had developed, I published an analysis of the mentational characteristics of Kennedy and Nixon (1963, 1969) and some of the logical gambit displayed in *Moby-Dick* (1963). More to the point of this chapter, I have also analyzed some of the logical characteristics contained in suicide notes (1969, 1981).

Every suicidal syllogism seems "reasonable" to the individual who is thinking it. Indeed, those syllogisms may be valid even by rigid Aristotelian standards, if one accepts that person's major premise as true.

To my mind the key part of any suicidal syllogism is the major premise. If the basic tenet of your current belief (from which your conclusions flow) starts you off on the wrong foot, then it is very likely that you may take steps in a disastrous direction. That is why in my clinical work with suicidal patients I somehow find a way—without argumentation or exhortation—to indicate that we must look closely at that mischievous major premise, challenge it, and modify it, even a little. Just as one does not collude with a suicidal person in fact, one should not collude with a suicidal person in his logic.

In some suicidal logic the reasoning is characterized not only by deductive fallacies (peculiarities in the form of the argument) but also by certain semantic turns, wherein the aberrance is dependent on the meanings of the terms occurring in the premise or conclusions. An example of a semantic fallacy is as follows: "Nothing is better than hard work. A small amount of effort is better than nothing. Therefore a small effort is better than hard work." Here the fallacy is not dependent upon the form of the argument but rather on the ambiguous meaning of the terms "nothing" and "better." Another example of a semantic fallacy, this time with suicidal content, is this: "If anyone kills himself, then he will get attention. I will kill myself. Therefore I will get attention"; or, "I hurt and desire freedom from this pain. If I am dead I will not have this pain. Therefore I shall kill myself and feel pain no longer."

The fallacy is concealed in the concepts contained in the word "I"; specifically, it is between the self as it is experienced by the individual himself, and the self as he feels himself thought of or experienced by others. Actually, this is not so much a fallacy in the words of the reasoning as it is a confusion about the self, a fallacious identification. It is a psycho–semantic fallacy that may well occur whenever an individual thinks about his own death, inasmuch as an individual has great difficulty really imagining his own complete cessation, for even as he thinks about it he imagines himself as a spectator–survivor in a world after his death. If an individual feels that as a result of his committing suicide, "I will be cried over; I will be attended to," then he is in a maelstrom of semantic confusion, for the "I" that he is talking about will no longer exist to receive those experiences. Another semantic fallacy has to do with the nature of existence and the confusion of the real world— our only world—with a possible existence in a timeless–spaceless concept of hereafter.

[VII]   *The common* cognitive state *in suicide is* constriction

I am not one who believes that suicide is best understood as a psychosis, a neurosis, or a character disorder. I believe that it is much more accurately seen as a more or less transient psychological constriction of affect and intellect. Synonyms for constriction are a tunneling or focusing or narrowing of the range of options usually available to *that* individual's consciousness when the mind is not panicked into dichotomous thinking: either some specific (almost magical) total solution *or* cessation; all or nothing; or *Caesar aut nihil*, Caesar or nothing (to quote from Binswanger's famous case of Ellen West). The range of choices has narrowed to two—not very much of a range. The usual life-sustaining images of loved ones are not disregarded; worse, they are not even within the range of what is in the mind.

Boris Pasternak (1959), writing of the suicidal deaths of several young Russian poets, described life-threatening constriction in this way:

> A man who decides to commit suicide puts a full stop to his being, he turns his back on his past, he declares himself to be bankrupt and his memories to be unreal. They can no longer help or save him, he has put himself beyond their reach. The continuity of his inner life is broken, and his personality is at an end. And perhaps what finally makes him kill himself is not the firmness of his resolve but the unbearable quality of his anguish which belongs to no one, of this suffering in the absence of the sufferer, of this waiting which is empty because life has stopped and no one can feel it.

One of the most dangerous aspects of a suicidal state (high lethality/high perturbation) is the presence of constriction. Any attempt at rescue or remediation has to deal, almost from the first, with the pathological constriction.

People are often critical, prejudiced, and unforgiving about suicide; they forget that, for the victim also, it is a narrow-minded decision. This fact, that suicide is committed by individuals who are in a special constricted condition, leads us to suggest that one should never commit suicide while disturbed. It is not a thing to do while one is not in one's best mind. Never kill yourself when you are suicidal. It takes a mind capable of scanning a range of options greater than two to make a decision as important as taking one's life. Dichotomous slogans in a patriotic context (like "Death before Dishonor," "Live Free or Die," "Better Red than Dead," "Give Me Liberty or Give Me Death") have emotional appeal, but they are not sensible or wide-ranged enough to be prescriptions for making it through life. It is vital to counter the suicidal person's constriction of thought by attempting to widen the mental blinders and to increase the number of options, certainly beyond the two options of either having some magical resolution or being dead.

The penchant toward dichotomous thinking (as an aspect of constriction) is commonly seen in the suicidal person. On the non-suicidal side, we need to say that the world is filled with dichotomies, paradoxes, contradictions, double meanings, inconsistencies, and double binds. One essence of good adjustment is to be able to view these apparently frustrating situations as existential dichotomies rather than historic dichotomies that have to be solved right away. Existential dichotomies—like the researcher's choice between relevance and precision—are always with us, but we can get along with them and live with aspects of both horns of the apparent dilemma, soothing, harmonizing, and resolving them in this way. Adjustment lies in the fundamental abilities to make subtle discriminations and distinctions, to wink at disparities, to sense what is appropriate to the moment, and on occasion to do what one thinks is right rather than act on one's principles.

Dichotomies abound in our everyday thinking. There are a number of psychological phenomena that easily express themselves in terms of opposites: doubt vs. certainty, insecurity vs. security, passivity vs. aggression, hope vs. despair, dependency vs. emancipation, chance vs. organization, sacred vs. profane love, right vs. wrong, good vs. bad, and—most relevant to the suicidal person—life vs. death. It is when the topic of death (or, more accurately, cessation) occurs as the *only* possible escape, as the *alternative*, that a pressured person falls into a suicidal state. The suicidal person is a desperate person who, thinking of cessation as an escape, is suddenly haunted by his own polarities.

Of course, one's notions of death and life, one's cosmology, philosophy of life, one's epistemology are all relevant to suicide. The *idea* of death (or of cessation or of the stopping of consciousness) is an essential ingredient of suicide; indeed, it is the igniting spark. However, while there is some idea of life and death in every suicidal complex, the particular form that it takes does not seem much to matter.

Stephen Pepper has provided us with the golden grid. In his indispensable book, *World Hypotheses* (1942), he argues, totally convincingly to me, that all philosophies ever enunciated—from Socrates and before to Sartre and after—can be subsumed under six rubrics, which he calls root metaphors or world hypotheses, a basic way of seeing the world. These are discussed in Part Three, "Basic Texts," above. To mention them again briefly, they are: *Animistic* world hypotheses, in which man and spirit are the primary root metaphors, and *mystical* world hypotheses, in which mystical experiences—unnatural conceptions and births (Venus, Eve, Jesus), resurrection, rebirth, reincarnation—are the root metaphors. Pepper considers these two to be inadequate world hypotheses because of their imprecision or limited scope. It is obvious that all the world's organized religions fall under these two categories. To what extent suicides fall under these categories is not known.

The four adequate world hypotheses, according to Pepper, are: *Formism*, also called Realism or Platonic Idealism, in which the root metaphor is similarity; *Mechanism*, also called Naturalism or Materialism, in which the root metaphor is a machine; *Contextualism*, also called Pragmatism, in which the root metaphor is the historical event; and *Organicism*, also called objective idealism, in which the root metaphor is historical process, especially the integration appearing in that process.

It is obvious that none of the six world hypotheses is an innoculation against suicide. One might conclude from this fact that the specific root metaphor would seem to be irrelevant to suicide. Nevertheless, it remains true that *some* concept of naughtment, oblivionation, death, or cessation is a sine qua non for the initiation of the suicidal drama. Although any credal religion has some life-enhancing implications, it also—especially when combined with elevated perturbation and constriction (which the creed may exacerbate)—often contains significant life-diminishing (and suicide promoting) components. In the long run, credal beliefs may hasten more deaths than they save lives.

Pepper concludes one of his articles, "Can a Philosophy Make One Philosophical?" (1967) with these reflections:

The rational guidance of a philosophy of life is available only to a relatively well-integrated personality whose unconscious conflicts (such as he has) do not overpower his voluntary actions. To such a man an adequate philosophy would be his safest guide through life. And to my mind, for all who are in a position to acquire it, an explicit philosophy is a guide greatly superior to a purely institutionalized ideology or creed. For even when not inadequate, the latter is rigid and dogmatic, whereas the former may be flexible and open to revision.

Inasmuch as suicides are distributed among adherents to these six hypotheses in currently unknown proportions, it remains for future empirical studies to tell us what these distributions are and, more importantly, if adherence to one or the other root metaphor has a significantly lower representation among suicides. All we know at present is that adherence to animism and mysticism (i.e., organized religion) is definitely not a philosophic innoculation against suicide.

P

Relational Aspects of Suicide

Who can deny that suicide often seems like a dyadic event between two unhappy people? Suicide commonly occurs in a dyadic context, seemingly as an almost direct result of rejection, abandonment, guilt, revenge, pity. Durkheim emphasized a person's relationship to his or her society; nowadays we talk much more about the relationship with the significant other. What we have not looked at so carefully are the common relational aspects of suicide other than specific psychodynamics or emotional states. Two of them, the common interpersonal act and the common action, are presented below.

[VIII] *The common* interpersonal act *in suicide is* communication of intention

Perhaps the most interesting finding from large numbers of retrospective psychological autopsies of unequivocal suicidal deaths is that in the vast majority there were clear clues to the impending lethal event. These clues to suicide are present in approximately

80% of suicidal deaths. Individuals intent on committing suicide, albeit ambivalently-minded about it, consciously or unconsciously emit signals of distress, indications of helplessness, pleas for response, and opportunities for rescue in the usually dyadic interplay that is an integral part of the suicidal drama. It is a sad and paradoxical thing to note that the common interpersonal act of suicide is not hostility, not rage or destruction, not even the kind of withdrawal that does not have its own intended message, but communication of intention.

Everyone in suicidology now knows the usual clues, verbal and behavioral: The statements are tantamount to saying: "I am going away [egression], you won't be seeing me, I cannot endure it [the pain] any longer;" the unusual acts for that person are putting affairs in order, giving away prized possessions and, more generally, behaving in ways that are different from his usual behaviors and betoken a bubbling (as a cauldron bubbles) in a perturbed psyche.

The communication of suicidal intention is not always a cry for help. First, it is not always a cry; it can be a shout or a murmur or the loud communication of unspoken silences. And it is not always for help; it can be for autonomy or inviolacy or any of a number of other needs. Nonetheless, in most cases of suicide, the common penultimate act is some interpersonal communicative exchange related to that intended final act.

[IX] *The common* action *in suicide is* egression

Egression is a person's departure or escape, often from distress. Egression means to leave, exit or escape. Suicide is the ultimate egression, besides which running away from home, quitting a job, deserting an army, leaving a spouse, seem to pale. Erving Goffman (1967) spoke of "killed moments" or "unpluggings" such as having a good read, darting into a movie, going for a weekend at Las Vegas or Atlantic City—benign expressions all. But we must distinguish between the wish to get away and the need to end it all, to stop it for real. The point of suicide is a radical and permanent change of scene; the action to effect it is to leave.

Here from Nicolson's *Portrait of a Marriage*, (1973, p. 179) is an excerpt from a letter, dated March 26, 1921, from Violet Keppel Trefusis to her lover Vita Sackville West, then in the eighth year of her unusual bisexual marriage to Harold Nicolson.

> I am dead with grief. I am utterly alone. You cannot want me to suffer so. You had to choose between me and your family, and you have chosen them. I do not blame you. But you must not blame me if one day I seek for what escape I can find.

In the only unnecessary line in that fascinating book, Nigel Nicolson informs us that that passage refers to suicide. Indeed, it is a pithy definition of what, at rock bottom, the suicidal person's point of view in suicide is: "... what escape I can find." In that brief quotation from the letter, one can see intimations of several common characteristics of suicide: the wish for cessation, the need to stop pain, the sense of hopelessness, the presence of constriction, the communication of the intent, and the search for escape.

In a special discussion of Melville and his egressions, Henry Murray (1967) discusses suicide and egression. Murray (pp. 22–23) alerts us to the fact that not only is suicide total egression, "... which may be defined for present purposes as a person's intended departure from a region of distress, chiefly with the aim of terminating with relief the pain he has been suffering therein," but that there are also egressions that can be partial or fractional, like partial deaths of the self "by the outcrossing of established boundaries of a territorial, social or cultural domain within which a person is conventionally expected or legally required to abide or play a role." This opens to us the vast topic of what I have called subintentioned deaths, those deaths—call them natural, accidental, or homicidal—in which the decedent has played a partial, covert, latent, or unconscious role in either effecting or hastening his death. Here is the key paragraph from Murray (p. 25):

. . . we can see that egression not only may be, as it is in many cases, the expedient substitute for total suicide (insofar as it results in a surcease of pain), but ultimately, in some rare cases, may constitute a wilful, partial suicide by taking the egressor beyond the tolerance of his fellowmen and of his own conscience, or, in other words, to the point where he is *as good as dead* in the affections of the world and *they* are as good as dead in *his* affections.

This kind of living death, death of parts of the self, social suicide, bringing one's death unnecessarily closer is a topic too large for our present discussion. Suffice it to say that the omnipresent feature of the act of overt suicide is egression. Suicide is a death in which the decedent removes himself from intolerable pain and simultaneously takes himself from others in the world in a precipitous fashion.

Q

Serial
Aspect
of Suicide

In a sense, the personality of an individual is his history; his history *is* his personality (Murray, 1938). In a concatenated way, there is a discernible history to every suicidal event; its scenario, its second by second development from the first moment of the thought of self-destruction to the death. In this scenerio one can see points at which it might have been interrupted and the lethal outcome prevented. There are threads or unity *thema* in each suicide; there are threads or unity *thema* in each life; and there are consistencies, in every case—it could not be otherwise—between certain aspects or features of a suicide and certain aspects or features of that life of which it is the ultimate part.

This section has only one common characteristic of suicide: its common consistency.

> [X] *The common* consistency *in suicide is with* life-long coping patterns

People who are dying over weeks or months of a disease (e.g., cancer) are very much themselves, even exaggerations of their normal selves. Contrary to some currently popular notions, there does *not* seem to be any standard set of stages in the dying process through which individuals are marched, lock-step, to their deaths. In terms of emotions displayed (rage, acceptance, etc.) or mechanisms of psychological defense manifested (projection, denial, etc.) one sees a full panoply of both of these arranged in almost every conceivable number and order. In almost every case what one does see are certain displays of emotions and use of defenses that are consistent with *that* individual's microtemporal, mesotemporal, and macrotemporal reactions to pain, threat, failure, powerlessness, impotence, and duress in previous episodes of that life. People who are dying have enormous consistency with themselves, a steadiness over time, an adherence to certain internal principles of behavior. So do suicidal people. So do people who are neither dying nor suicidal.

In suicide, we are initially thrown off the scent because suicide is an act which, by definition, that individual has never done before—so there is no precedent. And yet there are deep consistencies with lifelong coping patterns. We must look to previous episodes of disturbance, to capacity to endure psychological pain, and to the penchant for constriction and dichotomous thinking, for earlier paradigms of egression.

On this issue I speak with a tiny bit of experimental authority, at least with a sense of conviction that flows from some data I have examined (1970), specifically a study of 30 men who were about 55 years old, each of whom had been studied rather intensively on a continued basis since he was about 6 years old. The men were subjects in the well-known Terman longitudinal study of 1528 gifted male and female subjects, begun in 1921 and continuing to this date at Stanford University under the direction of Professor Robert Sears. In my bite-size study, two findings are relevant here. The first was the demonstration that it was possible (way beyond chance expectation) to select the five subjects who had committed suicide from the group of 30 cases. Second, and the main finding, was that—working as I did, from a detailed life-chart which I constructed for each individual—the determination that the person would (or would not) commit suicide at around age 55 could be made before the 30th birthday

in each man's life. There were already certain psychological consistencies within the life, certain characteristics or habitual patterns of
reaction for that person to threat, pain, pressure, and failure which
made dire predictions of a tragic suicidal outcome at 55 an almost
straightforward logical and psychological extrapolation.

In the sight of the enormous unpredictability of life, what im-
presses and excites me as a suicidologist is how much of a person's
life, in some of its more important aspects, is reasonably predictable.
In general, I feel that suicide, although enormously complicated, is
not totally random and it is amenable to a considerable amount of
prediction. That is our main handle on individual prevention.

Part Five

A Case Illustration

R

Headnote

In this Part, I wish to present an extensive illustration which focuses primarily on one aspect of the total suicidal picture, specifically the cognitive, mentational, and logical characteristics of suicide. I wish to do this by means of a study from literature, using Herman Melville's *non pareil* psychological masterpiece, *Moby-Dick*.

A similar analysis could, in theory, be made for each of the other nine common characteristics of suicide. It follows that a full explication or comprehensive assessment of any one suicide case ought to include an analysis in terms of all ten common characteristics, together with a summary or synthesizing statement and evaluation—a book in itself.

The contents of this sample part on logic will be presented under four headings: (1) Prologue; (2) case history data; (3) self-destructive patterns of logic; and (4) the role of hostility and the possible presence of insanity.

S

The Suicidal Psycho-Logics of *Moby-Dick*

PROLOGUE

From a tactical point of view, it is not necessary for the development of the flow of this book on suicide for me to engage in a disputation about the relative merits of the case history (idiographic) and statistical (nomothetic) approaches to knowledge. My attitude is: A blessing on both your houses—except that, unlike many dogmatic behaviorally oriented scientists who act as though only they have a strangle hold on science, I would wish that the idiographic study of man *also* be included.

Gordon Allport (1937, 1942) is generally credited with introducing Wilhelm Windelband's (1904) terms "idiographic" and "nomothetic" to American behavioral scientists. I, myself, tend to believe that the great impetus given to the intensive study of individual cases, and the necessary concomitant explicit stance against the specious accuracy of irrelevant numbers was trumpeted by Henry A. Murray, in 1938, in *Explorations of Personality*. Windelband, in his *Geschichte und Naturwissenschaft* (*History and Science*; 1904), proposed that there were two different approaches to knowledge. The tabular, statistical, demographic, nomothetic approach dealing with generalizations; and the idiographic approach, involving the intense study of individuals—the clinical methods, history, biography, Q-methodology, psychobiography and longitudinal studies of several or many individuals, for each of whom there is an enormous amount of data to be examined systematically. Runyan has provided us with an excellent summary of the idiographic–nomothetic discussions and debates of the 1950s and 1960s, citing the arguments and the words of over three dozen investigators, notably Allport, Holt, Meehl, Stephenson (Runyan, 1984; pp. 166–191).

As far as suicide is concerned, it did not seem necessary for me, in this volume, to reprint nomothetic data (tables and statistics) nor to repeat the usual tabular, epidemiological numbers, and assertions about suicide in relation to social class, gross national product, unemployment, or state of war. In relation to the last-named, we now know—since Korea and Viet Nam—that we must differentiate between suicide rate fluctuations with good (cathected) wars and bad (uncathected) wars.

I write primarily as a clinician, focally interested in the prevention of individual suicides and in the treatment of individual patients. In that sense I espouse an idiographic orientation to the study of suicidal lives, and thus it is almost natural for me to advance the flow of my thought in this book by means of an illustrative document, involving the explication of a single case.

The case that comes first to mind is my old Satanic self–destructive favorite, Captain Ahab of the *Pequod*. I shall use Herman Melville's monumental book, *Moby-Dick*—which I consider to be the greatest book written by an American—to illustrate some of the common cognitive characteristics of suicide as I have outlined them in this book. I shall try to do this by focusing on the logical gambits within *Moby-Dick*, particularly as they touch upon self-destruction. In this enterprise I am emboldened by my view that, at its heart, *Moby-Dick* is essentially a book about suicide, and that Melville had both the gifts and the temperament to know (and to interrelate) the inside workings of human self-destruction.

In Chapter 15 ("Chowder") of Melville's *Moby-Dick*, Ishmael, as a temporary guest of the Spouter Inn in New Bedford, is given the choice by Mrs. Hosea Hussey of two types of chowder: clam or cod. Ishmael's response merits repeating: " 'Both,' says I 'and let's have a couple of smoked herring by way of variety.' " I make much more of that seemingly innocuous word "both" in my discussion of *Moby-Dick*, below, but here I can say that I feel strongly about the idiographic–nomothetic matter. Of course I prize nomothetic data when they are useful, but I think it nonsensical to disregard idiographic data (as much of psychology seems to be bent on doing) on some silly principle that they are not sufficiently rigorous or scientific in terms of the standards of physiology or physics.

In taking this position, I am following what Murray has taught me: That a discipline can be no more scientific than its subject matter will allow. A suicidologist—at any rate, my kind of suicidologist—is essentially a personologist. The accuracies of other fields of science, like physics or chemistry, are not consistent with what we know today about the activities, conscious or unconscious, of the human mind. Of course the *person* is our legitimate subject matter. There is no point in achieving accuracy if one sacrifices relevance in the process. I am interested, not in what has specious accuracy, but in what is useful and what makes sense. I trumpet the virtues (and the excitements) inherent in such "personal documents" as diaries, logs, memoirs, autobiographies, letters, suicide notes, and anamnestic and catamnestic accounts. Murray says that the history of the personality *is* the personality. For me, a first-rate biography beats any case report. Much of the interesting part of life is inferential, attributive. (That is almost entirely what psychodynamic psychiatry and clinical psychology consist of.)

For Murray, the intensive, multifaceted study of the individual is the central enterprise for the personologist—and, from my view, for the suicidologist as well. Further, the individual to be studied need not be alive and present to qualify as a subject for interest. We can also fruitfully study individuals who are alive but not available, who are dead, or who are historical, fictional, aprocryphal, or mythological figures.

A brief survey of logic is now in order to establish the basis for my later discussion of the self-destructive patterns of logic to be found in *Moby-Dick*. The reason for this explication will, I trust, become obvious as one reads on.

The history of logic is a long and interesting one. Here, in an admittedly oversimplified view of Western deductive logic, I identify five major themes or sets of names:

1.   *Aristotle* dominates logic as Mt. Everest might dominate the plains of Kansas. He is the source of the concept of the syllogism. Refinement and improvement of his system have constituted the art and science of logic for the past 2000 years. Other than prayer, the principal occupation of the monasteries of the Middle Ages seems to have been a cerebral bead-counting of the Aristotelian syllogistic forms. What is considered to be correct, reasonable, sensible, or logical today is usually defined in terms of the traditional Aristotelian rules for reasoning.

2.   The bulk of Aristotle's logic is *deductive*, consisting of identifying all the statements (as either true or false) that are implied or imbedded in premises or syllogisms. Another rather different kind of reasoning, the *inductive* method flows from a number of actually observed facts to *one* empirical generalization or conclusion. Two giants are identified with this approach. First, *Francis Bacon*, who spoke of the kinds of rational lapses men are liable to make when they attempt these inductions, linked such errors to false gods and called them Idols—Idols of the Cave, of the Tribe, of the Marketplace, and of the Theater. Second, *John Stuart Mill* in *The System of Logic* propounded in 1843 a set of basic rules for establishing causality inductively. These are the Methods of Difference, of Agreement, of Agreement and Difference, of Residues, and of Concomitant Variation.

3.   Since the nineteenth century there has been a major refurbishing of Aristotelian logic, sparked in large part by the insight that mathematics is itself a form of logic. Associated with this development are Frege, Boole, De Morgan, Peirce, Peano, Russell, Whitehead, and the "Vienna Circle" (Carnap, Wittgenstein, Reichenbach), all of whom believed that the single proper function of philosophy was to clarify language. Their doctrine of *Logical Positivism*, which totally eschews the traditional topics of philos-

ophy (such as cosmology, epistemology, ethics, esthetics), has had an enormous impact on Western thought, perhaps, in part, because of the sanctified position in which we moderns hold mathematics and precision.

4. Not many people think of *Freud* as a giant logician. There are those of us, however, who believe that one of Freud's major contributions is to the world of thought and logic. His emphasis on unconscious processes and on the concept of ambivalence showed us that the dichotomy deemed to be absolutely basic to Aristotelian thinking (A vs. non-A) was not necessarily psychologically sound. One could both love and hate at the same time; a person could simultaneously wish to die and entertain fantasies of rescue and intervention. Freud changed Aristotle's monologic to a more psychologically sophisticated multilogic. For our purposes what is especially interesting is that Melville anticipated Freud in this important respect.

5. Most of us take it for granted that Western (Greek–European–American) logic is the only logic in the world. Of course, this is not so. There are ancient Eastern logics which are predicated on styles of thinking that are fundamentally different from Western ways of reasoning. Hajime Nakamura's monumental book, *The Ways of Thinking of Eastern Peoples* (UNESCO, 1967), for instance, explicates the dimensions of Japanese, Chinese, and Indian logics. Indeed, the Whorf–Sapir hypothesis (that our thinking is filtered through our language) should alert us that there are at least as many basic logics as there are language types, so we might expect a Standard Average European logic, and Arabic logic, a Chinese logic, a Hopi logic, an Eskimo logic, and so on.

There is much more, then, to deductive logic than classical Aristotelian syllogisms. Human beings employ many ways of coming to conclusions that are simply not accounted for in traditional logic. Further, many gambits of reasoning that receive poor marks in the Aristotelian system are better understood not as "errors" but as "idiosyncrasies of reasoning," that is, as part of cognitive style in which these idiosyncrasies seem to work quite well and to "make sense" to the person who employs them. In my own work I like to distinguish at least four kinds of deductive logic. I call these Denotative Deductive Logic, Connotative or Conditional Deductive Logic, Non-Summative Deductive Logic, and Paralogic. I shall discuss them in turn.

Denotative Deductive Logic

This is the traditional Aristotelian logic which depends solely on its formal structure. In this system, language sentences are represented by their denotated place. All subjects (S) are equal; all Predicates (P) are equal. Any P is equal to any other P. There is no flexibility about it. The well known syllogism about Socrates' mortality is equally and inflexibly true of Plato, Descartes, Smith, Jones, or anybody. It simply asserts that when all S is P (all men are mortal), then every S is P (any man is mortal).

Using S and P, four kinds of propositions can be generated: Universal affirmative (all S is P); universal negative (no S is P); particular affirmative (some S is P); and particular negative (some S is not P). These are labelled A, E, I, and O propositions, respectively.

A syllogism consists of two propositions and a conclusion, each being an A, E, I, or O statement. There are then 64 possible combinations or *moods* of the syllogism (AAA, AAE, AAI, etc.) of which only 16 are logically valid. The other combinations contain logical errors and are considered invalid.

Connotative or Conditional Deductive Logic

There is, of course, more to deductive logic than the classical textbooks say. There is a kind of logic—conditional logic—that purists would never admit. Connotative or Conditional Deductive Logic embodies the notion that the correctness of reasoning may depend on the time or place or circumstances. These circumstances may even include the emotional, psychological, or ethical state of mind of the logician. In other words, the logic depends, in part, on the connotative overtones of the words. Symbols alone will not do: Not all Ss or Ps are alike.

Logic itself is contextual or conditional. This idea is as unacceptable to Aristotelian logic as the idea that the meaning of a group of numbers depends on anything other than invariable addition. But reasoning is more complicated than mathematics precisely because it is touched by psychological and other contextual factors. All these notions lead us to a second, closer look at the seemingly least important word in the syllogism, the bridgeword "therefore."

At first, the most innocuous word in the syllogism is this simple conjunction. When someone says "therefore," we assume that person has come to some sort of decision or resolution. "Therefore" implies that the speaker has not only been thinking but, more than that, coming to conclusions. It is the pivotal word in the syllogism.

It is generally believed that not much need be said about "therefore." It is simply that automatic process—the colorless conjunction—between the premises and the conclusion. It is viewed as a sort of clearing of the throat after the "whereas," the signal before one gives the punch line (the conclusion) of the cognitive resolution. But "therefore" does not always indicate a totally automatic or innocuous operation, as we shall soon see when we examine the text of *Moby-Dick*. Sometimes the supposedly automatic "therefore" is tempered by qualifications and conditions that radically change its meaning and its impact within the flow of thought.

Apropos of conditional logic, Nicholas Reschler in his monograph *Temporal Modalities in Arabic Logic* (1967), quoting from the tenth–century Persian philosopher Avicenna and the thirteenth century Persian logician al-Qazwini-al-Katibi, points out that the Persians introduced temporal and quantitative qualifiers of the basic Aristotelian absolute categories of "all" and "none," such as "necessarily," "perpetually," "non-necessarily" and "non-perpetually." Thus, in the Persian logic of centuries ago, there were four basic modal relationships which reflected two dimensions that are not at all represented in Aristotelian logic: (1) a temporal dimension of ubiquity and occasionality; and (2) a possibility dimension of necessity (certainly) and mere probability.

Non-Summative Deductive Logic

This type of logic asserts that one thought can actually be a half, or two, and that the two can even be contradictory while embraced in the same thought. In other words, moieties, ambivalences, and oxymorons can all be integral parts of the flow of thought.

One or two key words can signal a major shift in emphasis. Words like "both" and "half" tell us that we are dealing with modes of logic that are clearly outside the ordinary Aristotelian mold. At the Try Pots Inn, when Ishmael answers Mrs. Hussey's query, "Clam or cod?" with "Both," he is asserting the possibility of the simultaneous presence of A and non-A. It is decidedly non-Aristotelian. On a much more profound level, the line "On life and death this old man walked" (Chapter 51) clearly asserts the possibility of psychological simultaneity of logical opposites. The use of "both" is critical in Melville's expanded logical style.

Paralogic

Paralogic is an openly flawed way of reasoning, a cryptologic, an illogic, a crazy logic. In a collection of nine brief essays edited by J. S. Kasanin entitled *Language and Thought in Schizophrenia* (1944/ 1964), there is a short piece by Elhard von Domarus entitled "The Specific Laws of Logic in Schizophrenia." He puts forth the view that, in terms of formal logic, schizophrenic thinking involves erroneous reasoning in terms of attributes of P (instead of correct thinking in terms of attributes of S) and it commits the error of the "undistributed middle term."

A few examples should clarify the principle. A female patient claims that she is the Virgin Mary. Elucidation of her thinking reveals that her basic syllogism is the following: The Virgin Mary was a virgin; I am a virgin; therefore I am the Virgin Mary. Another example: Certain Indians are swift; stags are swift; therefore—so reasons the paralogical thinker—certain Indians are stags.

Although I conceive the primary focus of this chapter to be the cognitive and logical aspects of suicide, I now need to comment briefly on the *psychodynamics* of suicide—the unconscious dramas of latent emotional or thematic forces within the psyche. But I need to precede such a discussion with two brief general comments.

1.   The traditional psychoanalytic position about the psychodynamics of suicide relates primarily to *hostility*. At the famous meeting of psychoanalysts (Freud, Jung, and others) in Vienna in 1910, Wilhelm Stekel said that "No one kills himself who has never wanted to kill another or at least wished the death of another" (Friedman, 1967). A more complicated way of saying this goes something like this: Suicide is to be understood as hostility directed toward the ambivalently viewed introjected love object; that is, suicide is the murder of the love–hatred psychological aspects within the self.

2.   I personally believe that Stekel's statement was much more a fine attempt at a brilliant aphorism than it was a universal psychological truth. We all know of contemporary psychoanalytically oriented theorists who believe that the core psychodynamic for suicide is not hostility, but guilt; others believe it to be shame, or fear, or depression, or mourning for a lost object, or spite. Objectively there is no way to demonstrate the primacy of any one of these as *the* universally irreducible dramatic theme. Indeed, these disagreements run the risk of degenerating into a fruitless sibling rivalry among the proponents of various emotions, without any one of them having a clear title for claiming primogeniture. My own way of dealing with this situation is to eschew this unnecessary fight, and to speak for the possibility of a number of basic emotions in different suicidal acts.

Now our challenge is to examine the text of *Moby-Dick*, looking especially at those aspects of cognitive style and psychodynamics which are consistent with self-destruction; in other words, to search out the psycho-logics of suicide.

CASE HISTORY DATA

From the first exciting moment that one looks at *Moby-Dick* as logic, it is startlingly clear that the book, as a living entity, and Melville–Ishmael, as driving intellects, have rich and textured *ways of thinking* that are consistent with and advance the main psychological thrust and message of the book. After dramatically telling us who the logician is—"Call me Ishmael"—Melville begins the journey with an extended syllogism, called a sorites. First he summarizes the argument in a rather straightforward and beguiling fashion:

> Some years ago—never mind how long precisely—having little or no money in my purse, and nothing particular to interest me on shore, I thought I would sail about a little and see the watery part of the world. It is a way I have of driving off the spleen, and regulating the circulation.

But then, Melville–Ishmael becomes explicit and reveals the bitter underlying meaning in this sorites:

> Whenever I find myself growing grim about the mouth;
> Whenever it is damp, drizzly November in my soul;
> Whenever I find myself involuntarily pausing before coffin warehouses, and bringing up the rear of every funeral I meet;
> and especially, whenever my hypos get such an upper hand of me, that it requires a strong moral principle to prevent me from deliberately stepping into the street, and methodically knocking people's hats off—
> Then, I account it high time to get to sea as soon as I can

In case any reader has lost sight of the argument (that getting away, egressing, is Ishmael's substitute for knocking people's heads in, for committing mayhem or *murder*), Melville–Ishmael tells us bluntly: "This is my substitute for pistol and ball. With a philosophic flourish Cato throws himself upon his sword: I quietly take to the ship."

The argument can be restated this way: When my humors (hypos) are such that I feel like committing murder, I (Melville) instead commit a partial or symbolic suicide by burying myself for an extended time in a ship at sea.

No one can miss the point: *Moby-Dick* is about suicide, specifically suicide as an alternative to murder (but not precluding murder–suicide). The first chapter is about it; the last chapter is about it. Self-destruction is the psychological topic which frames the entire work. All the glorious text in between is interstitial to the "book ends" of self-sought death.

And still further: *Moby-Dick* is about the covert, subintentioned, beneath-the-surface ways (". . . as if that infatuated man sought to run more than half way to meet his doom . . .") in which a person can demean, truncate, limit, narrow, or diminish himself. It is about the moieties of life, ". . . living on with half a heart and half a lung. . . ," short of death itself. It is about the unconscious elements, ". . . the gliding great demon of the seas of life. . . ," in self-induced destruction. The exploration of this world of the sub-surface stream of the mind makes this book an endlessly unfathomable excitement.

In order to understand man's logics, specifically the logics of his (accidentally suicidal) death, we must know something—as much as we can possibly learn—about his character, his personality, his life.

In *Moby-Dick* we must wait until almost the end (Chapter 132 of 135) to learn the bare-bone details of Ahab's life. From Ahab's anamnestic report we learn that: He is 58 years old; he has been at sea since he was a boy-harpooner of 18 (40 years of continuous whaling); at some age past 50 he married a young girl and sailed for Cape Horn on the next day; and he has a young child. Those are the bare facts.

But this book is about suicide and our main interest is in Ahab's death. What can we learn about that?

First, some facts: For Ahab's death, we have the following account (from Chapter 135) of his last actions:

The harpoon was darted; the stricken whale flew forward; with igniting velocity the line ran through the groove,—ran foul. Ahab stooped
to clear it; he did clear it; but the flying turn caught him round the
neck, and noiselessly as Turkish mutes bowstring their victims, he
was shot out of the boat, ere the crew knew he was gone.

On first thought, it might sound as though Ahab's death were
pure accident, an unintentioned death; but let us see where our second thoughts lead us. Could it be called a suicide? Or, more likely, a
subintentioned death?

If any case is to be made for subintention, then at the least, two
further background issues need to be involved: the concept of unconscious motivation and the concept of ambivalence. Ahab's chron-
icler would not have, in principle, resisted the concept of
subintention, on the grounds of its involving unconscious motivation. For, as Melville tells us about Ahab (Chapter 31):

... all this to explain, would be to dive deeper than Ishmael can go.
The subterranean miner that works in us all, how can one tell whither
leads his shaft by the ever shifting, muffled sound of his pick?

That which is most sharply and most accurately characteristic of
the subintentioned person—namely, the ubiquitous ambivalance, the
pervasive psychological coexistence of logical incompatibles—is seen
vividly in the following internal dialogue of life and death, of flesh
and fixture, within Ahab (Chapter 51):

Walking the deck with quick, side-lunging strides, Ahab commanded
the t'gallant sails and royals to be set, and every stunsail spread. The
best man in the ship must take the helm. Then, with every mast-head
manned, the piled-up craft rolled down before the wind. The strange,
upheaving, lifting tendency of the taff-rail breeze filling the hollows of
so many sails, made the buoyant, hovering deck to feel like air beneath the feet; while still she rushed along, as if two antagonistic influences were struggling in her—one to mount directly to heaven, the
other to drive yawingly to some horizontal goal. And had you

watched Ahab's face that night, you would have thought that in him also two different things were warring. While his one live leg made lively echoes along the deck, every stroke of his dead limb sounded like a coffin-tap. On life and death this old man walked.

And within Ahab, toward Moby-Dick, there were deep ambiguities.

In any psychological autopsy it is important to examine the method or the instrument of death and, especially, the victim's understandings and subjective estimations of its lethal works. Ahab was garroted by a free-swinging whale line. We are warned (in Chapter 60) that ". . . the least tangle or kink in the coiling would, in running out, infallibly take somebody's arm, leg, or entire body off . . ." We are forewarned ". . . of this man or that man being taken out of the boat by the line, and lost"; and we are warned again, "All men live enveloped in whale lines. All are born with halters round their necks; but it is only when caught in the swift, sudden turn of death, that mortals realize the silent, subtle, everpresent perils of life."

Ahab knew all this; nor was he a careless, accident-prone man. The apothecary knows his deadly drugs; the sportsman knows the danger of his weapons; the whaler captain—that very whaler captain who, instead of remaining on his quarterdeck, jumped to "the active perils of the chase" in a whale boat manned by his "smuggled on board" crew—ought to know his whale lines.

Having described the precise circumstances of Ahab's death, and having mentioned some background issues deemed to be relevant, I would now pose some questions concerning his demise: Was Ahab's death more than simple accident? Was there more intention than unintention? Was Ahab's orientation in relation to death entirely that of postponing death? Are there discernible subsurface psychological currents that can be fathomed and charted, and is there related information that can be dredged and brought to the surface? Specifically, can Ahab's death be described as victim-precipitated homicide; that is, is this an instance in which the victim stands up to subjectively calculated overwhelming odds, inviting destruction by the other?

Ahab led a fairly well–documented existence, especially insofar as the dark side of his life was concerned. *Moby-Dick* abounds with references to various funereal topics: coffins, burials, soul, life after death, suicide, cemeteries, death, and rebirth.

But—as in a psychological autopsy—we are primarily interested in interview data from everyone who had known the deceased, especially in what our informants can tell us about Ahab's personality, insofar as his orientations toward death are known. It should be recognized that in some important ways Captain Ahab's psychological autopsy will be a truncated and atypical one, especially with respect to the range of informants. There is no information from spouse, parents, progeny, siblings, collaterals, neighbors; there are only mates, some of the more articulate shipboard subordinates, captains of ships met at sea, and, with terrifying biblical certitude, Elijah.

As we know, all the possible informants, listed below, save Ishmael, perished with Captain Ahab and are technically not available for interview. Only Ishmael's observations are direct; all else is secondhand through Ishmael, colored by Ishmael, and perhaps with no more veridicality than Plato's reports of Socrates. We shall have to trust Ishmael to be an accurate and perceptive reporter.

Our primary informant, Ishmael, reflected about Captain Ahab in 25 separate chapters (specifically 16, 22, 27, 28, 30, 33, 34, 36, 41, 44, 46, 50, 51, 52, 73, 100, 106, 115, 116, 123, 126, 128, 130, 132, and 133). Starbuck, the chief mate of the *Pequod*, is next: There are nine separate encounters with, or reports about, his captain (in Chapters 36, 38, 51, 118, 119, 123, 132, 134, and 135). Next is Stubb, the second mate, with seven separate anecdotes (to be found in Chapters 26, 28, 31, 73, 121, 134, and 135). All the others are represented by one or two bits of information apiece: Elijah (in Chapters 19 and 21); Gabriel of the *Jeroboam* (Chapter 71); Bunger, the ship's surgeon of the *Samuel Enderby* (100); the blacksmith (113); the Captain of the *Bachelor* (115); Flask, the third mate (121); the Manxman (125); and the carpenter (127).

How can I summarize all the data? Perhaps my best course would be to concentrate on the general features that one would look for in a psychological autopsy. Thus, the information distilled from interviews with Ishmael, Starbuck, Stubb, and all the others, might, in a dialogue of questions and answers, take the following form.

1. Hidden psychosis? Not at the beginning of the voyage, but certainly at the end (and indeed from Chapter 36 on: "the chick that's in him picks the shell. 'Twill soon be out."), the madness in Ahab was blatant, open, known. His monomania was the official creed of his ship. Along with his other symptoms, his psychiatric syndrome was crowned with a paranoid fixation. But what matters in Ahab is not so much the bizarrely shaped psychological iceberg which many saw above the surface, but rather the hugeness of the gyroscopically immovable subsurface mass of other–destruction and self–destruction. We know the poems about fire and ice. Ahab is a torrid, burning, fiery iceberg.

2. Disguised depression? Ahab was openly morbid and downcast. His was not exactly psychotic depression, nor can we call it reactive depression for it transcended the bounds of that definition. Perhaps best it might be called a "character depression," in that it infused his brain like the let-go blood from a series of small strokes in the hemisphere.

3. Talk of death? The morbid talk of death and killing runs through reports about Ahab like an *idée fixe*.

4. Previous suicide attempts? None is reported.

5. Disposition of belongings? Ahab, after 40 solitary years at sea, had little in the way of possessions or personal belongings. His wife, he said, was already a widow; his interest in the possible profits from the voyage was nil; his withdrawal from meaningful material possessions (and his loss of joy with them) is perhaps best indicated by his flinging his "still lighted pipe into the sea" and dashing his quadrant to the deck—both rash acts for a sailor-captain.

In Ahab's conscious mind, he wanted to kill—but have we not said that self-destruction can be other-destruction in the 180th degree?

Figuratively speaking, the barb of the harpoon was pointed toward him, his brain thought a thrust, but his arm executed a retroflex. Was his death "accidental"? If he had survived his psychodynamically freighted voyage and had returned unharmed to Nantucket's pier, *that* would have been true accident. Men can die for nothing; most men do. But some few big-jointed men can give their lives for an internalized something: Ahab would not have missed this opportunity for the world.

What further evidence can be cited bearing on the issue of subintentioned cessation? With his three harpooners before him, with their harpoons turned up like goblets, Ahab (in Chapter 36) commands them, in this maritime immolation scene, as follows:

> Drink, ye harpooneers! drink and swear, ye men that man the death-ful whaleboat's bow—Death to Moby-Dick! God hunt us all, if we do not hunt Moby-Dick to his death!

Kill or be killed; punish or be retributed; murder or suicide. The two are intertwined.

In Ahab's case, we have no suicide note or other holograph of death, but, *mirabile dictu*, we do have Ahab's last thoughts (Chapter 135):

> I turn my body from the sun . . . Oh, lonely death on lonely life! Oh, now I feel my topmost grief. Ho, ho! from all your furtherest bounds, pour ye now in, ye bold billows of my whole foregone life, and top this one piled comber of my death! Towards thee I roll all-destroying but unconquering whale; to the last I grapple with thee; from hell's heart I stab at thee; for hate's sake I spit my last breath at thee. Sink all coffins and all hearses to one common pool! and since neither can be mine, let me now tow to pieces, while still chasing thee, though tied to thee, thou damned whale! *Thus*, I give up my spear.

What is to be particularly noted in this is the prescience of Ahab. "I spit my last breath at thee," he says. How does he know that it is to be his *last* breath? Where are the sources of his premonitions? What are the contents of his subintentions? Does this not remind us of Radney, the chief mate of the *Town-Ho* (Chapter 54) who behaved as if he "sought to run more than half-way to met his doom"? Is this not exactly what the tantalizer says to his "all-destroying but unconquering" executioner in cases of victim-precipitated homicide? And is that not rather close to our everyday use of the word "suicide"?

It is suggested that Captain Ahab's demise was goal-seeking behavior that made obsessed life *or* subintentioned death relatively unimportant to him, compared with the great press for the discharge of his monomania of hate. He dared, and made, that murderous death-white whale kill him. He could not rest until he was so taken. (Did Satan *provoke* God into banishing him?) Ahab invited cessation by the risks that he ran; he was a death-chancer. He permitted suicide. Consider Ahab's psychological position: What could he have done, to what purpose would any further voyages have been, if he *had* killed the symbol of his search?

Our present Death Certificate is inadequate to reflect the psychological facts. A certification of Ahab's death as "Accidental" would be blatantly superficial (and inaccurate); and a certification as "Suicidal" would be difficult to substantiate and would not reflect "suicide" as we currently use the word. What we are left with is our musings that the most accurate designation, "Subintentioned," is not currently available on the Death Certificate. Perhaps this is just as well, because Ahab's death was too special and too complicated to bury with a single word.

SELF-DESTRUCTIVE PATTERNS OF LOGIC

Let us turn now to some illustrations of logical gambits within *Moby-Dick*. We begin with the more simple examples.

Denotative Deductive Logic

Not unexpectedly, *Moby-Dick* has some interesting examples of straightforward Aristotelian syllogisms. Here, from Chapter 44 ("The Chart") is an AAA (or *Barbara*) syllogism. When Ishmael wishes to enter his room at the inn, he discovers Queequeg performing Ramadan.

The room was locked even though sufficient time has elapsed for Queequeg to have completed his ritual:

> Toward evening, when I felt assured that all his performances and rituals must be over, I went up to his room and knocked on the door; but no answer. I tried to open it, but it was fastened inside. "Queequeg," said I softly through the key-hole:—all silent. "I say, Queequeg! why don't you speak? It's I—Ishmael." But all remained still as before. I began to grow alarmed. I had allowed him such abundant time; I thought he might have had an apoplectic fit.

Through the key-hole, Ishmael espied the shaft of Queequeg's harpoon:

> I looked through the key-hole; ... I was surprised to behold resting against the wall the wooden shaft of Queequeg's harpoon ...

Ishmael knew that Queequeg never left his room without his harpoon:

> That's strange, thought I; but at any rate, since the harpoon stands yonder, and he seldom or never goes abroad without it ...

The syllogistic conclusion:

> Therefore he must be inside here, and no possible mistake.

But this straightforward syllogism is not totally straightforward. Curiously, it has a conditional quality about it. "He seldom or never

goes abroad without it." The word "seldom" introduces a continuum in the "always–never" dichotomy, but Melville treats the situation as though it were a dichotomy when he adds: "... and no
possible mistake."

Another, more dramatic example comes from the same chapter
("The Chart") and is quoted in its entirety:

> Often, when forced from his hammock by exhausting and intolerably
> valid dreams of the night, which, resuming his own intense thoughts
> through the day, carried them on amid a clashing of phrensies, and
> whirled them round and round in his blazing brain, till the very
> throbbing of his lifespot became insufferable anguish, and when, as
> was sometimes the case, these spiritual throes in him heaved his being
> up from its base, and a chasm seem opening in him, from which
> forked flames and lightnings shot up, and accursed fiends beckoned
> him to leap down among them; when this hell in himself yawned
> beneath him, a wild cry would be heard through the ship; and with
> glaring eyes Ahab would burst from his state room, as though escap-
> ing from a bed that was on fire. Yet these, perhaps, instead of being
> the unsuppressable symptoms of some latent weakness, or fright at
> his own resolve, were but the plainest tokens of its intensity. For, at
> such time, crazy Ahab, the scheming, unappeasedly steadfast hunter
> of the white whale; this Ahab had gone to his hammock, was not the
> agent that so caused him to burst from it in horror again. The latter
> was the eternal, living principle or soul in him; and in sleep, being for
> the time dissociated from the characterizing mind, which at other
> times employed it for its outer vehicle or agent, it spontaneously
> sought escape from the scorching contiguity of the frantic thing, of
> which, for the time, it was no longer an integral. But as the mind does
> not exist unless leagured with the soul, therefore it must have been
> that, in Ahab's case, yielding up all his thoughts and fancies to his one
> supreme purpose; that purpose, by its own sheer inveteracy of will,
> forced itself against gods and devils into a kind of self-assumed, inde-
> pendent being of its own. Nay, could grimly live and burn, while the
> common vitality to which it was conjointed, fled horror-stricken from
> the unbidden and unfathered birth. Therefore, the tormented spirit

that glared out of bodily eyes, when what seemed Ahab rushed from his room, was for the time but a vacated thing, a formless somnambulistic being, a ray of living light, to be sure, but without an object to color, and therefore a blankness in itself. God help thee, old man, thy thoughts have created a creature in thee; and he whose intense thinking thus makes him a Prometheus; a vulture feeds upon that heart for ever; that vulture the very creature he creates.

The syllogism in this chilling paragraph may be paraphrased as follows:

In each human being, there are these two aspects of the Self: the characterizing mind, and the eternal living principle or soul.

In times of great emotional intensity, these two—which should, in their normal functioning, be united—can become separated by a psychological chasm and thus become dissociated from each other.

In extreme cases of such dissociation (such as Captain Ahab's), by sheer power of will, one of the two elements, specifically the unsouled mind, can assume a grim (but empty) existence of its own.

Therefore, the manifestations of the tormented spirit that others see is but a hollow vessel; a man without a soul; an empty being. Such a man is a blankness, a nullity doomed by his self-created, self-destroying psychological vulture.

This extraordinary passage of Melville is pregnant with passages and prefigurings. In this one paragraph, Melville anticipates Bleuler (1857–1939), who coined the term "schizophrenia," implying a split personality, a schism between thought and feeling, a cleavage or fissure between the basic mental functions of intellect and emotion. Further, it presages Jung's (1875–1901) notions of the persona, the shadow, as well as existential ideas of the hollow man, the empty person, the meaningless life, the estranged individual, the affectless human: "All visible objects, man, are but as pasteboard masks. But in each event—in the living act, the undoubted deed—there, some unknown but still reasoning thing put forth the mouldings of its features from behind the unreasoning mask" (Chapter 36). It also anticipates the basic psychoanalytic concept of Freud (1856–1939) of the unconscious and, then necessarily, of various layers of personality functioning: "Hark ye yet again—the little lower layer" (Chapter 36); "How all this came to be . . . how to their unconscious understanding . . . all this to explain, would be to dive deeper than Ishmael can go" (Chapter 41). In all, this passage, like a frigate filled with a thousand ideas, is a rather fully packed syllogism.

These syllogisms give us some idea of Melville's deductive logical styles. *Moby-Dick* is filled with logical arguments. The book itself can be seen as one immense sorites.

The major premise of *Moby-Dick* might go something like this: There is a natural order in the universe, an order between man and man, and between man and nature. (By implication, there are strict limitations to any individual's autonomy and power.) The first minor premise would be: To depart from or to challenge this natural order always results in a corrective redress or balance by nature, usually retaliatory punishment of the offending individual. The second minor premise is that Ahab's monomaniacal, revengeful drive could have remained his own crazy business, but his overwhelming hubris openly taunted the Fates and thus became a matter between him and the natural order. Conclusion: Therefore, Ahab had to be punished; he had to be destroyed, even if it meant the death of almost everyone around him. Ishmael's admonition, "Look not too long in the face of the fire, O man!" (Chapter 96) can also be read as: Beware! Do not overtempt the Fates. You may go only so far—even (or especially) in your monomania.

Connotative or Conditional Deductive Logic

Among the 216,104 words in *Moby-Dick* there are 17,560 different word forms. From among these, I have looked at the "logical" words (conjunctions like "therefore" and "hence" and words like "both"

and "half") that reflect Melville's concern with simultaneous opposites, oxymorons, moieties, and ambivalences. The 12 "logical"
words used most frequently in *Moby Dick* (taken from *The Concor
dance*) are: then (629 times), half (137 times), both (124 times), because (92), therefore (67), since (65), hence (32), thinking (28),
concluded (19), thereby (18), whereas (18), and whenever (15). The
other words, with lesser frequencies, are: argument, conclude, con-
cluding, conclusion, deduction, denote, denoted, denotes, follows,
inasmuch, premised, and whereupon (Cohen & Cahalan, 1978).

We have said (in this section) that "therefore" does not always
indicate a totally automatic or innocuous operation. By examining
Melville's use of "therefore" and "hence," we can better understand
his style of thinking—the ways in which the author of *Moby-Dick* is
traditionally Aristotelian and the ways in which he is idiosyncratically, uniquely Melvillean in his thinking.

Not unexpectedly, most of Melville's usage of "therefore" is
straightforwardly syllogistic, as in the following example (Chapter
44):

> Now, the Pequod sailed from Nantucket at the very beginning of the
> Season-on-the-Line. No possible endeavor than could enable her com-
> mander to make the great passage southwards, double Cape Horn
> and then running down sixty degrees of latitude arrive in the equato-
> rial Pacific in time to cruise there. Therefore, he must wait for the
> next ensuing season.

There are many instances in *Moby-Dick* of this kind of not very exciting syllogism and sorites, all of them grist for any Schoolman's
mill.

But Melville was capable of a much more subtle kind of "therefor-
ing." And it is in these non-Aristotelian variations of syllogistic reasoning, specifically in his conditional, almost Persian ways of
thinking, that Melville creates a new language and a new logic and
adds to the tone of *Moby-Dick* that sense of special inevitability and
doom.

All this can be seen in Melville's conditional uses of "therefore" (and "hence"). Father Mapple provides a telling example of conditional thinking (Chapter 9):

> Shipmates, God has laid but one hand upon you; both his hands press upon me. I have read ye by what murky light may be mine the less than Jonah teaches to all sinners; and therefore to ye, and still more to me, for I am a greater sinner than ye.

In this case the "therefore" has more intensity (as if one had turned up the volume on a rheostat) for Father Mapple than it does for others. "still more to me." All men are sinners but some men are greater sinners than others. And what Jonah teaches to all sinners, he teaches much more to those who are the greatest sinners: "God has laid but one hand upon you; both his hands press upon me."

And reasoning can even depend on even more subjective states. From Chapter 42 ("The Whiteness of the Whale"), consider these:

> Can we, then, by the citation of some of those instances wherein this thing of whiteness thought for the time either wholly or in great part stripped of all direct associations calculated to impart to it aught fearful, but nevertheless, is found to exert over us the same sorcery, however modified;—can we thus hope to light upon some chance clue to conduct us to the hidden cause we seek?

> Let us try. But in a manner like this, subtlety appeals to subtlety, and without imagination no man can follow into these halls. And though, doubtless, some at least of the imaginative impressions about to be presented may have been shared by most men, yet few perhaps were entirely conscious of them at the time, and therefore may not be able to recall them now.

What is to be noted here is that what follows "therefore" relates to the state of consciousness of the individual *at that time,* an interesting example of conditional thinking specifically depending upon, of all things, the logician's state of mind.

In addition, there are philosophical elements which condition the logical flow. In Chapter 72 ("The Monkey-Rope") the narrator muses as follows:

So strongly and metaphysically did I conceive of my situation then, that while earnestly watching his motions, I seemed distinctly to perceive that my own individuality was now merged in a joint stock company of two: that my free will had received a mortal wound; and that another's mistake or misfortune might plunge innocent me into unmerited disaster and death. Therefore, I saw that here was a sort of interregnum in Providence; for its even-handed equity never could have sanctioned so gross an injustice. And yet still further pondering—while I jerked him now and then from between the whale and the ship, which would threaten to jam him—still further pondering, I say, I saw that this situation of mine was the precise situation of every mortal that breathes; only in most cases, he, one way or other has this Siamese connexion with a plurality of other mortals. If your banker breaks, you snap; If your apothecary by mistake sends you poison in your pills, you die.

All this is prologue to the main act: the psychological nuances in Melville's paragraphs on death and suicide and Melville's daring and original notion of partial suicide (like burying oneself in a whaling ship at sea) are a kind of subintentioned or unconscious way of cutting oneself off from life, short of overt death. Consider (Chapter 112):

Death seems the only desirable sequel for a career like this; but Death is only a launching into the region of the strange Untired; it is but the first salutation to the possibilities of the immense Remote, the Wild, the Watery, the Unshored; therefore, to the death longing eyes of such men, who still have left in them some interior compunctions against suicide, does the all-contributed and all-receptive ocean alluringly spread forth his whole plan of unimaginable, taking terrors, and wonderful, new-life adventures; and from the hearts of infinite Pacific, the thousand mermaids sing to them—'Come hither, brokenhearted; here is another life without the guilt of intermediate death; here are wonders supernatural, without dying for them. Come hither! bury thyself in a life which to your now equally abhorred and abhorring, landed world is more oblivious than death. Come hither! put up thy gravestone, too, within the churchyard, and come hither, till we marry thee!'

Hearkening to these voices, East and West, by early sunrise, and by fall of eve, the blacksmith's soul responded, Aye, I come! And so Perth went a-whaling.

Continuing to focus on this issue of subintentioned death—wherein the individual plays a latent or covert, an indirect or unconscious role in hastening his own demise—let us examine the final chapters of *Moby-Dick*, especially as they touch on Ahab's death.

There is a certain persuasive logic to the manner of Ahab's death, which might be called a victim-precipitated homicide; he dared, and made, that murderous death-white whale kill him. He could not rest until he was so taken. He invited death by the risks that he ran. His death by Moby-Dick on that voyage came at the right time, for in his unconscious wish it was perfect—the only death, the "appropriate" death.

Non-Summative Deductive Logic

Melville understood the importance of the non–Aristotelian coexistence of A and non-A. Was Socrates mortal or immortal? In a sense (by virtue, in part, of this very question), both. Was Ahab's goal survival or self-destruction? "On life and death this old man walked." Clam *and* cod. Life *and* death illustrate the close relationship between the style of logic and the basic theme in *Moby-Dick*. A suicidal person such as Ahab is basically ambivalent, thinking with simultaneity of opposites. He wants to flee unbearable circumstances and, at the same time, he has active fantasies of magical intervention to be like a Catskill eagle (Chapter 96):

And there is the Catskill eagle in some souls that can alike drive down into the blackest gorges, and soar out of them again and become invisible in the sunny spaces. And even if he forever flies within the gorge, that gorge is in the mountains; so that even in his lowest swoop the mountain eagle is still higher than other birds upon the plain, even though they soar.

In the Aristotelian sense, *Moby-Dick* is not a logical book and Ahab is not a logical character. We can reasonably conclude that Melville was not, himself, a logical person when he wrote it—for which we can be eternally grateful.

Part of Melville's marvelous illogicality stems from the fact that he was a self-taught depth psychologist. It may be as accurate to say that Melville was a pre-Freudian as it is to state that Freud was a post-Melvillean. Melville wrote about the unconscious in 1851, five years before Freud was born. When in *Moby-Dick* the author-narrator says, "What the white whale was to them or to their unconscious understanding . . ." (Chapter 41) or "through infancy's unconscious spell . . ." or the phrase "the little lower layer . . ." he is telling us that he understands the dualities, the admixtures, the contradictions, the ambivalences, the ambiguities, and the layers of the human mind.

Ambivalence is the non-Aristotelian idea that contradictions can coexist psychologically, like the simultaneous feelings of love and hate toward the same person. (Nowadays, ambivalence is considered to be an essential psychoanalytic idea.) In Melville's work one can get clues about his understandings of ambivalence by examining his use of the word "both." Melville knows that it is humanly possible, even if it is logically strained, that "even Christians could be both miserable and wicked" (Chapter 12); one can "boldly dip into the potluck of both worlds" (Chapter 12); and there is no rule of nature that one has to choose, as a rule of life, between clam or cod: "Both, say I" (Chapter 15). This seemingly innocuous statement projects more than gustatory greediness. It is a paradigm of life itself. In a single act, we can do something that has two different uses. Queequeg's tomahawk pipe can both brain his foes and soothe his soul

(Chapter 21); the whaleboat hull is both balanced and directed by one central keel (Chapter 134); and Ahab plunges his harpoon into Moby-Dick with both steel and curse (Chapter 135). The point is that Ahab and every one of us have within us warring forces: good and evil, light and dark, land and sea, order and disorder, love and hate, flesh and ivory limbs. Without these contradictory psychological richnesses, we would be as two-dimensional as pasteboard masks.

The first cousin of ambivalence is the oxymoron. It involves a union of opposites for epigrammatic effect. Among the best-known examples in English are from *Romeo and Juliet*: "Feather of lead, bright smoke, cold fire, sick health" and, of course, "parting is such sweet sorrow." Here is Melville's oxymoronic gem, his short poem, "Art":

> *In placid hours well–pleased we dream*
> *Of many a brave unbodied scheme.*
> *But form to lend, pulsed life create,*
> *What unlike things must meet and mate*
> *A flame to melt—a wind to freeze;*
> *Sad patience—joyous energies;*
> *Humility—yet pride and scorn;*
> *Instinct and study; love and hate;*
> *Audacity—reverence. These must mate,*
> *And fuse with Jacob's mystic heart,*
> *To wrestle with the angel—Art.*

Two points about the logic in this poem. The first is that it is from the juxtaposition of opposites—after conflict, sacrifices and struggle—that something tangible and worthwhile, art, is created. The second point reinforces the first. "Jacob" reminds us of the wrestling with the angel (Genesis XXXII:25–33) as a result of which he obtained both a blessing and a new name (Yisrael) as well as an injury in "the hollow of his thigh." Reflecting on the latter, we think of symbolic castration. So again: There are opposites of castrative injury, sacrifice, sweat, blood, tears, effort, pain, and loss on the one hand and, on the other, victory, creativity and almost everything that has value in life—as art and love have value. These values not only have their opposites, but, as part of a larger opposite, they have their "price." Ahab certainly wounded, perhaps even killed, "the stricken whale," (Chapter 135), the object of his hate, but at a price that a more rational man (one who is not crazy, not wildly vindictive, not obsessively hateful, not rigidly monomaniacal) would, long before, have prudently decided not to pay.

To exist with the knowledge of ambivalences, dualities, and oxymorons is a more complicated challenge than to live in the more simple world of the 16 valid moods of the Aristotelian syllogism. And even more frightening, for unlike the ordered Aristotelian world, there are no magic talismanic formulae to guide and save us. Melville tells us as much in his summation of the human course of life itself, and his reflection that there is no single set of fixed stages of life (Chapter 114)—see below.

Melville would seem to be open-minded—of two worlds—about the etiology of suicide. Some things are predictable and some things are not. Some suicides have their origin early in life and seem "diecast," while others are not at all of this type and seem much more tied to circumstances or even impulses that appear to have no precursors and no previous analogous patterns in that life.

In one of Melville's journeys at sea (either on his way to London or as a passenger around Cape Horn to San Francisco) he annotated his copy of *The Poetical Works of John Milton*. (These 1836 volumes, with Melville's written notes, came to light only in 1984.) To Milton's line ". . . the childhood shows the man, as morning shows the day," (*Paradise Regained*, Book IV) Melville wrote the following at the bottom of that page:

True, if all fair dawnings were followed by high noons and blazoned sunsets. But as many a merry moon precedes a dull and rainy day; so, often, unpromising mornings have glorious mid days and eves. The greatest, grandest things are unpredicted.

And it would follow that also unpredicted are the saddest, direst things, like some suicides.

This view of Melville's—of the unpredictability of some of life's events—is one that Melville could propound about life in general. In *Moby-Dick*, he states some of his "circular" ideas of the development of personality, a view sharply at odds with Shakespeare's view of the seven set "stages of life" (*As You Like It*) or in our own time, Erik Erikson's "linear" notion of eight psycho-social stages of life. Here is Melville speaking about a general, "spiral," repetitive view of human development (Chapter 114, "The Gilder"):

Oh, grassy glades: o, ever vernal endless landscapes in the soul; in ye—though long parched by the dead drought of the earthy life,—in ye, man yet may roll, like young horses in new morning clover; and for some few fleeting moments, feel the cool dew of the life immortal on them. Would to God these blessed calms would last. But the mingled, mingling threads of life are woven by warp and woof; calm crossed by storm, a storm for every calm. There is no steady unretracing progress in this life; we do not advance through fixed gradations, and at the last one pause;—through infancy's unconscious spell, boyhood's thoughtless faith, adolescence' doubt (the common doom), thence scepticism, then disbelief, resting at last in manhood's pondering repose of If. But once gone through, we trace the round again; and are infants, boys, and men, and Ifs eternally. Where lies the final harbor, whence we unmoor no more? In what rapt ether sails the world, of which the weariest will never weary? Where is the foundling's father hidden? Our souls are like those orphans whose unwedded mothers die in bearing them: the secret of our paternity lies in their grave, and we must there to learn it.

So we see that in *some* crises, suicide in an adult has its origin in the traumas of early childhood and it is to there that we must look if we wish to unravel the mystery of the tragic end. But, in others, the story is quite different, and, accordingly, so is the locus of origin.

I believe that the greatest oxymoronic passage in *Moby-Dick* is the stunning opening paragraph of "The Funeral" (Chapter 69):

'Haul in the chains! Let the carcass go astern!' The vast tackles have done their duty. The peeled white body of the beheaded whale flashes like a marble sepulchre; though changed in hue, it has not perceptibly lost anything in bulk. It is still colossal. Slowly it floats more and more away, the water round it torn and splashed by the insatiate sharks, and the air above viexed with rapacious flights of screaming fowls, whose beaks are like so many insulting poinards in the whale. The vast white headless phantom floats further and further from the ship, and every rod that it so floats, what seem roods of shark and cubic roods of fowls, argument the murderous din. For hours and hours from the almost stationary ship that hideous sight is seen. Beneath the unclouded and mild azure sky, upon the fair face of the pleasant sea, wafted by the joyous breezes, the great mass of death floats on and on, till lost in infinite perspectives.

What is to be noted especially in this superlative passage is the breathtaking shift in mood between the first eight lugubrious sentences and the last lilting sentence—from horror and rapaciousness to the most pacific calm. Indeed, the last sentence itself contains this same dramatic contrast in the shift in tone between the first three phrases and the last two. It is the connotative tension in this passage that rivets and chills us. The description is a paradigm, if not of the actualities, then of the omnipresent tensions (whatever their character) in our own lives. In *Moby-Dick* it is the logic of tension and the aberrant ways in which these tensions are reduced that, together, provide the central implicit drama beneath the surface of the written text.

Paralogic

As though all this were not enough, there is still one more kind of logic we must consider: paralogic. The topic of paralogical thinking in *Moby-Dick* has to be of some special interest to us—even though it may be somewhat painful to look at it too closely. Let us look briefly but open-mindedly at the issue.

"N.B.," wrote Melville in March of 1877, at the bottom of a letter to his brother-in-law John C. Hoadley, "*I ain't crazy.*" He underlined the words for emphasis. But his disclaimer has not prevented a whole swirl of controversy about his mental state; independent of this, the family tried to get him to see an alienist, the esteemed Dr. Oliver Wendell Holmes. Recently some newly found correspondence from Elizabeth Melville and Melville's brother-in-law, Samuel Shaw, has revealed rather explicitly that Melville was viewed as having more than ordinary perturbation (Kring & Carey, 1975; Yannella & Parker, 1981). While there is no evidence, in my opinion, that Melville suffered from what we today would call schizophrenia, it nonetheless provides an intellectually engaging exercise to turn to the topic of "language and thought in schizophrenia." In doing this I am not for a moment attempting to imply that over–simplistic notion that insanity and genius are identical, or that they are similar or just a hair's breadth apart. It is more sensible to say that they are "different." Both the insane person and the genius are, almost by definition, "different" from the sane and the ordinary; but they are different in radically diverse ways: Principally the genius is effective and makes sense, whereas the insane person is not and does not.

Not all examples of reasoning in terms of attributes of the predicate have wild or fervent content. In Chapter 82 ("The Honor and Glory of Whaling") there is a rather benign and innocuous example, in which Melville is clearly spoofing. He knows that the syllogism "St. George killed a whale; Nantucket whalers kill whales; therefore Nantucket whalers are equal with St. George" doesn't quite "hold water." But other times, Melville–Ahab uses an identical flawed logic in a totally serious way, filled with urgency and passion. What are we to make of the logic of this tirade by Ahab (Chapter 37): "Swerve me? The path to my fixed purposes is laid with iron rails, whereon my soul is grooved to run." A locomotive runs on rails; my soul runs on rails; therefore—it has a wild, Whitmanian ring—I am a locomotive.

And, again, in a great credo passage from Chapter 134 ("The Chase—Second Day"):

Starbuck, of late I've felt strangely moved to thee; ever since that hour we both saw—thou know'st what, in one another's eyes. But in this matter of the whale, be the front of thy face to me as the palm of this hand—a lipless, unfeatured blank. Ahab is for ever Ahab, man. This whole act's immutably decreed. 'Twas rehearsed by thee and me a billion years before this ocean rolled. Fool! I am the Fates' lieutenant; I act under orders. Look thou, underling! that thou obeyest mine.

The underlying syllogism of this passage takes its very strength from the attributes of the predicate: The Fates have grand designs and immutable needs; I have grand designs and immutable needs; therefore, I am part of the Fates, the Fates' lieutenant.

It is evident that while some of A is B, and some of C is B, A is not C. Paralogical thinking—reasoning in terms of attributes of the predicate—makes the mistake of believing that because A and C can be mentioned in the same breath (in relation to B) they are coequal. It is the *wish* to do so even in the absence of the necessary logical supports, that creates this fantasized bridge. It is the logic of yearning and of passion, not the logic of common sense.

Again in Chapter 133, "The Chase—First Day," just prior to the preceding passage, Ahab, in response to a statement by Starbuck about an omen, declaims:

Omen? omen?—the dictionary! If Gods think to speak outright to man, they will honorably speak outright; not shake their heads, and give an old wives' darkling hint.—Begone! Ye two are the opposite poles of one thing; Starbuck is Stubb reversed; and Stubb is Starbuck; and ye two are all mankind; and Ahab stands alone among the millions of this peoples earth, nor gods nor men his neighbors!

Confused in his logic, Ahab desires to be straightforward in his speech in order to communicate his deeper emotional needs. He does not seem to care that what he says contains a truly megalomaniacal bit of tortured reasoning. Here is what he implies: The extended universe—*all* that one can imagine—is made up of two and only two units: (1) *All* mankind (represented by their monotonous duplicated opposites, Starbuck and Stubb), and (2) one Ahab—"nor gods nor men his neighbors!" Does Ahab really mean that he is somehow outside mankind—that man makes one in the whole nation's census—"a mighty pageant creature formed for noble tragedies" (Chapter 16).

Ahab is so wrought up that he does not care how far he goes; he seems to have the need to show just how desperately he feels by making overextended assertions to the world: "Talk not of blasphemy, man; I'd strike the sun if it insulted me . . . Who's over me? Truth has no confines" (Chapter 36). And it does not matter if such a man has some defects (Chapter 16):

> Nor will it at all detract from him, dramatically regarded, if either by birth or other circumstances he have what seems a half wilful overruling morbidness at the bottom of his nature. For all men tragically great are made so through a certain morbidness. Be sure of this, O young ambition, all mortal greatness is but disease.

That passage speaks of morbidness and disease. Ahab surely suffered from a figurative disease, megalomania, but his core emotion was not morbidness; as we have seen above, it was hate.

THE ROLE OF HOSTILITY AND THE POSSIBLE PRESENCE OF INSANITY

We have no choice but to take the time to speak of Ahab's primary psychological emotion that influenced all his mental life, including his logical styles. "Monomania" is Melville's accurate label for Ahab's focused, single–minded, narrowed, negative passion toward Moby-Dick. That passion—pure and univalent—was *hate*. When one speaks of Captain Ahab, one cannot avoid talking about hostility as *the* central gesture of his drive toward death. To the extent that his death was a suicide, it was certainly one that can be understood in terms of hostility.

We know that Stekel, in 1910, stated the famous psychoanalytic dictum about suicide: That suicide—all suicide—was essentially *hostility directed inwardly* in order to rid the self of the hated introjected figure. Further, we know that since 1910, suicidologists have come to believe that there can be many key emotions that motivate suicide, other than hostility.

But *Moby-Dick* is different. It makes the legitimate case for that particular kind of suicide that genuinely *is* based on hate. Melville, who wrote *Moby-Dick* in 1851 at age 32 (six years before Freud was born), anticipated both Stekel and Freud. The white whale's torment at the hands of Captain Ahab is an open and shut case of hostility: attempted murder with malice. And, psychologically, we have to say the following about Ahab's death: It is a more than accidental death; he "sought to run more than half way to meet his doom" (Chapter 54); it is what I have called a subintentioned death, and now would also call a "miscalculated *suicide*." In the vendetta between Moby-Dick and Ahab, Ahab's death is a true murder–suicide, where neither party coerces the other into committing suicide, but where one party is totally willing to kill the other even though he knows it may cost him his life.

Ahab's behavior toward Moby-Dick is a classical illustration of the traditional psychoanalytical position of suicide, which propounds the view that the central core of the suicidal drama is hostility. Melville tells us not a word about Ahab's mother or father or his psychological relations with either of them (and he tells us barely a few words— nothing really descriptive—about Ahab's wife and young son); but Melville does treat us to a full, psychologically insightful clinical report about Ahab's hostility. At the very end of the drama, in the few seconds before his death, as Ahab hurtles his harpoon into Moby-Dick, he screams this hate–filled oath: ". . . from hell's heart I stab at thee; for hate's sake I spit my last breath at thee . . . thou damned whale!"

The case for Ahab's hostility is fully made in the great chapter entitled "Moby-Dick" (Chapter 41). A sampling will suffice. There are probably no half-dozen paragraphs in the English language so suffused with hate. They constitute a white-hot, minutely detailed, totally accurate psychodynamic description of *one kind* of suicide, the one in which murder and suicide are inextricably linked. Ponder these words (Chapter 41):

I, Ishmael, was one of that crew; my shouts had gone up with the rest; my oath had been welded with theirs; and stronger I shouted, and more did I hammer and clinch my oath, because of the dread in my soul. A wild, mystical, sympathetical feeling was in me; Ahab's quenchless feud seemed mine. With greedy ears I learned the history of that murderous monster against whom I and all the others had taken our oaths of violence and revenge . . .

His three boats stove around him, and oars and men both whirling in the eddies; one captain, seizing the line-knife from his broken prow, had dashed at the whale, as an Arkansas duellist at his foe, blindly seeking with a six inch blade to reach the fathom-deep life of the whale. That captain was Ahab. And then it was, that suddenly sweeping his sickle-shaped jaw beneath him, Moby-Dick had reaped away Ahab's leg, as a mower a blade of grass in the field. No turbanned Turk, no hired Venetian or Malay, could have smote him with more seeming malice. Small reason was there to doubt, then, that ever since that almost fatal encounter, Ahab had cherished a wild vindictiveness against the whale, all the more fell for that in his frantic morbidness he at last came to identify with him, not only all his bodily woes, but all his intellectual and spiritual exasperations. The White Whale swam before him as the monomaniac incarnation of all those malicious agencies which some deep men feel eating in them, till they are left living on with half a heart and half a lung. That intangible malignity which has been from the beginning; to whose dominion even the modern Christians ascribe one-half of the worlds; which the ancient Ophites of the east reverenced in their statue devil;—Ahab did not fall down and worship it like them; but deliriously transferring its idea to the abhorred White Whale, he pitted himself, all mutilated, against it. All that most maddens and torments; all that stirs up the lees of things; all truth with malice in it; all that cracks the sinews and cakes the brain; all the subtle demonisms of life and thought; all evil, to crazy Ahab, were visibly personified, and made practically assailable in Moby-Dick. He piled upon the whale's white hump the sum of all the general rage and hate felt by his whole race from Adam down; and then, as if his chest had been a mortar, he burst his hot heart's shell upon it.

It is not probable that this monomania in him took its instant rise at the precise time of his bodily dismemberment. Then, in darting at the monster, knife in hand, he had but given loose to a sudden, passionate, corporal animosity; and when he received the stroke that tore him, he probably felt the agonizing bodily laceration, but nothing more. Yet, when by this collision forced to turn towards home, and for long months of days and weeks, Ahab and anguish lay stretched together in one hammock, rounding in mid winter that dreary, howling Patagonian Cape; then it was, that his torn body and gashed soul bled into one another; and so interfusing, made him mad. That it was only then, on the homeward voyage, after the encounter, that the final monomania seized him, seems all but certain from the fact that, at intervals during the passage, he was a raving lunatic; and though unlimbed of a leg, yet such vital strength yet lurked in his Egyptian chest, and was moreover intensified by his delirium, that his mates were forced to lace him fast, even there, as he sailed, raving in his hammock. In a straitjacket, he swung to the mad rockings of the gales. And, when running into more sufferable latitudes, the ship, with mild stun' sails spread, floated across the tranquil tropics, and, to all appearances, the old man's delirium seemed left behind him with the Cape Horn swells, and he came forth from his dark den into the blessed light and air; even then, when he bore that firm, collected front, however pale, and issued his calm orders once again; and his mates thanked God the direful madness was now gone; even then, Ahab, in his hidden self, raved on. Human madness is oftentimes a cunning and most feline thing. When you think it fled, it may have but become transfigured into some still subtler form. Ahab's full lunacy subsided not, but deepeningly contracted; like the unabated Hudson, when that noble Northman flows narrowly, but unfathomly through the Highland gorge. But, as in his narrow-flowing monomania, not one jot of Ahab's broad madness has been left behind; so in that broad madness, not one jot of his great natural intellect had perished. That before living agent, now became the living instrument. If such a furious trope may stand, his special lunacy stormed his general sanity, and carried it, and turned all its concentrated cannon upon its own mad mark; so that far from having lost his strength, Ahab, to that one end, did now possess a thousand fold more potency than ever he had sanely brought to bear upon any one reasonable object . . .

. . . But be this as it may, certain it is, that with the mad secret of his unabated rage bolted up and keyed in him, Ahab had purposely sailed upon the present voyage with the one only and all-engrossing object of hunting the White Whale. Had any one of his old acquaintances on shore but half dreamed of what was lurking in him then, how soon would their aghast and righteous souls have wrenched the ship from such a fiendish man! They were bent on profitable cruises, the profit to be counted down in dollars from the mint. He was intent on an audacious, immitigable, and supernatural revenge.

Here, then, was this grey-headed, ungodly old man, chasing with curses a Job's whale round the world, at the head of a crew, too, chiefly made up of mongrel renegades, and castaways, and cannibals—morally enfeebled also, by the incompetence of mere unaided virtue or right-mindedness in Starbuck, the invulnerable jollity of indifference and recklessness in Stubb, and the pervading mediocrity in Flask. Such a crew, so officered, seemed specially picked and packed by some infernal fatality to help him to his monomaniac revenge. How it was that they so aboundingly responded to the old man's ire— by what evil magic their souls were possessed, that at times his hate seemed almost theirs; the White Whale as much their insufferable foe as his; how all this came to be—what the White Whale was to them, or how to their unconscious understandings, also, in some dim, unsuspected way, he might have seemed the gliding great demon of the seas of life,—all this to explain, would be to dive deeper than Ishmael can go. The subterranean miner that works in us all, how can one tell whither leads his shaft by the ever shifting, muffled sound of his pick?

Who does not feel the irresistible arm drag? What skiff in tow of a seventy-four can stand still? For one, I gave myself up to the abandonment of the time and the place, but while yet all a rush to encounter the whale, could see naught in that brute but the deadliest ill.

Considering all this hate, what can we say about the kind of morbidness or disease or madness that Ahab had? In the Preface to Kasanin's *Language and Thought in Schizophrenia* (1942), the noted American psychiatrist Nolan D. C. Lewis, speaking of schizophrenia says (pp. viii-ix):

Among those presented features repeatedly emphasized in this connection are (1) fundamental or fancy-born inconsistencies more or less foreign to normal or average life; (2) shut-in tendencies, with a sense of something wrong or unusual going on in the environment; (3) indulgence in vague artistic fantasies, with daydreaming and partial withdrawal from reality, or at least lack of concentration on the tangible realities of the present life situation; (4) automatic and dissociated thought processes, often with projection . . .; (5) odd mental influences, with transformation experiences; (6) grotesque incongruities of judgment, with accounts of fantastic episodes; (7) scatterings of thought and speech, with curious condensations and complaints of unnatural interference with thought, combined with oddities of statement and fantastic action; (8) impulsive episodes and vagueness, with shifts of emotional reactions; responses with opposites and 'word hash,' or with other evidence of marked disorganization in language such as neologisms and distortions of content.

With a few slight shifts of emphasis, this explication of schizophrenic language and thought sounds like a harsh description of the goings on in *Moby Dick*. Some examples of all eight of the symptoms are present. On these grounds, a schizophrenic "syndrome" might be said to be present in *Moby-Dick*. But we would be illogical to say so.

I certainly will not be so careless as to say that the language and thought in *Moby-Dick* are schizophrenic. There are a thousand differences, but the vital difference is that what Melville says, albeit in his idiosyncratically bold and lofty way, *makes sense*. From a strictly traditional point of view, the text of *Moby-Dick* is filled with grammatical and logical mistakes, but it does not make aesthetic or psychological errors; rather it uses all these devices to heighten tension, to create grand efforts, and to *further communication*. It is the opposite of schizophrenic gibberish; it is art which, by taking risks and stretching the limits of governable wisdom, communicates projectively with each active and eager listener.

Melville tells us that Ahab is special; Melville knew that *he* was special. Further, a special person creates a special "bold and nervous lofty language," a language that obviously is different from the common talk and yet enables him to communicate while retaining some important measures of independence; to speak and think his own way. It is a language-and-logic which is especially effective precisely because of the precise modes of thought and persuasive logic that it so cunningly employs.

That is what a great writer is: A person who creates a new language, a fresh way of thinking and talking, a different style of language and thought; one who possesses an idiosyncratic way of seeing the world and reports his vision in a unique way. More even than a fresh-sounding cadence, a different accent, or a dialect of his own, he needs the unhesitating talent to be his own Aristotle and to forge a style of *logic* copyrighted in a private patent office of which he is the sole proprietor and the most enthusiastic spokesman. Every great author is his own logician, eligible to be included in the company of Aristotle, Avicenna, Bacon, Mill, and Whitehead. There are many styles of logic in the world, most of them yet to be formulated. Any textbook of logic would, if read, cripple the mind of a potential Proust or Joyce. Melville knew that standard philosophy and logic had to be diluted to meet individual tastes: "Adler & Taylor came into my room ... We talked metaphysics continually, & Hegel, Schlegel, Kant & c were discussed under the influence of whiskey" (*Journal*, Oct. 22, 1849). More importantly, Melville also knew the larger corollary truth: "There are some enterprises in which a careful disorderliness is the true method" (Chapter 82). A great writer must forge a new genre; be a true "original." The names are few. In nineteenth century America we have Whitman, Poe, Clemens, Dickinson, and rising above all, "like a snow hill in the air," Herman Melville.

Part
Six

Definitional
Issues

T

Headnote

In the beginning was the word, and toward the end is the word again. At this point, before I proceed, I can venture one further definition of suicide, beyond the one in the 1973 *Encyclopaedia Britannica* ("Suicide is the human act of self-inflicted, self-intentioned cessation"). I am now prepared to offer an operational definition of suicide, an improvement on the one just cited. It is quite brief in the statement of it. My operational definition of suicide is: *All of the above* (in Part Four). The system *is* the definition. Taken together, the preceding 10 sets of statements about the common characteristics of suicide are what I believe suicide to be, how committed suicide can be understood, what it is like on the inside and, by implication, how individuals who are on the brink of self-inflicted termination can be brought back from the precipice.

Part Six consists of three sections, all on definition: A definition of suicide in terms of an empirical study of genuine and simulated suicide notes; a rather lengthy section on a proposed definition of suicide with an exigesis of every key word; and a very brief section on clarifying the definition of suicide by contrasting suicidal behaviors with parasuicidal behaviors. This book on the essentials of suicide is largely an essay on the definition of suicide. It begins (and ends) with the belief that meaningful definition is propaedeutic to effective remediation and that what the field of suicidology most desperately requires is a clarifying discussion of the definitions of suicide—definitions that can usefully be applied to needful persons.

U

Definition
in Terms
of Suicide Notes

Antoon Leenaars (in press) has taken my work and done an original thing. He carefully examined 12 pieces of my writings on suicide (books, chapters, and articles) and produced some 50 protocol sentences which he believed reflected the theoretical perspectives and implications in them. (He had previously done something similar from Freud's writings on suicide [1984] and from those of Binswanger and George Kelly [1984]). Some of these 50 protocol statements are reproduced in Table 1.

Two judges were then asked independently to verify each of the 50 statements for a set of 66 suicide notes (Shneidman & Farberow, 1957), all written by individuals who were male, Caucasian, Protestant, native–born, and between the ages of 25 and 59, where half the notes were genuine suicide notes (obtained from the office of the Los Angeles County Coroner) and the other half were simulated notes obtained from non-suicidal note writers. In Leenaars' study the coefficient of concordance between his two judges indicated substantial inter–judge reliability (at the .01 level of confidence).

Ten of the 50 protocol sentences appeared significantly more often in the genuine notes as compared with the simulated notes. Table 1 (on the following page) reproduces those 10 sentences.

Table 1. Leenaars' Protocol Sentences Derived From Shneidman's Formulations Regarding Suicide

3. In the suicide note, the person communicated ambivalence (e.g., complications, concomitant contradictory feelings, attitudes and/or thrusts toward the same person).[a]

17. In the suicide note, the person communicated evidence of a crucial role of the significant other who seemed to doom him to a suicidal outcome (e.g., a wife who is hostile, independent, competitive or non-supporting).[a]

21. In the suicide note, the person communicated evidence of adult trauma (e.g., poor health, rejection by the spouse, being married to a competing wife).[b]

28. In the suicide note, the person communicated that he feels helpless and confused emotionally and feels pessimistic about the possibilities of making meaningful interpersonal relationships.[c]

32. In the suicide note, the person seems to be figuratively intoxicated or drugged by his overpowering emotions and constricted logic and perception.[a]

44. In the suicide note, the person communicated the active withdrawal by a key "significant other" which plunges him even deeper into a state of despair.[a]

45. In the suicide note, the person communicated calamitous relationships (e.g., rejecting father, hostile mother, spiteful aunt, exploiting lover, unloving husband, unresponsive friend, disapproving nurse).[b]

46. In the suicide note, the person communicated the simultaneous presence of both love and hate as well as other emotions.[b]

49. In the suicide note, the person communicated that a root cause of his self-destruction was the sense of total rejection, in a personality that already depreciated itself.[b]

50. In a suicide note, the person's communications appear to have unconscious psychodynamic implications.[b]

[a]Significant at the .01 level of confidence.
[b]Significant at the .05 level of confidence.
[c]Significant at the .07 level of confidence.

Briefly, the 10 significant statements indicate the following: feelings and attitudes of ambivalence; the crucial role of the significant other; evidence of ill health; rejection of a competitive spouse; feelings of helplessness, confusion, and pessimism about possibilities of establishing meaningful interpersonal relationships; the presence of overpowering emotions and constricted logic and perception; active withdrawal of support by the significant other; some earlier calamitous relationship; the simultaneous expression of love and hate—ambivalence; a deep sense of total rejection; and the presence of important unconscious psychodynamic forces.

In addition, Leenaars found that there were 12 protocol sentences which occurred in at least two-thirds of the genuine suicide notes. (Only two of these occurred significantly more often than in the simulated notes, which may be taken to mean that individuals who are asked to simulate a suicide note can effectively empathize with the suicidal person and capture these same elements of the suicidal situation.) These dozen protocol sentences were: many different emotions are cited; an acute crisis is indicated; there is ambivalence toward the same key person; a dyadic event is involved; there are pressures which are not handled well; the individual is in a state of heightened perturbation; there is statement of trauma (ill health, rejection, a poor marriage) as an adult; there are fixed purposes and constriction of the mind; the suicidal behavior is intentional; the person is in a state of heightened disturbance and helplessness; there is a narrowing of the range of perception; and there is a sense of shame or disgrace.

Leenaars' findings lend themselves to a number of theoretical speculations. He muses:

> Our results suggest that the active withdrawal by a key significant other, that is described in most notes, plunges the suicidal individual into despair. In the genuine notes, the person states that one is not "able to go on" or that one cannot "be" or "do" anything without the lost person. This state of despair is described in one note in the following manner: "This is the last note I shall ever write. No one should feel bad about my going as I am not worth it. I don't want to go but

there is nothing else to do." The person is not only in despair but appears to have overly depreciated himself

Suicidal individuals describe the cause of the suicide as a loss, rejection and/or trauma, e.g., a calamitous relationship, a physical illness. External sources, e.g., spouse, friends, etc., have been noted to concur with these observations. However, based on Shneidman's formulations and the current results, the suicidal individuals appear to be preoccupied with the perceived loss, rejection or other aspects of the precipitating event, but they have limited insight into their own dynamics or reaction patterns. . . . Since not everybody kills themselves after a rejection or other trauma, it appears that Shneidman's belief that: "Each individual tends to die as he or she has lived, especially as he or she has previously reacted in the periods of threat, stress, failure, challenge, shock and loss" is most important in understanding the suicidal person. Suicidal individuals appear to be so preoccupied with the trauma that they are unaware of their own developmental history and how they have previously adjusted to stress. The suicidal individuals are also unaware of the unconscious dynamics that appear to be related to their suicide.

V

A Formal
Definition,
with Explication

My principal assertion about suicide has two branches. The first is that suicide is a multifaceted event and that biological, cultural, sociological, interpersonal, intrapsychic, logical, conscious and unconscious, and philosophical elements are present, in various degrees, in each suicidal event.

The second branch of my assertion is that, in the distillation of each suicidal event its essential element is a *psychological* one; that is to say, each suicidal drama occurs in the *mind* of a unique individual. Suicide is purposive. Its purpose is to respond to or redress certain psychological needs. I have said before that there are many pointless deaths but there are no needless suicides. Suicide is a concatenated, complicated, multidimensional, conscious and unconscious "choice" of the best possible practical solution to a perceived problem, dilemma, impasse, crisis, desperation.

To use an arborial image: The psychological component in suicide is the "trunk" of it. An individual's biochemical states, for instance, are the roots. An individual's method of suicide, the contents of the suicidal note, the calculated effects on the survivors, and so on, are the branching limbs, the flawed fruit and the camouflaging leaves.

But the psychological component, the problem-solving choice—the best solution to the perceived problem—is the main trunk.

We may now proceed to my proposed definition of suicide.

Currently in the Western world, suicide is a conscious act of self-induced annihilation, best understood as a multidimensional malaise in a needful individual who defines an issue for which the suicide is perceived as the best solution.

Now I shall attempt an exegesis of this definition by clarifying the meaning of each word.

Currently.   What is meant to be implied in this study of suicide is a contextual endeavor, embedded in the historical epic or era in which it occurs and in which it is either historically or concurrently studied. For example, if it were possible it would not be enough simply to contrast suicide rates in pre-Christian Rome with suicide rates in Rome today. The whole meaning of this act for the person who did it and the contemporary witnesses is vastly different from that time to now. I would believe that the definition of suicide offered in this book will have to become out of date in time and would not be applicable to apply without appropriate modification even to suicidal occurrences as recent as the nineteenth century.

Western World.   There are publications of studies of suicides in Africa (Bohannan, 1960), in Hong Kong (Yap, 1958), and other places around the world. I believe that this proposed definition is applicable only to the Western world (which may very well, in certain circumstances, include Japan and other countries.) But this cautionary needs to be cited so that cross-cultural comparisons do not make the error of assuming that a suicide is a suicide.

Suicide.   Two comments about this word. First is that after much thought I have concluded we are well advised to use this word rather than to venture on a substitute for it or to create a neologism. The use of the word admittedly has some disadvantages, but it has such wide usage that it is tactically best to employ it.

The second point is that an examination of a number of previous definitions of suicide reveals that the word is often (perhaps typically) used with not one, but two meanings. These two meanings are: The definition of the *act* of self-destruction, and some delineation of the *person* who commits that act. I have followed this practice in my proposed definition.

Conscious.   What is implied here is that first of all suicide—at least the kind of suicide we are talking about—is limited to *human* acts. We shall not be concerned at all with migrating lemmings or mourning dogs in as much as (as we shall see) suicide devolves in part on reportable intention.

A second important issue reflected in this word is the entire domain of the unconscious mind. The use of the word conscious in this definition is not meant to gainsay or to deny the notion that there may be important (even vital or anti-vital) unconscious elements in a total suicidal scenario. Rather it is meant to indicate that, by definition, suicide can occur only when an individual has some conscious mediation or, better, some conscious intention to stop his or her own life. There is always an element of some awareness and conscious intentionality in suicide.

This is not to say there are not many deaths—I would venture to assert even a majority of all deaths—that do not have a *subintentioned* quality to them. A subintentioned death is any death other than a suicidal death (accidental, natural, or homicidal) in which the decedent has played some significant covert, latent, unconscious role in hastening his or her demise. No suicide is a subintentioned death. Rather, every suicide is an intentioned death with a conscious advertent element in it.

Act.   This word is meant to carry some special meanings. One direct implication is, I believe, that we should totally eschew the words "attempt" or "threat" when they are preceded by the adjective "suicidal." (I am now obviously discussing other than lethal suicidal acts.) I make this suggestion because the words attempt and threat are often used in either a judgmental pejorative way, impuning even the worthlessness of the person or the seriousness of the personal crisis which in part impelled the act, as in the phrase "We sewed her up and sent her home. It was only a suicide attempt." My suggestion is that we reject the words "attempt" and "threat" and try to describe every suicidal act. Instead, we should use words like suicidal act, event, occurrence, deed, maneuver, phenomenon, and indicate our *lethality rating*. The lethality rating that might run, say, from 1 to 9, is the common-sense ascription of the probability of that act or deed or event having a lethal outcome. (In this sense *any* act, deed, or event in the world can be rated on a lethality dimension.) The main merit of the use of the word "act" is that it clarifies and appropriately simplifies what suicide is; namely, a behavior which leads to death.

Two ratings should be made for each suicidal act or event or deed: Lethality, as indicated above, and *perturbation*; as discussed below. The rating of perturbation—also from 1 to 9—is an indication of how upset, agitated, depressed, psychotic, or perturbed the individual was deemed to be at the time of doing the act. It is very important in assessing a suicidal act (or treating a suicidal person) to distinguish between how perturbed the individual is and how lethal that individual is.

No one has ever died from elevated perturbation alone. It is elevated lethality which is dangerous to life. The two concepts need to be separated in order to have a clear understanding of the total event and the chief protagonist in it.

Self-Inflicted.   The fulcrum word in the definition of suicide is the word self-inflicted. If suicide is anything, it is a *mort ius dese*, a death by oneself. This would seem to be clear enough although there are problems with the biblical incident in which Saul asked another soldier to kill him and in cases of what are now called assisted suicides. But in these instances the suicidal person changes only the voice of the grammar of the event and instead of killing himself directly has himself killed at one remove only by the asked for action of another agent.

In the same sense the suicide is also self-inflicted even in the instance when Seneca was ordered by the mad Roman emperor Nero to kill himself. We can reasonably assume that until the moment of that imperial order, Seneca had no intention of killing himself but after the order he then consciously intended to kill himself when he did because the alternative—disgrace, enforced death, or punishment to his family—was worse.

Annihilation.   This word is meant to imply that the life of an individual is the life as that individual experiences it. It is the life of the mind. (The activities of the mind are the products of a living brain. No brain, no mind; no mind, no life.) One's life is the history—the introspective history—of one's mind. Suicide is the stopping or cessation of consciousness. It is redundant to say "forever." Cessation is thus distinguished from interrupted states (i.e., sleep, coma, anesthetic unconsciousness) and altered continuation states (i.e., intoxication, fugue states, psychotic states). Termination is what others see to have happened to your body. You can never experience cessation—being dead. A committed suicide results in cessation but we know that often the person who does it wants only a stopping of the flow of unbearable anguish or intolerable emotion or a change of "locale" from this world to a hoped for other existence. But operationally speaking, suicide is a conscious act of self-inflicted cessation. Synonyms are cessation, nothingness, oblivionation, and naughtment.

These seven terms above, especially terms three to seven, define the *act* of suicide. The remaining eight terms define the *actor*, the person who does the act.

We have already defined what suicide is. It is the consciously intended act of self-inflicted cessation. Every definition is a tautology and it turns upon itself in a more or less obvious way. A definition is like an equation in which the word and its meaning have equal weight on the two sides of the copula. (usually the word "is"). Now having defined the act, we shall go on and explicate some of the omnipresent characteristics of the actor (limited, of course, to "currently in the Western world").

Multidimensional.   No single learned discipline is sufficient to explain any individual suicidal event. I believe it is most accurate to define (in addition to the definition above) suicide as a biological/ biochemical/sociocultural/sociological/interpersonal/intrapsychic/ philosophic/existential event. It is certainly possible to write about suicidal phenomena from, say, a sociological point of view (as Durkheim has done with great success) or from a psychodynamic point of view (as Menninger has done, also with great success). But those are simply elaborations of one point of view and cannot be thought to tell the whole story. The main point is that suicide is a multidimensional event and requires, for its understanding, a multidisciplinary approach.

Malaise.   The history of suicide is a record that involves words like sin, crime, and disease. Battin, in her recent book (1982), reminds us that even today "the narrower definition used in the Catholic tradition" (which emphasizes the moral signification under which the act is done synonymous with "morally repugnant self-killing") "seems closest to much ordinary usage." The notion of suicide as sin is very much present in current talk of it. A contemporary scientist, on the other hand, eschewing religion, has attempted to express suicide in medical terms, insisting that suicide is best understood not as a sin, not as a crime, and certainly not as a disease. From everything we know about a human event as complicated as suicide, we can be certain that such human disorders as malaria, syphilis, and tuberculosis are not accurate paradigms of suicide. In this sense suicide is more akin to delinquency or prostitution or craziness. I believe it is best conceptualized as a malaise, not a disease (for which we might hope to find a virus, coccus). It is a state of being, a human malaise.

Perturbed.   In the assessment of any (living) potentially suicidal person, evaluations along two continuum should be made: How oriented toward death the individual is (lethality), and how upset or disturbed the individual is (perturbation). By its very definition no one commits suicide who is not highly lethal. We know, of course, it is possible to be highly perturbed and not to be highly lethal at the same time—the living presence of many disturbed individuals attests to this. But our clinical observations affirm to us that no one commits suicide who is unperturbed. Consider: If a totally unperturbed individual were to commit suicide (so to speak "for no reason at all,") that, in itself would be an aberrant act. There are several implications and corollaries of the above statements. It is not implied that all, or even most, individuals who commit suicide are insane or psychotic. It is implied that some elevated state of perturbation is necessarily present. This could be as relatively "innocuous" as the truncated scope of choices induced by severe psychical pain, sudden threat of torture, loss of health, or loss of status. The point is that an individual in his or her normal or modal state of being-in-the-world (by which is meant being in his or her accustomed world) does not ever commit suicide. Some elevated perturbation is the trigger, the *sine qua non*, the omnipresent component of the suicidal act.

One obvious and important implication (supported by the totality of my clinical experience) is that the most effective way to treat a potentially suicidal (highly lethal) person is for the helping person to address not the lethality directly, but the perturbation. The most effective way to treat a suicidal person is to do whatever is humanly possible to decrease the lethality to a point below its critically explosive level. This means that one is not limited to addressing the suicidal individual's psyche. Instead, one attempts to make whatever changes are required in that individual's inter-personal relationships (especially with his or her significant others) and with other aspects of that person's environment, job, jail, cancer, and so on.

Needful.   It is difficult to conceptualize an individual's committing suicide apart from that individual's seeking to satisfy certain inner-felt needs (of course, these needs always operate within the context of a surrounding psychological situation—and there is something to be said for the subsidiary role of the environmental determinants of action). The reader will recall the discussion of suicide in relation to Murray's classification of human needs. That approach is not the be all and end all but it certainly is a good beginning and perhaps the very best set of useable terms now available. I dare to repeat my own dictim in this matter: There are many pointless deaths but there can never be a needless suicide.

It might be argued that the word "needful" is unnecessary (almost redundant) in this definition in that every living individual is needful. The point of including this word in the definition of suicide is to focus on the fact that aside from whatever else suicide represents, it focally involves the attempt to fulfill some urgently felt psychological needs. Operationally, these heightened unmet needs make up, in large part, what the suicidal person feels (and reports) as his or her perturbation.

Individual.   Fedden (1938) distinguishes between two kinds of suicide: personal and institutional (or sacrificial) suicide. In this he is simply wrestling, as Deshaies and others have, with the tag end of sacrificial suicide, not knowing where to put it and needing to create a separate category for it. Just as we do not believe in the "mob mind" or in the "collective unconscious," so we do not believe in institutional suicide. All suicides are individual acts. Granted that they reflect degrees of social or societal or group pressure. At the furthest remove, all suicide might be considered institutional or social to some degree in the sense that the individual has learned about it. There is no history of a feral person (that is, a person raised by animals) ever committing (i.e., inventing) suicide.

The task of the suicidologist who wishes to understand or to assess a suicidal act, whether that of a samurai warrior, a traditional Hindu widow that has practiced suttee, or a child at Jonestown, is no different from assessing a suicide of a middle class Westchester teenager who kills herself by taking an excessive amount of barbiturates and permits herself to drown in her swimming pool.

In each case what is to be rated is the intention of the decedent vis-à-vis death. We can now answer the question that was discussed by European intellectuals during World War II. That question was: If you kill yourself when the Gestapo knocks on your door, have you,—without any moral judgment in it (except, perhaps, about the Gestapo)—committed suicide? What else would you call it? (Accident? Natural death? Homicide?) In a terrible sense all suicides—

every suicide—is committed because the real or figurative or imagined or hallucinated "Gestapo" is knocking at the psychic door.

If one could arrange it—and one cannot—it would be "appropriate" to die at one of the apogees of one's life; but it would be pointless if it were done. To commit suicide at the high point (when one is healthy, successful, happy, etc.) would be pointless and aberrant. The examples in Durkheim of individuals who kill themselves on the occasion of attaining sudden wealth are always referred to as being "overwhelmed" by their "good fortune." One man's apogee is another man's perigee.

It seems sensible to say that no person left entirely to his or her own devices would commit suicide. A feral adult would not have the conceptualization of suicide and, more importantly, that concept without which suicide has absolutely no meaning, death. In that sense and in the further sense that many, perhaps most, suicidal events are intensely dyadic (involving some significant other), suicide may be said to be an interpersonal and certainly an intracultural event. But in its essence suicide is always an individual occurrence. It is separate people who kill themselves (albeit on occasion in a group setting) and always, as I have indicated, within a cultural nexis. All this may sound fairly obvious but those readers whose orientations are tenaciously sociological may well take umbrage at the seemingly rather innocuous, words. To do so would be to misunderstand what I wish to say: Suicide is always an individual event, *but* (or *and*) it always occurs in an individual who, willy-nilly, holds one or more citizenships in one or more cultures and who can never emigrate to *no where* (there is *no where* in suicide). In addition, there can be no suicide without some independent conceptualization of death, nullity, naughtment, cessation, and surcease and their opposites survival, continuance, and immortality. The emphasis on the individual does not at all preclude interest and concern with social (including economic) and especially cultural forces as they reside or swirl within the individual psyche.

Defines.   Psychic life is perception (and imagining and thinking and feeling). Perception involves, by its very nature, distortion by the living brain which performs the act of perceiving. We are "defining" our world all the time, misperceiving it in our own idiosyncratic way—albeit with such commonplace agreements that no one but a sophist would quibble over a vast percentage of our perceptions. All this is to say that the word "defines" and the subsequent key word "issue" need to be discussed together since an issue is always defined by someone; that is, the very act which makes some matter in the world an image in the first place.

Inasmuch as the various words in this definition are organically related to one another, an additional point can be made about the word "defines." We have already indicated that the individual who commits suicide is perturbed. More specifically that perturbation is manifested by a constriction and narrowing of the perceptional "diaphragm" in the camera of the mind. There is a narrowing and a tunneling and a closing down—much more light is needed for an ordinary common–sense "picture" of what is going on. This means that the very act of defining is done with some constriction and is not done in the relatively more open way of which that individual is capable. Operationally it means that fewer options than would ordinarily occur to that individual are present for the perturbed mind's consideration. A suicidal individual who is defining any issue is not at his etymological best. He is rather like Dr. Samuel Johnson might have been if he had worked on his famous *Dictionary* with a mind truncated by drugs, fatigue, or extraordinary emotional stress.

Issue.   There is a notion in the watered-down popular misconception of psychoanalytic theory that if the individual (usually in the course of psychotherapy) need only discover that one traumatic incident or moment in the earlier life at which point the complexes were fixed. We can call this "the magic moment" theory of the neuroses. It is a point of view that looks for *the* cause of relatively complex next of human behaviors. In the same sense there is some danger of focusing on the issue in a suicidal drama. At the outset we are aware that the causes of suicide are multiple and layered. We can speak of primary causes, sustaining causes, resonating causes, exacerbating causes, and precipitating causes. (Most discussions of the causes of suicide—for instance, ill health, financial failure, emotional rejection—deal only with precipitating situations.) Nonetheless it makes sense in the linguistic analysis of the typical suicidal scenario to speak of *the* issue which is paramount in the consciousness of the suicidal person. The implication of this view is that the unconscious factors (the psychodynamics) which admittedly do play an important role in the entire suicidal drama play their role indirectly by making what could be an issue in an individual's life *the issue* around which that individual then conducts a life-or-death debate.

Perceived.   No brain, no life. Everything we experience is processed through our living brain. In that sense all perception has some idiosyncratic components. The words "perceive" and "misperceive" are synonymous. There is some distortion, by definition, in all perception. In the cases of suicidal individuals, the issue is the extent of this distortion. Our definition of suicide could have as easily read ". . . for which the suicide is misperceived as the best solution." The pathology in suicidal perception is linked most directly with the *constriction* of the individual's then-present perceptual processes. This tunneling or focusing of the mind's set seems stimulated by the increase in perturbation. It is a commonplace observation that when one is upset, one does not (or is unable to) think clearly. Operationally, "clearly" implies capacity internally to scan and to choose among several viable options. Confusion is not so much a jumbling of possible options as it is a falling away of viable options and an arbitrarily operational focusing on only one seemingly possible solution (i.e., suicide) where more than one solution is realistically possible.

Best.   Suicide is an act done by a perturbed individual who (with a somewhat truncated perception of the options possible in the world) decides that cessation is the *best* possible solution that he can choose. Pascal, in his *Pensèes*, talked about the Bet Situation (in which he asserted each individual must bet his soul on whether or not God exists). In a comparable way we can say that the suicidal person places himself in a Bet Situation where, under duress, he jumps to what he considers to be the best choice among the possible options—all of which may be noxious or offensive in some degree; an *aristos*, the best one can do under the circumstances. One implication of this view is that the treatment of the suicidal person almost always involves an effort to broaden the scope or range of his perceptions—"to widen his blinders" and to increase the number of more or less onerous options available in his consciousness.

Solution.   We have described suicide as an act or a deed. We have said that it is an event done in the service of certain unfilled psychological needs. It is all purposeful; its purpose is to solve a problem. In the mind of the chief protagonist suicide is a solution—*the* solution—to a perceived problem, dilemma, challenge, difficulty, seemingly inescapable, intolerable situation. "It was the only thing I could do. What else could I do? It was the best way out of that terrible situation." In this sense every suicide is not only a solution; it is an *aristos*—the best that one can do.

In this definition, "suicide" has an adaptive and a self–serving function. Suicide is always done in the individual's "best interests;" that is, in the service of the individual's most pressing yearnings (to be free of intolerable emotion). In this sense, suicide can be said to be a selfish act. The individual's first fealty is not to his own preservation, but to himself. In this paradoxical sense, we are reminded of Richard Dawkin's brilliantly reasoned (but not totally convincing) presentation, *The Selfish Gene* (1976), whose major thesis is "that a predominant quality to be expected in a successful gene is ruthless selfishness" (p. 2). Neither for Dawkins (in his book), nor for me (in this context), is it a moral judgment to say that both successful evolution and "successful" suicide are ruthlessly committed self processes—the "best" that can be done under the circumstances.

W

Parasuicide

All that I have said to this point in the book has to do with *suicidal* behavior, that is, committed suicide. Earlier, in Part One, I touched briefly on behaviors which were suicide–like but were less than lethally intended, or indecisively intended—what is commonly called attempted suicide, but which more accurately is now called parasuicide (Kreitman et al., 1969). (A medical meaning of *para* is "similar but not identical with a true condition.") I hope that it is immediately obvious that a set of observations similar to the 10 common characteristics of (committed) suicidal behaviors can also be made for parasuicidal behaviors. This book is about *suicide:* I consider parasuicide—self-assaultive behavior, suicidal attempts, self–mutilation (Simpson, 1976) and inimical behaviors which diminish, punish, wound, and work against the self, to be a topic for a separate work. However, simply to illustrate how this might be done, I shall briefly indicate what some of the common characteristics of parasuicidal behavior are. These are summarized in Table 2. One can see that suicide and parasuicide are, by and large, operationally quite different and are defined, respectively, by their common characteristics.

These differences can be briefly cited, without attempting a full explication of them:

1. Whereas the common *stimulus* of suicide is unendurable psychological pain, the common stimulus of parasuicidal behavior is psychological pain that is quantitatively different. It is severe; it is endurable *if* the individual feels that he is truly not alone and can evoke some response in a significant other. If those efforts fail, then the pain may seem unendurable and the person may become suicidal.

2. The common *stressors* in both suicide and parasuicide are frustrated psychological needs, but how the nature and intensity of the unfulfillment differ between the two has not been empirically determined. We have yet to ascertain the typical patterns of needs in suicidal and parasuicidal persons. The current suspicion is that one would find a heterogeneity of patterns and the individuals in the two groups which would not distinguish with this criterion alone. The determination of what the disposition of needs is and which needs within any given disposition are, at the moment, painfully unfulfilled, will probably have to be done—because of the very nature of the problem—on an individual by individual basis.

3. Whereas the common *purpose* is to seek a solution to an overwhelming problem, in parasuicidal behavior the common purpose is to evoke a response. Suicide is conclusive; parasuicide is evocative. Suicide is autistic (beyond thinking of the response of others); parasuicidal behavior is enacted on an interpersonal stage. The target of the evocation in parasuicidal behavior can be a specific "other" or it can be generalized "others," even society or the world in general.

Table 2. Comparisons of the Common Characteristics of Suicidal and Parasuicidal Acts[a]

Aspect	Common Characteristic	Suicide (is)	Parasuicide (is)
Situational	1. Stimulus	Unendurable psychological pain	Intense, potentially endurable, psychological pain
	2. Stressor	Frustrated psychological needs	Frustrated psychological needs[b]
Conative	3. Purpose	To seek a solution to an overbearing problem	To reduce tension and to evoke a response
	4. Goal	Cessation of consciousness	Reordering of the life space
Affective	5. Emotion	Hopelessness–helplessness	Loss and rejection; disconnectedness and disenfranchisement
	6. Internal Attitude	Ambivalence	Trivalence among living (life), suffering, and dying (death)
Cognitive	7. Cognitive State	Constriction	Obsessional, with some planfulness
Relational	8. Interpersonal Act	Communication of intention	Communication of unhappiness; a call to rescue; evocation
	9. Action	Egression	Communication; importuning
Serial	10. Consistency	With lifelong adjustment patterns	With lifelong adjustment patterns[b]

[a]The assistance of Mark Goulston, M.D. with Parasuicidal Behaviors is gratefully acknowledged.

[b]Even when the Common Characteristics are the same in the two columns, the *content* of the characteristics is quite different.

4.   Whereas the common *goal* of suicidal behavior is cessation of consciousness, the common goal of parasuicidal behavior is to re-order the life space and, in the process, to decrease discomfort. The goal of one is the stopping of life; of the other, the changing of it.

5.   Whereas in suicide the common *emotion* is of hopelessness–helplessness, in the parasuicidal person it is more disconnectedness and disenfranchisement. The former has the banked emotions of the living dead; the second is experiencing loss and rejection. There is a curious paradox relating to the intensity of the emotions, as seen in the intensity of general perturbation; specifically, the parasuicidal person may be *more* perturbed than the suicidal one who, after all, has made a decision which will allow him to solve his most pressing problems. The picture is further complicated in that the perturbation level of suicidal persons themselves changes noticeably as they move through their suicidal scenario, becoming less severely perturbed when the suicidal plan is formed. Obviously, the rather swift reduction of perturbation in a highly lethal person needs to be viewed as a possibly serious portent and not necessarily as an indication that the storm is over.

6.   Whereas the common *internal attitude* in suicide is ambivalence (essentially between continuation and cessation), the common internal attitude in the parasuicidal situation is, in a sense, trivalent. These tripartite pulls are among life, suffering, and death; not only between life and death, but also with suffering (in life) as a middle term.

7.   Whereas the common *cognitive state* in suicide is one of intellectual and perceptual constriction, this is not to say that this state does not occur in the parasuicidal situation, but that it does not have

the closed-ring, tightly focused characteristic; there is rather an obsessional quality with some ruminative planfulness.

8.   Whereas the common *interpersonal act* in suicide is communication of an irrevocable conclusion, the common interpersonal act in parasuicidal behavior is the communication of a state of unhappiness and, in general, a call to rescue and a plea for nurturance. It is meant to evoke helping behavior from others; the suicidal act, obviously, is meant to do no such thing. They are quite different on this score.

9.   Whereas the common *action* in suicide is egression—escape, leaving life, the common parasuicidal action is communication itself, with the not so latent content of importuning the other person. We ought, on therapeutic principle, eschew such words as "coercion," "manipulation," and "blackmail" (Baechler, 1979) for they seem to add only an emotional, even pejorative, tone to the discussion, without, in an even-handed way, simply describing accurately what is going on or, in any way, furthering any therapeutic efforts.

10.   The common *consistency* is the same in both suicidal and parasuicidal behavior. That consistency is with the individual's lifelong behavior patterns in "comparable" life situations. It is difficult to say exactly what these are, but in a very general way the parasuicidal person, in moments of crisis, tends to throw himself on the mercy of the court (of society, of significant others), whereas the suicidal person would throw himself out of the window—some precipitous, often irrevocable act. In a work situation where both were let go, the suicidal person might say, "You can't fire me, I quit;" whereas the parasuicidal person might say, "Please don't fire me, I've just become sick." The inner consistencies within a life as re-

lated to suicidal or parasuicidal behaviors are not as superficial as these examples might indicate; In each case they resonate to certain subtleties of habitually unconscious ways of coping under great duress. °

°"Suicide" and "parasuicide" are not the only possible categories along a dimension of lethality. Six kinds of "suicidal" behaviors can be distinguished along, say, a nine-point continuum of lethality. They are: (1) *Simulated suicide.* with a low lethality rating; no deaths; an individual who pretends to be dead (by his own hand) or who "vanishes" or assumes a different identity and is given up for dead; (2) *pseudo-suicide,* with a low lethality rating; no deaths; an example would be an individual who swallows a small amount of sodium bicarbonate after claiming it is arsenic powder; (3) *parasuicide,* with medium lethality ratings (3 to 6); behaviors that use some methods traditionally associated with suicide such as overdosing or wrist cutting, where the intention is not to effect cessation of consciousness (death) but rather to effect some changes in the on-going life space especially with significant others; (4) *equivocal suicide,* with medium-high lethality ratings (6, 7, 8), where the chief protagonist is unclear, indecisive, or equivocal, leaving his survival to chance or to significant others; certain cases of "accident," victim-precipitated homicide and subintentioned deaths are in this category; (5) *attempted suicide,* with a high lethality rating (8, 9) where, in effect, the individual has committed suicide but against all odds has fortuitously survived, such as jumping from the Golden Gate bridge; no deaths; and (6) *suicide,* by any method; deaths; by definition, with a high (8 or 9) lethality rating.

Part Seven

Implications and Coda

X

Headnote

The two main components (and purposes) of this book lie in the presentation of the common characteristics of suicide (in Part Four) and in the discussion (in this part) of the implications of this view of suicide for saving lives. As much as the next person, I enjoy and value knowledge—in this case, understanding suicidal phenomena—for its own sake, but as a clinical suicidologist my deepest belief is that the kind of knowledge that is best worth knowing is that which also improves the human condition, which, in this case, *helps* suicidal people. If Part Four was the "head" of the book, then this part is the "heart" of the matter. The listing (and discussion) of the 10 common characteristics of suicide is the "theory;" the presentation of the implications for response and therapy is the *praxis*.

There is one more matter, not yet discussed in this book, that I need to mention. In spite of some urgent temptations to do otherwise, I have resisted including, I think correctly, a chapter on what I believe to be the possible wider, global applications of my view of individual suicide. However, I would be unfair to myself if I did not at least voice, in this headnote, my suggestion that we need quickly to *psychologize* the serious falling out between Uncle Sam and Uncle Ivan—the indisputable brothers on this one indivisible globe—and begin to address the frustrated psychological needs of each of them (i.e., their needs not to be villified, threatened, blackmailed, or bamboozled) before one or the other (or some equally or more disturbed juvenile relative) involves us in a mutually suicidal catastrophe. Even though I have not dwelt upon this matter in this book, I need to say that from the beginning of my career, my working with and helping each potentially suicidal individual was, for me, a tiny paradigm of the possible prevention of global suicide. If we do not prevent that, then all the other items on our life-saving agenda will not matter because the agenda itself, and the agenda makers along with it, will have disappeared.

Y

Implications
for Prevention
and Response

Those readers who are looking under this section heading for some simple prescription as to how to treat suicidal persons ("easy steps for little feet") have, I am afraid, missed the main message of this book. It should now be clear that we cannot hope to find a single cause for human phenomena as complex as self–destruction.

It also follows that there is, equally, a contextual implication for the *kind* of research efforts we should pursue. Specifically, we should abandon our use of oversimplified, two-term, equations of cause and effect and instead use more applicable research designs employing procedures of path analysis and attention to the multiple variables in developmental changes over time.

I would protest that it is not I who obfuscates the issue; the phenomena of suicides themselves are complicated and it is only responsible to report them so. Past methodologically oversimplified efforts have not worked because they were not methodologically relevant.

Not unexpectedly, there are also implications in this point of view for therapy with suicidal persons. I shall state a few of them.

The first implication is that I do not believe, in principle, in the individual private practice of suicide prevention. (I know that it is done and often done well, but I am speaking here in terms of a general rule.) And, of course, I am not speaking about one therapist seeing one patient. It is the setting I am talking about. Suicide prevention should optimally be practiced in consultation with a number of colleagues representing various disciplines. Suicide can best be understood in terms of concepts from several points of view. It follows that treatment of a suicidal individual should reflect the learnings from these same several disciplines.

A further implication for therapy, following from the above, is that, optimally, treatment of a suicidal person should be handled by more than one therapist. Here, I obviously have in mind the inter-disciplinary Diagnostic Council at the Harvard Psychological Clinic directed by Dr. Henry A. Murray some years ago (roughly between 1930 and 1960). I would propose that the treatment of a suicidal person would optimally be done by a *Therapeutic Council*. Such a council would be concerned with the biological, sociological, developmental, philosophical, and cognitive aspects of its patients. It might include a biologically oriented psychiatrist, a psychoanalytically oriented therapist, a sociologist, a logician–philosopher, a marriage and family counselor, and an existential social worker.

It may be that the skills of these several specialties can, on rare occasions, be found in one individual—the rare, so-called "Renaissance Man." I believe I have known a few of them in my life: Drs. Henry A. Murray, Avery Weisman, James G. Miller, Franz Alexander. A Renaissance Man nowadays is hard to find. But the concept is that an individual therapist who gives deep interpretations of childhood memories, prescriptions for medications for depression, or a behavior modification regime is, by himself, not enough.

Practically (when working with suicidal persons), we do what we can. We see people in consultation. We make interpretations. We write prescriptions, and so on. We force the concept of suicide into the templates of our own theoretical bias about personality, its vicissitudes and their remediation. That is not what it ought to be; but we also throw in our energies on the side of life and that often seems to be life-saving.

No efforts at remediation or therapy (however benignantly intended) can be effective unless there is some willing participation on the part of the individual who is defined as the patient. One implication of this is that we must now extend our previous definition of suicide to add the phrase (in our description of the suicidal person) ". . . in an ambivalent individual . . ." Granted there are some people who are, for all practical purposes, unambivalent (univalent) about killing themselves—we first hear about these people as coroner's cases—but most living people who are seen in consultation in relation to their "being suicidal" have the deepest ambivalences between wanting (needing) to be dead and yearning for possible intervention or rescue. The rescue often takes the form of improvement or a change in one of the major details in the patient's world such as the wish to be free of cancer, to be loved, and so on. In general, we can assume that a suicidal patient whom we are seeing, however lethally oriented, is deeply ambivalent about the crucial life-and-death issue. Obviously, the therapist should work with the life-directed aspects of the ambivalence (without, of course, being timorous to touch upon the death-oriented elements in that patient).

Having said the above, I do not think it a contradiction to indicate some further implications for individual psychotherapy, if individual psychotherapy is done. (We can assume that it will be.) Our definition of suicide (focusing on the problem-solving aspect of the act) implies that the therapist should try to understand not only the hurt that the patient is feeling but, centrally, the "problem" that the individual is trying to solve. Concomitantly, the therapist needs to appreciate what psychological needs the individual is trying to satisfy. The focus should not be on "why" suicide has been chosen as the method for solving life's problems, but rather on solving the problems, so that suicide—chosen for whatever reasons—becomes unnecessary (in that the problems are addressed and that the person sees some hope of at least partially satisfying, or redirecting, the urgently felt needs which were central to his suicidal scenario). In part, the treatment of suicide is the satisfaction of the unmet needs. One does this not only in the consultation room but also in the real world. This means that one talks to the significant others, contacts social agencies, and is concerned about practical items such as job, rent, and food. The way to save a suicidal person is to cater to that individual's infantile and realistic idiosyncratic needs. The suicidal therapist should, in addition to other roles, act as an existential social worker, a practical person knowledgeable about realistic resources and aware of philosophic issues—a speciality which should be encouraged.

I have said that a clinical rule is to address the frustrated needs in order to decrease the patient's psychological discomfort. One does this task by focusing on the thwarted needs. Questions such as "What is going on?" "Where do you hurt?" and "What would you like to have happen?" can usefully be asked by a therapist helping a suicidal person.

The psychotherapist can focus on feelings, especially such distressing feelings as guilt, shame, fear, anger, thwarted ambition, unrequited love, hopelessness, helplessness, and loneliness. The key is the improvement of the external *and* internal situations—a J.N.D. (Just Noticeable Difference). This can be accomplished through a variety of methods: ventilation, interpretation, instruction, behavior modification, *and* realistic manipulation of the world outside the consultation room. All this implies—when working with a highly lethal person—a heightened level of therapist-patient interaction during the period of elevated lethality. The therapist needs to work diligently, always giving the suicidal person realistic transfusions of hope until the perturbation intensity subsides enough to reduce the lethality to a tolerable, life-permitting level.

Another implication for individual therapy: The suicidal individual typically has a (transient) tunneling of perception manifested specifically in a narrowing or shrinking of the options for behavior which occur in his mind. The options have often been narrowed to only two: To live a certain specific way (with changes on the part of significant others) *or* to be dead. It follows that the therapist's task is to extend the range of the patient's perceptions, "to widen his blinders," to increase the number of choices, including, of course, the number of viable options. I have, on more than one occasion, in the presence of a suicidal patient, written a list of things which might be done, including suicide. All of the items on the list are more or less onerous. But it is precisely in the adjective (more or less) that life-saving opportunities lie. The patient is then asked to rank, in order from least to most odious, this list of realistic options including suicide—and then to discuss the least onerous ones.

An example may be useful. A young college student, single, attractive, demure, well-to-do, filled with Victorian moralities, and highly distressed, was encouraged to come to see me. She was pregnant and suicidal, with a formed suicide plan. Her challenge to me was that I somehow, magically, had to arrange for her to be the way she was before she became pregnant—virginal—or she would have to commit suicide. Her being pregnant was such a mortal shame to her, combined with her strong religious feelings of rage, piety, and guilt, that she simply could not, to quote her, "bear to live." At that moment suicide was the *only* alternative for her.

I did several things. For one, I took out a single sheet of paper and began to "widen her blinders." Our conversation went something on these general lines: "Now, let's see: You could have an abortion here locally." ("I couldn't do that.") (It is precisely the "can'ts" and the "won'ts" and "couldn'ts" and "have to's" and "nevers" and "always" and "onlys" that are negotiated in psychotherapy.) "You could go away and have an abortion." ("I couldn't do that.") "You could bring the baby to term and keep the baby." ("I couldn't do that.") "You could have the baby and adopt it out." ("I couldn't do that.") "We could get in touch with the young man involved." ("I couldn't do that.") "We could involve the help of your parents." ("I couldn't do that.") "You can always commit suicide, but there is obviously no need to do that today." (No response.) "Now, let's look at this list and rank them in order of your preference, keeping in mind that none of them is perfect."

The very making of this list, my non-hortatory and non-judgmental approach, had already had a calming influence on her. Within a few minutes her lethality had begun to de-escalate. She actually ranked the list, commenting negatively on each item. What was of critical importance was that suicide was now no longer first or second. We were then simply "haggling" about life—a perfectly viable solution.

The point is not how the issue was eventually resolved or what interpretations were made as to why she permitted herself to become pregnant, other aspects of her relationships with men, and so on. What is important is that it was possible to achieve the assignment of that moment—to lower her lethality by reducing her perturbation through widening her range of visable and realistic options (from only the choice between suicide and one other choice).

The immediate antidote for suicide lies in reduction of perturbation. Suicide is best understood not so much in terms of some sets of nosological boxes (e.g., depression or any of the often sterile labels in *DSM-III*) but rather in terms of two continua of general personality functioning: perturbation and lethality. Everyone is rateable (by oneself or others) on how disturbed or distressed or upset (perturbation) he or she is and, additionally, on how deathfully suicidal (lethality) he or she is.

To say that an individual is "disturbed" and "suicidal" simply indicates that there is an elevation in that individual's perturbation and lethality levels, respectively. Experience has taught us the important fact that it is neither possible nor practical in an individual who is highly lethal and highly perturbed to attempt to deal with the lethality directly, either by moral suasion, confrontatory interpretations, exhortation, or whatever. (It does not work any better in suicide than it does in alcoholism.) The most effective way to reduce elevated lethality is by doing so indirectly; that is, by reducing the elevated perturbation. Reduce the person's anguish, tension, and pain and his level of lethality will concomitantly come down, for it is the elevated perturbation that drives and fuels the elevated lethality.

With a highly lethal suicidal person the main goal is, of course, to reduce the elevated lethality. The most important rule to follow is that *high lethality is reduced by reducing the person's sense of perturbation.* One way to do this is by addressing in a practical way those in-the-world things that can be changed if ever so slightly. In a sensible manner, the therapist should be involved with such significant others as the patient's spouse, lover, employer, and government agencies. In these contacts the therapist acts as ombudsman for the patient, promoting his or her interests and welfare. The sub-goal is to reduce the real-life pressures that are sustaining or increasing the patient's sense of perturbation. To repeat: In order effectively to decrease the individual's lethality, one does what is necessary to decrease the individual's perturbation.

A psychotherapist can try to decrease the elevated perturbation of a highly suicidal person by doing almost everything possible to cater to the infantile idiosyncrasies, the dependency needs, the sense of pressure and futility, and the feelings of hopelessness and helplessness that the individual is experiencing. In order to help a highly lethal person, one should involve others and create activity around the person; do what he or she wants done; and, if that cannot be accomplished, at least move in the direction of the desired goals to some substitute goals that approximate those which have been lost. Remind the patient that life is often the choice among undesirable alternatives. The key to well-functioning is often to choose the least awful alternative that is practically attainable.

The intermediate response to potential suicide is to increase awareness of other adjustment processes. The key to intermediate and long-range effectiveness with a suicidal person is to increase the options for action available to the person; in a phrase, to widen the angle of the blinders. We should keep in mind that the suicidal act is an effort to stop unbearable anguish or intolerable pain by the individual's "doing something." Knowing this usually guides us to what treatment should be. In the same sense, the way to save a person's life is by doing something.

The common characteristics of suicide (described earlier) have direct implications for saving lives. Here are some practical measures for helping highly suicidal persons, following the previously presented outline:

1. Stimulus (unbearable pain): *reduce the pain.*
2. Stressor (frustrated needs): *fill the frustrated needs.*
3. Purpose (to seek a solution): *provide a viable answer.*

4. Goal (cessation of consciousness): *indicate alternatives.*
5. Emotion (hopelessness–helplessness): *give transfusions of hope.*
6. Internal attitude (ambivalence): *play for time.*
7. Cognitive state (constriction): *increase the options.*
8. Interpersonal act (communication of intention): *listen to the cry, involve others.*
9. Action (egression): *block the exit.*
10. Consistency (with life–long patterns): *invoke previous positive patterns of successful coping.*

An example may be clarifying: Given that the omnipresent action in committed suicide is to leave the scene (egression), then it follows that, when possible, the means of exit should be blocked. A practical application of this view is to "get the gun" in a suicidal situation where it is known that the individual intends to shoot himself and has a weapon. I have, admittedly on rare occasions, made an arrangement with a patient for him or her (and there have been instances of both) to bring the gun (in a bag or box) into the office for me to put in a safe place (including the local police station). Those guns were never reclaimed. The explosive situation had been defused and the person no longer had the need for a suicidal weapon.

Finally, I wish to say a few words about "locus of action"; that is, *where* (or *between what*) the suicidal drama is supposed to take place. Briefly: The early Christians, St. Augustine (354–430) and St. Thomas Aquinas (1225–1274), made suicide a crime and a sin; the site of the fault was in man's "heart," his soul. Jumping a good bit, the French philosopher Jean Jacques Rousseau (1712–1778) emphasized the natural state of man and thereby transferred the blame from man to society, making man generally good (and innocent) and asserting that it is society that makes him bad. The disputation as to the locus of blame, whether in man or in society, is a major theme that dominates the history of suicidal thought. David Hume (1711–1776) was one of the first Western philosophers to discuss the topic in the absence of the concept of sin. His famous essay "On Suicide" (published posthumously in 1777) refuted the view that suicide is either a sin or a crime by arguing that suicide is not a transgression of our duties toward God or State. ("If it be no crime in me to divert the Nile or Danube from its course, were I able to effect such purposes, where then is the crime in turning a few ounces of blood from their natural channel?") In the twentieth century, the two great suicidological theorists played rather different roles: Durkheim focused on society's inimical effects on the individual (without asserting that man was innately innocent), while Freud—eschewing the notions of either sin or crime—gave suicide back to man but put the locus of action in man's unconscious mind, for which man could hardly be blamed.

What are the implications of the view propounded in this volume in relation to the locus of action? It is certainly one of less unity than that of Rousseau, Hume, Durkheim, or Freud. Like them, it does not talk of crime or sin in relation to suicide, but it implies that the locus of action is in the individual—in *both* his conscious *and* unconscious mind—*and*—as he lives *within* his social "surround"—*with* his significant others, *in* his political and social times. Murray and Miller especially would not permit us to think of an individual not bathed in an environment, or of an organism that was not made up of smaller constituent systems behaving in the context of larger surrounding ones.

It is obvious that it is an *individual* who commits suicide, so that the locus of action can be said to be in their minds. (There are unconscious components in probably every conscious movement of the mind and each suicide contains both.) Furthermore, each mind interacts with other persons and is mightily influenced by them, and by social mores, folkways, fads, cults, injunctions, advertisements, importunings, and even transient events. Inasmuch as each suicide is a socially and interpersonally influenced intrapsychic event, efforts at individual prevention of a suicidal act are most effectively directed at transmuting the course of the mind and aided by making beneficent changes in the surroundings, where these changes are practical and can be made quickly.

The therapeutic message of this book is not to eschew the ordinary, common-sense gambits of response simply on account of their direct relationship to the nature of suicide itself. Of course, one should use *all* measures that work (for the therapist and the patient). These include support, psychodynamic interpretation, medication, the involvement of others including social agencies, and so on—all of which serve directly or indirectly to mollify one or more of the common characteristics of suicide.

In order to come back from a suicidal abyss and to stay on relatively firm ground, one needs to employ adjustment processes not prominent in one's armamentarium of techniques. In this regard I have a rather catholic view: I certainly embrace the suicide prevention centers of this country—you would hardly expect me to do otherwise; I endorse psychotherapy, counseling, outreach groups and agencies. I have become tolerant of behavior modification techniques and role modeling—anything that increases the person's awareness of choosing between living with a variety of miseries (and possible unhappinesses) and the ambivalently viewed awful escape.

A highly suicidal state is characterized by its transient quality, its pervasive ambivalence, and its dyadic nature. Psychotherapists are well-advised to minimize, if not totally to disregard, those probably well-intentioned but shrill writings in this field which naively speak of an individual's "right to commit suicide"—a right which in actuality cannot be denied.

Several other special features in the management of a highly lethal patient can be mentioned. Some of these special therapeutic stratagems or orientations reflect the transient, ambivalent and dyadic aspects of almost all suicidal acts.

1. Monitoring. A continuous (preferably daily) monitoring of the patient's lethality.
2. Consultation. There is almost no instance in a psychotherapist's professional life when consultation with peers is as important as when one is dealing with a highly suicidal patient.
3. Attention to transference. The successful treatment of a highly suicidal person depends heavily on the transference. The therapist can be active, show his concern, increase the

frequency of the sessions, invoke the magic of the unique therapist–patient relationship, be less of a *tabula rasa*, give transfusions of (realistic) hope and nurturance. In a figurative sense I believe that Eros can work wonders against Thanatos.

4. The involvement of significant others. Suicide is often a highly charged dyadic crisis. It follows from this that the therapist, unlike his or her usual practice of dealing almost exclusively with the patient (and even fending off the spouse, lover, parents, or grown children) should consider the advisability of working directly with the significant others.

Working with highly suicidal persons borrows from the goals of crisis intervention: Not to take on and attempt to ameliorate the individual's entire personality structure and cure all the neuroses but simply to keep the person alive. This is the *sine qua non* without which all other psychotherapy and efforts to be helpful could not have the opportunity to function.

Of course, the actual practice of suicide prevention "in the trenches" is often not as "clean" as I have described it, for in dealing with the walking wounded and the desperately stricken the situation—to quote from a personal communication of Robert E. Litman (perhaps the most experienced clinical suicidologist in the country)—is often one of working "in the smoke and heat and hassle of everyday living, sometimes ourselves among the wounded, and in doubt of what is feasible, not to say what is optimal. We need to be reminded that to work in suicide prevention is risky and dangerous and there are casualties and that is to be expected." To which, without feeling at all inconsistent in my own mind, I can fully say "Amen."

Z

Some Observations About the Topic of Suicide

Up to this point I have been writing about suicide; that is, the *act* of suicide and how best to understand that act. But there are also a few things that I wish to say about the *topic* of suicide; that is, suicide in the round, a few observations about suicide as an intellectual subject matter.

The universal psychodynamic formulation for suicide is non-existent. I do not regret that suicidology is a different discipline from physiology or physics. I simply note that it is and reflect upon it: Different subject matter, different relevant methodologies, and different degrees of ultimate veridicality. I have spoken of the possibilities for some prediction but never, I believe, with the precision that the physiologist or physicist has, nor do I aspire to that level. Our subject matter is the mind and we can be no more accurate or scientific than the relevant ways of investigating our subject matter will currently permit us.

And yet the yearning for universal suicidological laws understandably persists. A sweeping psychological statement with the ring of psychodynamic truth in it becomes a dictum. I believe, and not sadly, that the search for a single universal psychodynamic formulation for suicide is a chimera, an imaginary and non-existent conceptual monster. There should be no sense of loss in this. This view simply redefines who we are, what our legitimate business is, and what our sensible goals ought to be.

A common psychodynamic thread—probably ubiquitous in cases in which a parent of the suicidal person has committed suicide—is the problem of *negative identification*. Negative identification has to do with the powerful unconscious emulation, patterning, modeling or copying of "negative" or generally undesirable traits or features in the person who is being copied. For example, in order for a son to feel that he is loyal and is returning the love (in order to deserve to continue to receive it) of his father who is alcoholic or schizophrenic, does that mean that he must, in his own life, "be a good (obedient) boy" by being alcoholic or schizophrenic like his father? More to the point of this context, the issue arises when one or the other parent has committed suicide. Then the psychological question is whether or not the child feels that he "has to" emulate *that* pattern in order to show total fealty to the parent.

There is, of course, no patent answer to this issue. But in cases where there is suicide in the family, the likely presence of the psychodynamic problem of negative identification should always be recognized.

If there are common psychodynamic themes in suicide, they probably relate to omnipotence and loss. In the unconscious, every suicide is psychodynamically related, directly or indirectly, to feelings of omnipotence–impotence; to feelings of being all-powerful and powerless–helpless. Suicide is an effort to do *something*, to do something effective, impactful, dramatic, memorable, noteworthy, special. A suicide would not be a suicide if it were unknown as a suicide.

Being known as a suicide is an integral part of the act. If, for example, a person has an extramarital affair and then tells the spouse about it, there are then two events: the affair and the telling. (That is why many—not all—suicide notes seem poignantly redundant. They unnecessarily restate what is instantaneously obvious to the survivor on sighting the dead body.)

Suicide, like all deaths, while occurring in a dyadic setting, is, at bottom, an egotic (individual, solo, private) act. It is a one-person deed relating to that person's conscious and unconscious concern with active mastery—which, at its furthermost remove, is related to omnipotence. At the moment of committing suicide, the individual may feel he controls the world—and by his death can bring it down. At least he controls his own destiny, and realistically typically touches and influences the destinies of at least several others.

The great loss in suicide is the loss of the self. The main psychological focus of every formed person is with himself or herself. We are endlessly taken with the process of our own minds, even if we do not reflect upon them. Our greatest fealty and loyalty is to ourselves. (This is not identical to narcissism, as we currently understand it.) The great mourning of the suicidal person is premourning, the mourning for the potential loss of the best-known and best-loved person in the world, the self.

A handsome young man—who happened to be a homosexual prostitute by profession—dying of leukemia, said to me, "Now a perfectly good person is going to die and the world will be poorer for it." He spoke a universal truth.

The ultimate prevention of suicide lies in public education specifically about the clues to suicide. Most people would agree that the best prevention is primary prevention; here, perhaps more than anywhere else, an ounce of prevention can be priceless, life–saving. The primary prevention of suicide lies in education. The route is through teaching one another and that large, amorphous group known as the public, that suicide can happen to anyone, that there are verbal and behavioral clues that can be looked for (if one but has the threshold to see and hear them when they occur), and that help is available. Perhaps the main task of suicidologists lies in the dissemination of information especially about the clues to suicide: in the schools, in the workplace, and by means of the public media.

In the last analysis, the prevention of suicide is everybody's business.

Bibliography

Achille-Delmas, F. (1932). *Psychopathologie du suicide*. Paris: Felix Alcan.

Allport, G. (1937). *Personality: A psychological interpretation*. New York: Holt.

Allport, G. (1942). *The use of personal documents in psychological science*. New York: Social Science Research Council.

Alvarez, A. (1970). *The savage god*. New York: Random House.

Aries, P. (1981). *The hour of our death*. New York: Alfred A. Knopf. (Original work published in France 1977.)

Arieti, S. (1974). *Interpretation of schizophrenia* (Rev. ed.). New York: Basic Books. (Original work published 1955.)

Attwater, D. (1965). *The Penguin dictionary of saints*. Baltimore: Penguin Books.

Aubert, V., & White, H. (1959). Sleep: A sociological interpretation. *Acta Sociologica, 4*, 2, 3, 1–16, 46–54.

Bacon, F. (1620). *Novum organum*. (First published in 1620.)

Baechler, J. (1979). *Suicides*. New York: Basic Books. (Original work published 1975 as *Les Suicides*.)

Battin, M. P. (1982). *Ethical issues in suicide*. Englewood Cliffs, NJ: Prentice-Hall.

Battin, M. P., & Maris, R. W. (Eds.) (1983). Special issue: Suicide and ethics. *Suicide and Life-Threatening Behavior 13*, 7–129.

Battin, M. P., & Mayo, D. J. (Eds.). (1980). *Suicide: The philosophical issues*. New York: St. Martin's Press.

Beauchamp, T. L. (1978). What Is Suicide? In T. Beauchamp & S. Perlin (Eds.), *Ethical issues in death and dying*. Englewood Cliffs, NJ: Prentice-Hall.

Berman, J. (1977). *Joseph Conrad: Writing as rescue*. New York: Astra Books.

Bertalanffy, L. von. (1969). *General systems theory*. New York: Brazillier.

Binswanger, L. (1958). The Case of Ellen West. In R. May et al. (Eds.), *Existence*. New York: Basic Books.

Bohannan, P. (1960). *African homicide and suicide*. Princeton: Princeton University Press.

Bridgman, P. (1938). *The intelligent individual and society*. New York: MacMillan.

Caillois, R. (1961). *Man, play and games*. New York: The Free Press.

Camus, A. (1955). *The myth of Sisyphus and other essays*. New York: Alfred A. Knopf.

Cassedy, J. H. (1969). *Demography in early America: Beginnings of the statistical mind, 1600–1800*. Cambridge, MA: Harvard University Press.

Cavan, R. (1928). *Suicide*. Chicago: University of Chicago Press.

Choron, J. (1972). *Suicide*. New York: Scribners.

Church, A. (1973). Logic, History of: Modern Logic. *Encyclopaedia Britannica*. Chicago: William Benton Publishers.

Cohen, H., & Cahalan, J. (1978). *A concordance to Meville's Moby-Dick*. Ann Arbor, MI: University Microfilms International.

Daube, D. (1977). The linguistics of suicide. *Suicide and Life-Threatening Behavior, 7*, 132–182. (Reprinted from *Philosophy and Public Affairs*, 1972, *1*, 387–437).

Davis, M. R., & Gilman, W. W. (Eds.) (1960). *The letters of Herman Melville*. New Haven, CT: Yale University Press.

Dawkins, R. (1976). *The selfish gene*. New York: Oxford University Press.

Deshaies, G. (1947). *Psychologie du suicide*. Paris: Presses Universitaires de France.

Douglas, J. D. (1967). *The social meanings of suicide*. Princeton: Princeton University Press.

Draper, G., Dupertuis, C. W. & Caughley, J. L. (1944). *Human constitution in clinical medicine*. New York: Hoeber.

Dublin, L. I. (1963). *Suicide: A sociological and statistical study*. New York: Ronald Press.

Dublin, L. I., & Bunzel, B. (1933). *To be or not to be*. New York: Random House.

Durkheim, E. (1951). *Suicide* (J. A. Spaulding & G. Simpson, Trans.). Glencoe, IL: The Free Press. (Original work published 1897 as *Le suicide*.)

Erikson, E. (1950). *Childhood and society*. New York: W. W. Norton.

Farberow, N. L., & Shneidman, E. S. (Eds.) (1961). *The cry for help*. New York: McGraw-Hill.

Farberow, N. L. (1972). *Bibliography on suicide and suicide prevention: 1897–1970*. Washington, D.C.: Department of Health, Education and Welfare.

Farberow, N. L. (Ed.) (1980). *The many faces of suicide*. New York: McGraw-Hill.

Fedden, H. R. (1938). *Suicide. A social and historical study*. London: Peter Davies.

Fowles, J. (1975). *The aristos*. New York: New American Library. (Original work published 1964.)

Fox, R. (1976). The recent decline of suicide in Britain: The role of the Samaritan suicide prevention movement. In E. S. Shneidman (Ed.), *Suicidology: Contemporary developments*. New York: Grune and Stratton.

Freedman, A., Kaplan, H. I., & Sadock, B. J. (Eds.) (1975). *Comprehensive textbook in psychiatry* (2nd ed.). Baltimore: Williams & Wilkins Co.

Frey, R. G. (1980). Did Socrates commit suicide? In M. P. Battin & D. J. Mayo (Eds.), *Suicide: The philosophical issues*. New York: St Martin's Press.

Friedman, P. (Ed.). (1967). *On suicide*. New York: International Universities Press.

Gibbon, E. (1776–1788). *The decline and fall of the Roman Empire.*

Gibbs, J. P., & Martin, W. T. (1964). *Status integration and suicide: A sociological study.* Eugene, OR: University of Oregon Press.

Goffman, E. (1967). *Interaction ritual.* New York: Anchor Books.

Graber, G. C. (1981). The rationality of suicide. In S. E. Wallace & A. Eser (Eds.), *Suicide and euthanasia: The rights of personhood.* Knoxville, TN: University of Tennessee Press.

Halbwachs, M. (1930). *Les causes du suicide.* Paris: Felix Alcan.

Henry, A. F., & Short, J. E., Jr. (1954). *Suicide and homicide.* Glencoe, IL: The Free Press.

Hill, T. E., Jr. (1983). Self-regarding suicide: A modified Kantian view. *Suicide and Life-Threatening Behavior 13,* 254–275.

Hinton, J. (1967). *Dying.* Baltimore: Penguin Books.

Hinton, J. (1975). The Influences of previous personality on reactions to having terminal cancer. *Omega 6,* 95–111.

Huizinga, J. (1938). *Homo ludens: A study of the play element in culture.* Boston: Beacon Press.

Hume, D. (1777). *On suicide.* (Original work published 1777.)

James, W. (1890). *Principles of psychology.* New York: Henry Holt & Co.

James, W. (1902). *The varieties of religious experiences.* New York: Longmans, Green & Co.

Kasanin, J. S. (Ed.) (1964). *Language and thought in schizophrenia.* Berkeley: University of California Press. (Original work published 1944).

Kleitman, N. (1963). *Sleep and Wakefulness* (rev. ed.). Chicago: University of Chicago Press.

Kreitman, N., Philip, A. E., Green, S., and C. R. Bagley. (1969). Parasuicide. *British Journal of Psychiatry 115,* 746.

Kring, W. D., & Carey, J. S. (1975). Two discoveries concerning Herman Melville. *Proceedings of the Massachusetts Historical Society, 87,* 137–141.

Leenaars, A., & Balance, W. D. G. (1981). A predictive approach to the study of manifest content in suicide notes. *Journal of Clinical Psychology 37,* 50–52.

Leenaars, A., & Balance, W. D. G. (in press). A predictive approach to Freud's formulations regarding suicide. *Suicide and Life Threatening Behavior.*

Leenaars, A., & Balance, W. D. G. (in press). A logical empirical approach to the study of suicide notes. *Canadian Journal of Behavioral Science.*

Leenaars, A., Balance, W. D. G., & Wenckstern, S. (in press). An empirical investigation of Shneidman's formulations regarding suicide. *Suicide and Life-Threatening Behavior.*

Leites, N. (1953). Trends in affectlessness. In C. Kluckhohn, H. A. Murray, & D. M. Schneider (Eds.), *Personality in nature, society and culture.* New York: Alfred A. Knopf.

Lifton, R. J. (1979). *The broken connection.* New York: Simon and Schuster.

Litman, R. E. (1967). Sigmund Freud on suicide. In E. S. Shneidman (Ed.), *Essays in self–destruction.* New York: Science House.

Maris, R. (1981). *Pathways to suicide.* Baltimore: The Johns Hopkins University Press.

Maris, R. (1983). Suicide: Rights and rationality. *Suicide and Life-Threatening Behavior 13,* 223–230.

Mayo, D. J. (1983). Contemporary philosophical literature on suicide. *Suicide and Life-Threatening Behavior 13,* 313–245.

Melville, H. (1849). *Mardi.* (Original work published 1849.)

Melville, H. (1851). *Moby-Dick.* (Original work published 1851.)

Menninger, K.A. (1938). *Man against himself.* New York: Harcourt, Brace and Co.

Miller, J. G. (1978). *Living systems.* New York: McGraw-Hill.

Murray, H. A. (1938). *Explorations in personality.* New York: Oxford University Press.

Murray, H. A. (1981). This I believe. In E. S. Shneidman (Ed.), *Endeavors in psychology: Selections from the personology of Henry A. Murray.* New York: Harper and Row. (Original work published 1954.)

Murray, H. A. (1967). Dead to the world. In E. S. Shneidman (Ed.), *Essays in self-destruction.* New York: Science House.

Naegele, K. (1961). *Sociological observations on everyday life: First and further thoughts on sleep.* Unpublished manuscript, University of British Columbia.

Nakamura, H. (1967). *The ways of thinking of Eastern peoples.* New York: UNESCO.

Nicolson, N. (1973). *Portrait of a marriage.* New York: Atheneum.

Ogilvie, D. P., Stone, P. G., & Shneidman, E. S. (1976). Some characteristics of genuine versus simulated suicide notes by use of the general inquirer. In P. G. Stone et al. (Eds.), *The general inquirer: A computer approach to content analysis.* Cambridge, MA: MIT Press.

Pascal, B. (1658). *Pensèes.* (Original work written 1657–1658.)

Pasternak, B. (1959). *I remember: Sketch for an autobiography.* New York: Pantheon.

Pavese, C. (1961). *Il mestiere di vivere.* (A. E. Murch, Trans.), *The burning brand.* New York: Walker.

Pavese, C. (1961). *This business of living.* London: Peter Owen.

Peirce, C. S. (1955). *Collected papers of Charles Sanders Peirce* (C. Hartshorne & P. Weiss, Eds.). Cambridge, Mass.: Harvard University Press.

Peplau, L. A., & Perlman, D. (Eds.) (1982). *Loneliness: A sourcebook of current theory, research and therapy.* New York: Wiley-Interscience.

Pepper, S. C. (1942). *World hypotheses.* Berkeley: University of California Press.

Pepper, S. C. (1967). Can a philosophy make one philosophical? In E. S. Shneidman (Ed.), *Essays in self-destruction.* New York: Science House.

Pepper, S. C. (1970). *The sources of value.* Berkeley: University of California Press.

Reschler, N. (1967). *Temporal modalities in Arabic logic.* New York: The Humanities Press.

Romanyshyn, R. D. (1982). *Psychological life: From science to metaphor.* Austin, TX: University of Texas Press.

Rosenblatt, P. C. (1983). *Bitter, bitter tears: Nineteenth–century diarists and twentieth century theories.* Minneapolis: University of Minnesota Press.

Runyan, W. M. (1982). *Life histories and psychobiography: Explorations in theory and method.* New York: Oxford University Press.

Russell, B. (1967). *Autobiography* (Vol. 1). Boston: Little, Brown and Co.

Sainsbury, P. (1955). *Suicide in London: An ecological study.* London: Chapman and Hall.

Schmid, C. F. (1928). *Suicides in Seattle, 1914–1925.* Seattle: University of Washington Publications in Social Science.

Schmid, C. F. (1939). Suicide in Minneapolis, 1928–1932. *American Journal of Sociology 39,* 30–48.

Shaffer, T. L. (1976). Legal views of suicide. In E. S. Shneidman (Ed.), *Suicidology: Contemporary developments.* New York: Grune and Stratton.

Shneidman, E. S. (1959). The logic of suicide. In E. Shneidman & N. Farberow (Eds.), *Clues to suicide.* New York: McGraw-Hill.

Shneidman, E. S. (1963). Orientations toward death: A vital aspect of the study of lives. In R. W. White (Ed.), *The study of lives.* New York: Atherton.

Shneidman, E. S. (1963). The logic of politics. In M. May & L. Arons (Eds.), *Television and human behavior.* New York: Appleton-Century-Crofts.

Shneidman, E. S. (1968). The deaths of Herman Melville. In H. P. Vincent (Ed.), *Melville and Hawthorne in the Berkshires.* Kent, OH: Kent State University Press.

Shneidman, E. S. (1968, July). Classifications of suicidal phenomena. *Bulletin of Suicidology,* 1–9.

Shneidman, E. S. (1969). Logical content analysis: An explication of styles of concludifying. In G. Gerbner et al. (Eds.), *The analysis communication content.* New York: Wiley.

Shneidman, E. S. (1973). Suicide. *Encyclopaedia Britannica.* Chicago: William Benton.

Shneidman, E. S. (1973). Suicide notes reconsidered. *Psychiatry 36*, 379–393.

Shneidman, E. S. (1976). Some psychological reflections on the death of Malcolm Melville. *Suicide and Life-Threatening Behavior 6*, 231–242.

Shneidman, E. S. (1976). The components of suicide. *Psychiatric Annals 6*, 51–66.

Shneidman, E. S. (1979). A bibliography of suicide notes: 1856–1979. *Suicide and Life-Threatening Behavior 9*, 57–59.

Shneidman, E. S. (1979). Risk writing: A special note about Cesare Pavese and Joseph Conrad. *Journal of the American Academy of Psychoanalysis 7*, 575–592.

Shneidman, E. (Ed.) (1980). *Endeavors in psychology: Selections from the Personology of Henry A. Murray.* New York: Harper and Row.

Shneidman, E. S. (1981). *Suicide thoughts and reflections, 1960–1980.* New York: Behavioral Science Press.

Shneidman, E. S. (1982). On "Therefore I must kill myself." *Suicide and Life–Threatening Behavior 12*, 52–55.

Shneidman, E. S. (1982). The suicidal logic of Cesare Pavese. *Journal of the American Academy of Psychoanalysis 10*, 547–563.

Shneidman, E. S. (1982). *Voices of death.* New York: Bantam Book. (Original work published 1980.)

Shneidman, E. S. (1983). *Deaths of man.* New York: Jason Aronson. (Original work published 1973.)

Shneidman, E. S., Farberow, N. L., & Litman, R. E. (Eds.) (1970). *The psychology of suicide.* New York: Science House.

Shneidman, E. S., & Farberow, N. L. (1961). *Some facts about suicide.* (PHS Publication No. 852). Washington, D.C.: U.S. Government Printing Office.

Shneidman, E. S., Farberow, N. L., & Litman, R. E. (Eds.) (1970). *The psychology of suicide.* New York: Science House.

Silving, H. (1957). Suicide and the law. In E. S. Shneidman & N. L. Farberow (Eds.), *Clues to suicide.* New York: McGraw-Hill.

Simpson, M. A. (1976). Self-mutilation and suicide. In E. Shneidman (Ed.), *Suicidology: Contemporary developments.* New York: Grune and Stratton.

Stekel, W. (1967). Discussion. In P. Friedman (Ed.), *On suicide.* New York: International Universities Press. (Original work stated 1910.)

Stengel, E. (1974). *Suicide and attempted suicide* (rev. ed.). New York: Jason Aronson. (Original work published 1964.)

Sullivan, H. S. (1953). *The interpersonal theory of psychiatry.* New York: W. W. Norton.

Tyler, L. (1984). *Thinking creatively.* San Francisco: Jossey-Bass.

Von Domarus, E. (1964). The specific laws of logic in schizophrenia. In J. S. Kasanin (Ed.), *Language and thought in schizophrenia.* Berkeley: University of California Press. (Original work published 1944.)

Weisman, A. D. (1974). *The realization of death.* New York: Jason Aronson.

Williams, G. (1957). *The sanctity of life and the criminal law.* New York: Alfred A. Knopf.

Windelband, W. (1904). *Geschichte und naturwissenchaft* (3rd ed.). Strassburg: Heitz.

Windt, P. (1980). The concept of suicide. In M. P. Battin & D. J. Mayo (Eds.), *Suicide: The philosophical issues.* New York: St. Martin's Press.

World Health Organization (1968). *Prevention of suicide.* Geneva: World Health Organization.

Yannella, D., & Parker, H. (1981). *The endless, winding way in Melville: New charts by Kring and Carey.* Glassboro, NJ: The Melville Society.

Yap, P. M. (1958). *Suicide in Hong Kong.* London: Oxford University Press.

Zilboorg, G. (1937). Considerations on suicide. *American Journal of Orthopsychiatry 7*, 15–31.

Name Index

Subject Index